AF417571

CBSE X 2022

Term II

20 Sample Papers

5 Mathematics-Standard | 5 Science
5 Social Science | 5 English Language & Literature

CBSE X 2022

Term II

20 Sample Papers

5 Mathematics-Standard | 5 Science
5 Social Science | 5 English Language & Literature

Career Launcher

Title : CBSE 2022 : Class X Term II - 20 Sample Papers

Language : English

Editor's Name : Amit Singh

Typeset & Published by :

Career Launcher Infrastructure (P) Ltd.

A-45, Mohan Cooperative Industrial Area, Near Mohan Estate Metro Station, New Delhi - 110044

Marketed by :

G.K. Publications (P) Ltd.

Plot No. 9A, Sector-27A, Mathura Road, Faridabad, Haryana-121003

ISBN : **978-93-92837-48-7**

Printer's Details: Made in India, New Delhi.

For product information :

Visit ***www.gkpublications.com*** or email to ***gkp@gkpublications.com***

CONTENTS

PREFACE

To ace the Board exams, it is crucial to get your basics right. This book has, therefore, been designed to help you maximize your score in Class X Boards. There are 20 exhaustive Sample Question papers in the book developed by experienced teachers at Career Launcher. 5 Sample Papers each on Mathematics (Standard), Science, Social Science and English Language and Literature will help you practice in the most efficient manner possible.

The Sample Papers are followed by a detailed marking scheme, which will provide you with clarity on how to go about writing answers, as well as gauge where exactly you stand, in terms of marks obtained.

We hope you enjoy studying this book, as much as we enjoyed creating it.

On behalf of every one of us at Career Launcher, we wish you success in the Class X Term II Board exams, and a glorious career ahead!

Blueprint & Marks Distribution

Class 10th Mathematics Standard Term II Analysis Unit Wise 2021-22

Unit No.	Name	Marks
I	Algebra (Cont.)	10
II	Geometry (Cont.)	9
III	Trigonometry (Cont.)	7
IV	Mensuration (Cont.)	6
V	Statistics & Probability (Cont.)	8
	Total	**40**
	Internal Assessment	**10**
Grand Total		**50**

Class 10th Science Term II Analysis Unit Wise 2021-22

Units	Name of Units	Marks Distribution
I	Chemical Substances-Nature and Behaviour	10
II	World of Living	13
IV	Effects of Current	12
V	Natural Resources	05
	Total	**40**
	Internal assessment	**10**

Social Science Course Structure Term II 2021-22

Theory Paper

		Max. Marks : 40
No.	Units	Marks
I	India and the Contemporary World – I	10
II	Contemporary India – I	10
III	Democratic Politics – I	10
IV	Economic	10
	Total	40

Class 10th English Language and Literature Term II Analysis Unit Wise 2021-22

Unit No.	Name	Marks
I	Reading Skills	10
II	Writing Skills with Grammar	10
III	Literature Textbook and Supplementary Reading Text	20
Total		40
Internal Assessment		10
Grand Total		50

Mathematics Standard

UNIT I: ALGEBRA

1. QUADRATIC EQUATIONS

Standard form of a quadratic equation $ax^2+bx+c=0$, $(a \neq 0)$. Solution of the quadratic equations (only real roots) by factorization, by completing the square and by using quadratic formula. Relationship between discriminant and nature of roots.

Situational problems based on quadratic equations related to day to day activities (problems on equations reducible to quadratic equations are excluded)

2. ARITHMETIC PROGRESSIONS

Motivation for studying Arithmetic Progression Derivation of the nth term and sum of the first n terms of A.P. and their application in solving daily life problems.

(Applications based on sum to n terms of an A.P. are excluded)

UNIT II: GEOMETRY

3. CIRCLES

Tangent to a circle at, point of contact

i. (Prove) The tangent at any point of a circle is perpendicular to the radius through the point of contact.

ii. (Prove) The lengths of tangents drawn from an external point to circle are equal.

4. CONSTRUCTIONS

i. Division of a line segment in a given ratio (internally).

ii. Tangent to a circle from a point outside it.

UNIT III: TRIGONOMETRY

5 . SOME APPLICATIONS OF TRIGONOMETRY

HEIGHTS AND DISTANCES-Angle of elevation, Angle of Depression. Simple problems on heights and distances. Problems should not involve more than two right triangles. Angles of elevation / depression should be only 30°, 45°, 60°.

UNIT IV: MENSURATION

6. SURFACE AREAS AND VOLUMES

(i) Surface areas and volumes of combinations of any two of the following: cubes, cuboids, spheres, hemispheres and right circular cylinders/cones.

(ii) Problems involving converting one type of metallic solid into another and other mixed problems. (Problems with combination of not more than two different solids be taken).

UNIT V: STATISTICS AND PROBABILITY

7. STATISTICS

Mean, median and mode of grouped data (bimodal situation to be avoided). Mean by Direct Method and Assumed Mean Method only.

Science

Course Structure

THEME: MATERIALS

Unit I: Chemical Substances - Nature and Behaviour

Chapter – 4 Carbon and its compounds

Carbon compounds: Covalent bonding in carbon compounds; Versatile nature of carbon; Homologous series.

Chapter – 5 Periodic classification of elements

Periodic classification of elements: Need for classification, Early attempts at classification of elements (Dobereiner's Triads, Newland's Law of Octaves, Mendeleev's Periodic Table), Modern periodic table, gradation in properties, Valency, Atomic number, Metallic and Non-metallic properties.

THEME: THE WORLD OF THE LIVING

Unit II: World of Living

Chapter – 8 How do organisms reproduce?

Reproduction: Reproduction in animals and plants (asexual and sexual) reproductive health-need and methods of family planning. Safe sex vs HIV/ AIDS. Child bearing and women's health.

Chapter – 9 Heredity and Evolution

Heredity and Evolution: Heredity; Mendel's contribution- Laws for inheritance of traits: Sex determination: brief introduction;

THEME: NATURAL PHENOMENA

Unit IV: Effects of Current

Chapter – 12 Electricity

Ohm's law; Resistance, Resistivity, Factors on which the resistance of a conductor depends. Series combination of resistors, parallel combination of resistors and its applications in daily life. Heating effect of electric current and its applications in daily life. Electric power, Interrelation between P, V, I and R.

Chapter – 13 Magnetic effects of current

Magnetic effects of current : Magnetic field, field lines, field due to a current carrying conductor, field due to current carrying coil or solenoid; Force on current carrying conductor, Fleming's Left Hand Rule, Electric Motor, Electromagnetic induction. Induced potential difference, Induced current. Fleming's Right Hand Rule.

THEME: NATURAL RESOURCES

Unit V: Natural Resources

Chapter – 15 Our Environment

Our environment: Eco-system, Environmental problems, Ozone depletion, Waste Production and their solutions. Biodegradable and Non-biodegradable substances.

Social Science

Unit 1: India and the Contemporary World - II	
Themes	**Learning Objectives**
Section 1: Events and Processes **2. Nationalism in India** • The First World War, Khilafat and Non - Cooperation • Differing Strands within the Movement • Towards Civil Disobedience • The Sense of Collective Belonging	• Recognize the characteristics of Indian nationalism through a case study of Non-Cooperation and Civil Disobedience Movement. • Analyze the nature of the diverse social movements of the time. • Familiarize with the writings and ideals of different political groups and individuals. • Appreciate the ideas promoting Pan Indian belongingness.
Section 2: Livelihoods, Economies and Societies Note: Any one theme of the following. The theme selected should be assessed in the periodic test only and will not be evaluated in the board examination:	
3. The Making of a Global World • The Pre-modern world • The Nineteenth Century (1815-1914) • The Inter war Economy • Rebuilding a World Economy: The Post-War Era	• Show that globalization has a long history and point to the shifts within the process. • Analyze the implication of globalization for local economies. • Discuss how globalization is experienced differently by different social groups.
4. The Age of Industrialization • Before the Industrial Revolution • Hand Labour and Steam Power • Industrialization in the colonies • Factories Come Up • The Peculiarities of Industrial Growth • Market for Goods	• Familiarize with the Pro- to-Industrial phase and Early - factory system. • Familiarize with the process of industrialization and its impact on labour class. • Enable them to understand industrialization in the colonies with reference to Textile industries.

Unit 2: Contemporary India - II	
Themes	**Learning Objectives**
5. Minerals and Energy Resources • What is a mineral? • Mode of occurrence of Minerals • Ferrous and Non-Ferrous Minerals • Non-Metallic Minerals • Rock Minerals • Conservation of Minerals • Energy Resources o Conventional and Non-Conventional • Conservation of Energy Resources Note: The theoretical aspect of chapter 'Minerals and Energy Resources' to be assessed in the Periodic Tests only and will not be evaluated in Board Examination. However, the map items of this chapter as given in the Map List will be evaluated in Board Examination	• Identify different types of minerals and energy resources and places of their availability • Feel the need for their judicious utilization
6. Manufacturing Industries • Importance of manufacturing • Contribution of Industry to National Economy • Industrial Location • Classification of Industries • Spatial distribution • Industrial pollution and environmental degradation • Control of Environmental Degradation	• Bring out the importance of industries in the national economy as well as understand the regional disparities which resulted due to concentration of industries in some areas. • Discuss the need for a planned industrial development and debate over the role of government towards sustainable development.
7. Life Lines of National Economy • Transport – Roadways, Railways, Pipelines, Waterways, Airways • Communication • International Trade • Tourism as a Trade	• Explain the importance of transport and communication in the ever-shrinking world. • Understand the role of trade and tourism in the economic development of a country.
Unit 3: Democratic Politics - II	
Themes	**Learning Objectives**
6. Political Parties	
	• Analyze party systems in democracies.

• Why do we need Political Parties? • How many Parties should we have? • National Political Parties • State Parties • Challenges to Political Parties • How can Parties be reformed?	• Introduction to major political parties, challenges faced by them and reforms in the country.
7. Outcomes of Democracy • How do we assess democracy's outcomes? • Accountable, responsive and legitimate government • Economic growth and development • Reduction of inequality and poverty • Accommodation of social diversity • Dignity and freedom of the citizens	• Evaluate the functioning of democracies in comparison to alternative forms of governments. • Understand the causes for continuation of democracy in India. • Distinguish between sources of strengths and weaknesses of Indian democracy.
Unit 4: Economics	
Themes	**Learning Objectives**
3. Money and Credit • Money as a medium of exchange • Modern forms of money • Loan activities of Banks • Two different credit situations • Terms of credit • Formal sector credit in India • Self Help Groups for the Poor	• Understand money as an economic concept. • Understand the role of financial institutions from the point of view of day-to-day life.
4. Globalization and the Indian Economy • Production across countries • Interlinking production across countries • Foreign Trade and integration of markets • What is globalization? • Factors that have enabled Globalization • World Trade Organization • Impact of Globalization on India • The Struggle for a fair Globalization	• Explain the working of the Global Economic phenomenon.

English Language and Literature

SECTION A: READING (10 Marks)

Question based on the following kinds of unseen passages to assess inference, evaluation, vocabulary, analysis and interpretation:

I. Discursive passage (400-450 words)

II. Case based Factual passage (with visual input/ statistical data/ chart etc. 300-350 words)

SECTION B: WRITING AND GRAMMAR (10 Marks)

WRITING SKILL

I. Formal letter based on a given situation
   - Letter of Order
   - Letter of Enquiry

II. Analytical Paragraph (based on outline/chart/cue/map/report etc.)

GRAMMAR

1. Tenses
2. Modals
3. Subject Verb Concord
4. Determiner
5. Reported Speech
6. Commands and Requests
7. Statements
8. Questions

SECTION C: LITERATURE (20 Marks)

Questions based on extracts / texts to assess interpretation, inference, extrapolation beyond the text and across the texts.

FIRST FLIGHT

1. Glimpses of India
2. Madam Rides the Bus
3. The Sermon at Benares
4. The Proposal (Play)

POEMS

1. Amanda
2. Animals
3. The Tale of Custard the Dragon

FOOTPRINTS WITHOUT FEET

1. The Making of a Scientist
2. The Necklace
3. The Hack Driver
4. Bholi

Mathematics Standard

CBSE

Sample Question Paper 1

TERM II

CLASS X

MATHEMATICS- STANDARD

Time Allowed: 2 Hours *Maximum Marks: 40*

General Instructions

1. *The question paper consists of 14 questions divided into 3 sections A, B, C.*
2. *All questions are compulsory.*
3. *Section A comprises of 6 questions of 2 marks each. Internal choice has been provided in two questions.*
4. *Section B comprises of 4 questions of 3 marks each. Internal choice has been provided in one question.*
5. *Section C comprises of 4 questions of 4 marks each. An internal choice has been provided in one question. It contains two case study based questions.*

Section-A

6 × 2 = 12

1. The angles of a triangle are in A.P., the least being half the greatest. Find the angles.

OR

Find whether -150 is a term of the A.P. 17, 12, 7, 2, ... ?

2. Determine whether the given quadratic equation has root(s). If so, find the root(s) of $y^2 - 4y - 1 = 0$.

3. In the given figure, O is the centre of a circle, AB is a chord and AT is the tangent at A. If $\angle AOB = 100°$, then calculate $\angle BAT$.

4. The diameter of the base of a right circular cylinder is 28 cm and its height is 21 cm. Find the:

   (i) Curved surface area of the cylinder

   (ii) Total surface area of the cylinder

5. The median of the following observations 11, 12, 14, (x – 2), (x + 4), (x + 9), 32, 38, 47 arranged in ascending order is 24. Find the value of x.

6. Divide 12 into two parts such that the sum of their squares is 74.

OR

If the roots of the quadratic equation: $hx^2 + 21x + 10 = 0$ $(h \neq 0)$ are in the ratio 2:5. Find the possible values of h.

Section-B

4 × 3 = 12

7. Find the value of p, if the mean of the following distribution is 20:

x :	15	17	19	20 + p	23
f :	2	3	4	5p	6

8. Draw a line segment of length 7 cm. Find a point P on it which divides it in the ratio 3 : 5.

9. The following table shows the marks scored by 140 students in an examination of a certain paper:

Marks:	0-10	10-20	20-30	30-40	40-50
Number of students:	20	24	40	36	20

Calculate the average marks by using the direct method.

10. The angle of elevation of the top of a hill from the foot of a tower is 60° and the angle of elevation of the top of the tower from the foot of the hill is 30°. If the tower is 50 m high, find the height of the hill.

OR

An electric pole is 10 m high. A steel wire tied to top of the pole is affixed at a point on the ground to keep the pole up right. If the wire makes an angle of 45° with the horizontal through the foot of the pole, find the length of the wire.

Section-C

4 × 4 = 16

11. The internal and external diameters of a hollow hemispherical vessel are 24 cm and 25 cm respectively. Find the cost of painting the vessel all over, at the rate of 5 paise per sq.cm.

12. In the given figure, a circle is inscribed in a quadrilateral ABCD touching its sides AB, BC, CD and AD at P, Q, R and S respectively. If the radius DA of the circle is 10 cm, BC = 38 cm, PB = 27 cm and AD $\perp$ CD, then calculate the length of CD.

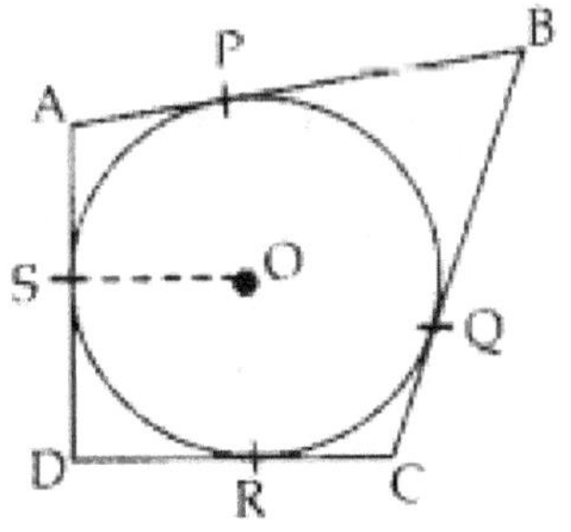

OR

Two concentric circles are of radii 7 cm and r cm respectively, where r > 7. A chord of the larger circle, of length 48 cm, touches the s7maller circle. Find the value of r.

Case study–1

13. A group of students of class X visited India Gate on an education trip. The teacher and students had interest in history as well. The teacher narrated that India Gate, official name Delhi Memorial, originally called All-India War Memorial, monumental sandstone arch in New Delhi, dedicated to the troops of British India who died in wars fought between 1914 and 1919.The teacher also said that India Gate, which is located at the eastern end of the Rajpath (formerly called the Kingsway), is about 138 feet (42 metres) in height.

(i) What is the angle of elevation if they are standing at a distance of 42 m away from the monument? Also, they want to see the tower at an angle of 60°. So, they want to know the distance where they should stand and hence find the distance.

(ii) ii) If the altitude of the Sun is at 60°, then find the height of the vertical tower that will cast a shadow of length 20 m. The ratio of the length of a rod and its shadow is 1 : 1 .Find the angle of elevation of the Sun.

Case study–2

14. Your friend Veer wants to participate in a 200m race. He can currently run that distance in 51 seconds and with each day of practice it takes him 2 seconds less. He wants to set his target to do it in 31 seconds.

(i) Form an A.P. for the given situation and also find the minimum number of days he needs to practice till his goal is achieved.

(ii) (a) If n^{th} term of an A.P. is given by $a_n = 2n + 3$, then find the common difference of the A.P.

(b) Find the value of x for which $2x$, $x + 10$, $3x + 2$ are three consecutive terms of an A.P.

SOLUTION

Section-A

1. Let the angles be a – d, a, a + d

$\because$ Sum of angles = 180°

$\therefore$ a – d + a + a + d = 180° (a > 0, d > 0)

$\Rightarrow$ 3a = 180° $\therefore$ a = 60° ...(i)

By the given condition

$$a - d = \frac{a+d}{2}$$ **[1]**

$\Rightarrow$ 2 = 2a – 2d = a + d

$\Rightarrow$ 2a – a = d + 2d $\Rightarrow$ a = 3d

$\Rightarrow$ $d = \frac{a}{3} = \frac{60°}{3} = 20°$ ...[From (i)]

$\therefore$ Angles are : 60° – 20°. 60°, 60° + 20° **[1]**

i.e., 40°, 60°, 80°

OR

Given: 1st term, a = 17

Common difference, d = 12 – 17 = – 5

n^{th} term, a_n = 150 (Let)

$\therefore$ a + (n – 1)d = –150 **[1]**

17 + (n – 1) (–5) = – 150

(n – 1) (–5) = – 150 – 17 = – 167

$$(n-1) = \frac{-167}{-5}$$

$$n = \frac{167}{5} + 1 = \frac{167+5}{5} = \frac{172}{5}$$

$n = \frac{172}{5}$ ...[Being not a natural number] **[1]**

$\therefore$ – 150 is not a term of given A.P.

2. Given equation is,

$$y^2 - 4y - 1 = 0$$

We know, $D = b^2 - 4ac$ **[½]**

$$a = 1,\ b = -4,\ c = -1$$

$$D = (-4)^2 - 4(1)(-1)$$

$\therefore$ $$D = 20$$ [½]

Since, D > 0 hence, the roots are real and unequal.

Using quadratic formula, the value of y gives us:

$$y = \frac{4-\sqrt{20}}{2} = 2-\sqrt{5} = -0.236$$ [½]

$$y = \frac{4+\sqrt{20}}{2} = 2+\sqrt{5} = 4.236$$ [½]

3.

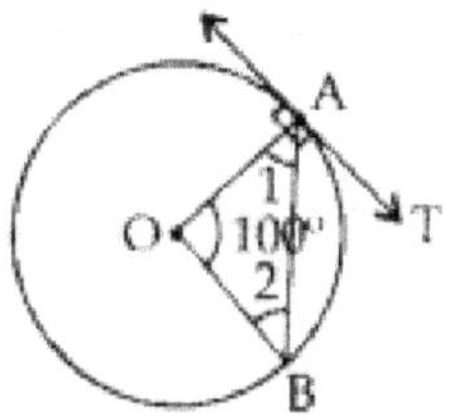

$$\angle 1 = \angle 2$$ [1]

$$\angle 1 + \angle 2 + 100° = 180°$$

$$\angle 1 + \angle 1 = 80°$$

$\Rightarrow$ $$2\angle 1 = 80°$$

$\Rightarrow$ $$\angle 1 = 40°$$

$$\angle 1 + \angle BAT = 90°$$

$$\angle BAT = 90° - 40° = 50°$$ [1]

4. Diameter of base (d) = 28 cm

$\therefore$ Radius of the base (r) = $\frac{28}{2}$ cm = 14 cm

Height (h) = 21 cm [½]

(i) Curved surface area = $2\pi rh$

$$= 2 \times \frac{22}{7} \times 14 \times 21 = 1848 \text{ cm}^2$$ [½]

(ii) Total surface area = $2\pi r(h + r)$ [½]

$$= 2 \times \frac{22}{7} \times 14 \times (21 + 14)$$ [½]

$$= 2 \times \frac{22}{7} \times 14 \times 35 = 3080 \text{ cm}^2$$

5. As, $N = 9$ **[½]**

$\therefore$ $\text{Median} = \left(\frac{9+1}{2}\right)^{th}$ item = 5th item **[½]**

$\Rightarrow$ $24 = x + 4 \Rightarrow x = 20$ **[1]**

$\therefore$ Observations are 11, 12, 14, 18, 24, 29, 32, 38, 47

6. Let the first number be 'x', so the other number will be '(12 – x)'.

$\because$ $x^2 + (12 - x)^2 = 74$

$$x^2 + 144 + x^2 - 24x = 74$$

On simplifyling further,

$$2x^2 - 24x + 70 = 0$$

$$x^2 - 12x + 35 = 0$$

$$\frac{-b \pm \sqrt{b^2 - 4ac}}{2a}$$ **[1]**

$$\frac{-(-12) \pm \sqrt{(-12)^2 - 4(1)(35)}}{2(1)}$$

$$\frac{12 \pm \sqrt{144 - 140}}{2(1)}$$

$$\frac{12 \pm \sqrt{4}}{2}$$

$$\frac{12 \pm 2}{2}$$

$\therefore$ x = 5 or x = 7.

Then other numbers will be (12 – x) = {12 – 5} & {12 – 7} i.e., 7 or 5. **[1]**

$\therefore$ The number 12 is divided into two parts namely 5 & 7.

OR

The given quadratic equation is:

$$hx^2 + 21x + 10 = 0$$

Let the roots be 2p & 5p,

$$2p + 5p = \frac{-21}{h}$$

and $10p^2 = \frac{10}{h}$ (sum and product of roots) **[1]**

$\Rightarrow$ $7p = \frac{-21}{h}$ and $p^2 = \frac{1}{h}$

$$p = \frac{-3}{h}$$

$\Rightarrow$ $$\frac{9}{h^2} = \frac{1}{h}$$ **[1]**

$\Rightarrow$ $$h = 9.$$

Section-B

7. Given that

Mean of the distribution is 20

x	f	fx
15	2	30
17	3	51
19	4	76
20 + P	5P	100 P + 5P^2
23	6	138

[1]

We know (By direct method of mean)

$$\text{Mean} = \frac{\sum fx}{\sum f} \quad ...(1)$$ **[½]**

$\Rightarrow$ $$\sum f = 15 + 5P$$

$$\sum fx = 295 + 100P + 5P^2$$

$\therefore$ from (1)

$$20 = \frac{295 + 100P + 5P^2}{15 + 5P}$$

$\Rightarrow$ $$295 + 100P + 5P^2 = 20(15 + 5P)$$ **[1]**

$\Rightarrow$ $$295 + 100P + 5P^2 = 300 + 100P$$

$$5P^2 = 300 - 295$$

$$5P^2 = 5$$

$$P^2 = 1$$

$\therefore$ $$P = 1$$

Value of P = 1. **[½]**

8. Draw a line segment, AB = 7 cm.

Step 2 : Draw a ray, AX, making an acute angle downward with AB. **[1]**

Step 3 : Mark the points A_1, A_2, A_3 ... A8 on AX.

Step 4 : Mark the points such that $AA_1 = A_1A_2 = A_2A_3 = ...,\ A_7A_8$.

Step 5 : Join BA_8. **[1]**

Step 6 : Draw a line parallel to BA_8 through the point A_3, to meet AB on P.

Hence AP: PB = 3 : 5 **[1]**

9. **[1]**

size	x_i	f_i	x_if_i
0-10	5	20	100
10-20	15	24	360
20-30	25	40	1000
30-40	35	36	1260
40-50	45	20	900

$$\text{mean} = \frac{\sum f_i x_i}{\sum f_i}$$ **[1]**

$$= \frac{3620}{140} = 25.857$$ **[1]**

10. **[1]**

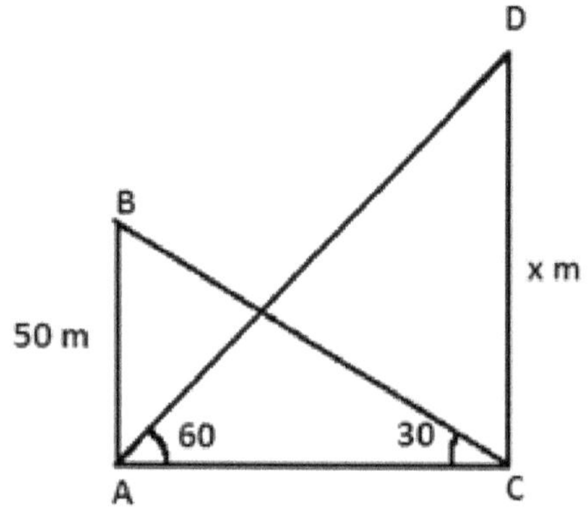

Let AB be the tower and CD be the hill. Then, $\angle ACB = 30°$, $\angle CAD = 60°$ and AB = 50 m.

Let CD = xm

In right ΔBAC, we have,

$$\cot 30° = \frac{AC}{AB}$$

$$\sqrt{3} = \frac{AC}{50}$$ [½]

$$AC = 50\sqrt{3} \text{ m}$$

In right ΔACD, we have

$$\tan 60° = \frac{CD}{AC}$$ [½]

$$\sqrt{3} = \frac{x}{50\sqrt{3}}$$ [1]

$$x = 50 \times 3 = 150 \text{ m}$$

Therefore, the height of the hill is 150 m.

OR

[1]

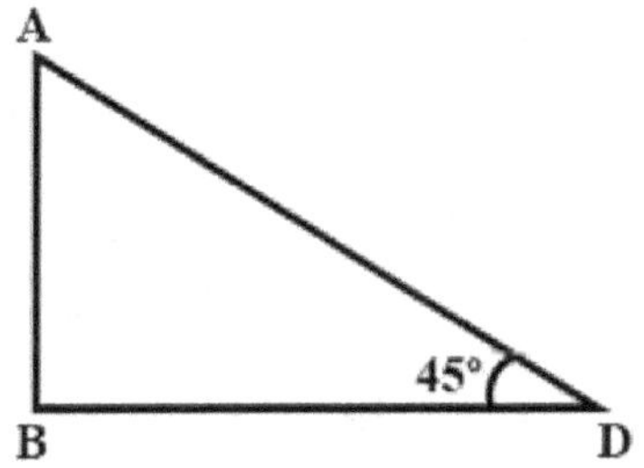

Let AB = 10 = Height of Pole

and AD be the length of the wire

From ΔABD

$$\sin 45° = \frac{AB}{AD} \Rightarrow \frac{1}{\sqrt{2}} = \frac{10}{AD} \Rightarrow AD = 10\sqrt{2}$$ [1]

$\Rightarrow$ $10 \times 1.414 \left(\text{Take } \sqrt{2} = 1.414\right)$ [1]

Section-C

11. Internal diameter of spherical vessel = 24 cm

External diameter of hemispherical vessel = 25 cm

Internal radius = r = 12 cm and External radius = R = 12.5 cm

Total surface area of be painted

$= \text{External curved surface} + \text{Internal curved surface} + \text{Area of ring}$

$= 2\pi R^2 + 2\pi r^2 + \pi(R^2 - r^2)$ **[1+½]**

$= \pi(2R^2 + 2r^2 + R^2 - r^2)$

$= \pi(3R^2 + r^2)$

$= \frac{22}{7}(3 \times 12.5^2 + 12^2)$

$= \frac{22}{7}(468.75 + 144)$

$= \frac{22}{7} \times 612.75$

$= 1925.75$ sq. cm **[1]**

Rate of painting = 5 paise per sq.cm

Thus, cost of painting = Area × Rate = $\frac{1928.78 \times 5}{100}$ = Rs. 96.29 **[1+½]**

12. Const. Join OR **[1]**

Proof. $\angle 1 = \angle 2 = 90°$ ...[Tangent is $\perp$ to the radius throughthe point of contact]

$\angle 3 = 90°$ ...[Given] **[1]**

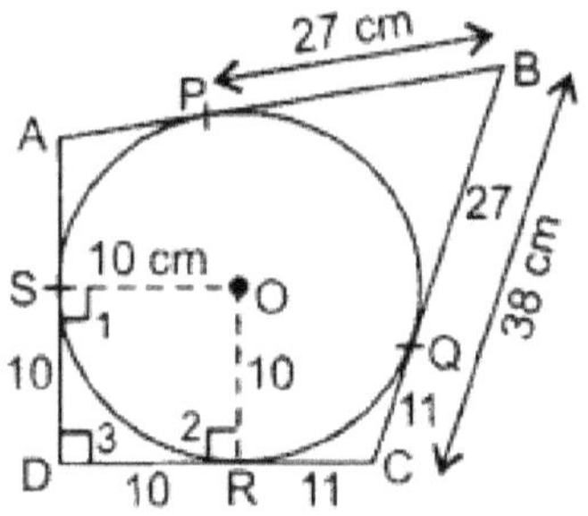

∴ ORDS is a square. **[1]**

DR = OS = 10 cm ...(i)

BP = BQ = 27 cm ...[Tangents drawn from an external point]

∴ CQ = 38 – 27 = 11 cm

RC = CO = 11 cm ...[Tangents drawn from an external point] **[1]**

DC = DR + RC = 10 + 11 = 21 cm. ...[From (i) and (ii)]

OR

Given : OC = 7 cm, AB = 48 cm

To find : r = ? **[1]**

$\angle OCA = 90°$ ...[Tangent is $\perp$ to the radius through the point of contact]

$\therefore$ $OC \perp AB$

$AC = \frac{1}{2}(AB)$ ...[$\perp$ from the centre bisects the chord]

$\Rightarrow$ $AC = \frac{1}{2}(48) = 24$ cm **[1]**

In rt. ΔOCA, $OA^2 = OC^2 + AC^2$ ...[Pythagoras' theorem]

$r^2 = (7)^2 + (24)^2 = 49 + 576 = 625$ **[1]**

$\therefore$ $r = \sqrt{625} = 25$ cm **[1]**

13. (i) 45° and 25.24 m **[1+1]**

(ii) $20\sqrt{3}$ and 45° **[1+1]**

14. (i) The A.P. will be 51, 49, 47 .... **[1]**

The minimum number of days will be 11 days. **[1]**

(ii) (a) The common difference will be 2. **[1]**

(b) The value of x will be 6. **[1]**

CBSE

Sample Question Paper 2

TERM II

CLASS X

MATHEMATICS- STANDARD

Time Allowed: 2 Hours *Maximum Marks: 40*

General Instructions

1. *The question paper consists of 14 questions divided into 3 sections A, B, C.*
2. *All questions are compulsory.*
3. *Section A comprises of 6 questions of 2 marks each. Internal choice has been provided in two questions.*
4. *Section B comprises of 4 questions of 3 marks each. Internal choice has been provided in one question.*
5. *Section C comprises of 4 questions of 4 marks each. An internal choice has been provided in one question. It contains two case study based questions.*

Section-A

6 × 2 = 12

1. Which term of the progression 4, 9, 14, 19,... is 109?

OR

Which term of the progression 20, 192, 183, 17... is the first negative term?

2. Determine the nature of the roots of the following equations from their discriminants.

$$2y^2 + 5y - 3 = 0$$

3. In the given figure, O is the centre of a circle, PQ is a chord and PT is the tangent at P. If $\angle POQ = 70°$, then calculate $\angle TPQ$.

4. If the volume of a vessel in the form of a right circular cylinder is 448 πcm^3 and its height is 7 cm, then the curved surface area of the cylinder is?

5. Find the median of the data : 19, 25, 59, 48, 35, 31, 30, 32 and 51. If 2 is replacement by 52 what will be the new median?

6. The sum of a natural number and its reciprocal is 10/3. Find the number.

OR

Find the roots of the following equation:

$$\frac{1}{x+3} - \frac{1}{x-6} = \frac{9}{20}; x \neq -3, 6$$

Section-B

4 × 3 = 12

7. If the median of a distribution given below is 28.5 then, find the value of an x and y.

Class Interval	Frequency
0-10	5
10-20	x
20-30	20
30-40	15
40-50	y
50-60	5
Total	60

8. Draw a circle of radius 3 cm. Take two points P and Q on one of its extended diameters, each at a distance of 7 cm from its centre. Draw tangents to the circle from these two points P and Q.

9. Find the mean marks from the following data:

Marks	Number of students
Below 10	5
Below 20	9
Below 30	17
Below 40	29
Below 50	45
Below 60	60
Below 70	70
Below 80	78
Below 90	83
Below 100	85

10. There is a small island in the middle of a 100 m wide river and a tall tree stands on the island. P and Q are points directly opposite to each other, two banks and in the line with the tree. If the angle of elevation of the top of the tree from P and Q are respectively 30° and 45°, find the height of the tree.

OR

A flag staff stands upon the top of a building. At a distance of 40 m. the angles of elevation of the tops of the flag staff and building are 600 and 300 then the height of the flag staff in metres is?

Section-C

4 × 4 = 16

11. The diameter of a metallic sphere is 6 cm. The sphere is melted and drawn into a wire of uniform circular cross-section. If the length of the wire is 36 m, find the radius of its cross-section.

12. Prove that the parallelogram circumscribing a circle is a rhombus.

OR

In figure, a quadrilateral ABCD is drawn to circumscribe a circle, with centre O, in such a way that the sides AB, BC, CD and DA touch the circle at the points P, Q, RA and S respectively. Prove that:

AB + CD = BC + DA.

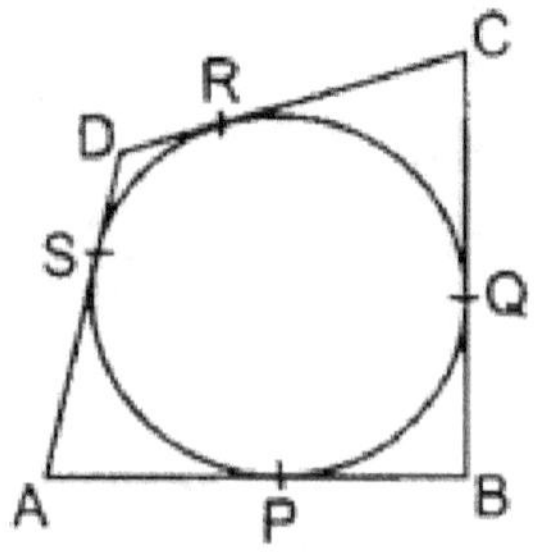

Case study–1

13.

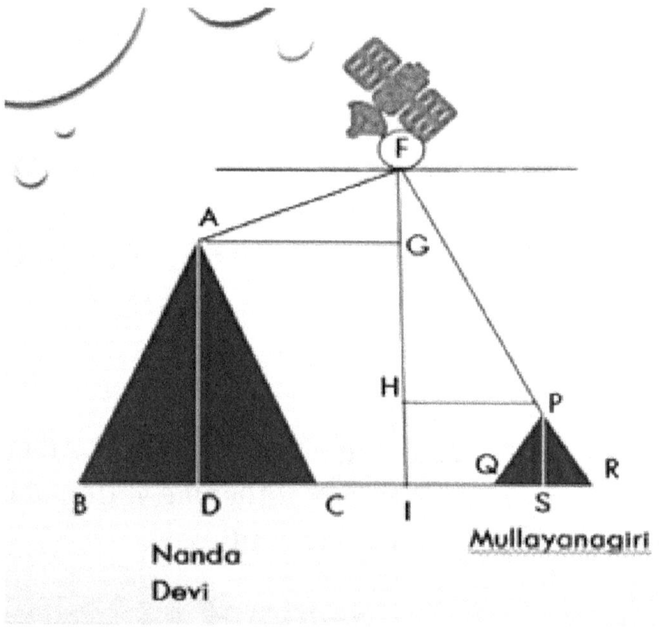

A Satellite flying at height h is watching the top of the two tallest mountains in Uttarakhand and Karnataka, them being Nanda Devi (height 7,816m) and Mullayanagiri (height 1,930 m). The angles of depression from the satellite, to the top of Nanda Devi and Mullayanagiri are 30° and 60° respectively. If the distance between the peaks of two mountains is 1937 km, and the satellite is vertically above the midpoint of the distance between the two mountains.

(i) Find the distance of the satellite from the top of Nanda devi and mullayanagiri.

(ii) If a mile stone very far away from, makes 45° to the top of Mullanyangiri mountain .So, find the distance of this mile stone form the mountain.

Case study–2

14. Your elder brother wants to buy a car and plans to take loan from a bank for his car. He repays his total loan of Rs 1,18,000 by paying every month starting with the first instalment of Rs. 1000. If he increases the instalment by Rs 100 every month, then answer the following:

(i) Find the amount paid by him in 30th instalment and also find the amount does he still have to pay offer 30th instalment.

(ii) Find the ratio of the 1st instalment to the last instalment.

SOLUTION

Section-A

1. Here, $d = 9 - 4 = 14 - 9 = 19 - 14 = 5$ **[½]**

$\therefore$ Difference between consecutive terms is constant.

Hence it is an A.P.

Given : First term, $a = 4$, $d = 5$, $a_n = 109$ (Let) **[½]**

$\therefore \quad a_n = a + (n - 1)d$ ...[General term of A.P.]

$\therefore \quad 109 = 4 + (n - 1)5$

$\Rightarrow \quad 109 - 4 = (n - 1)5$

$\Rightarrow \quad 105 = 5(n - 1)$

$\Rightarrow \quad n - 1 = \frac{105}{5} = 21$ **[½]**

$\Rightarrow \quad n = 21 + 1 = 22$

$\therefore$ 109 is the 22nd term **[½]**

OR

Given : A.P. : $20, \frac{77}{4}, \frac{37}{4}, \frac{71}{4}$

Here $a = 20$, $d = \frac{77 - 80}{4} = -\frac{3}{4}$ **[½]**

For first negative term, $a_n < 0$

$\Rightarrow \quad a + (n - 1)d < 0$

$\Rightarrow \quad 20 + (n - 1)\left(-\frac{3}{4}\right) < 0$

$\Rightarrow \quad -\frac{3}{4}(n - 1) < -20$

$\Rightarrow \quad 3(1 - 1) > 80$ **[1]**

$\Rightarrow \quad 3n - 3 > 80$

$\Rightarrow \quad 3n > 83$

$n > \frac{83}{4}$ **[½]**

$\Rightarrow \quad n > 27.5$

$\therefore$ Its negative term is 28th term.

2. Given equationis, $2y^2 - 5y - 3 = 0$

$D = b^2 - 4ac$ **[1]**

$a = 2, b = 5, c = -3$

$D = (-5)^2 - 4(2)(-3)$

$\therefore$ $D = 49$

Since, D > 0, hence, the roots are real and unequal. **[1]**

3.

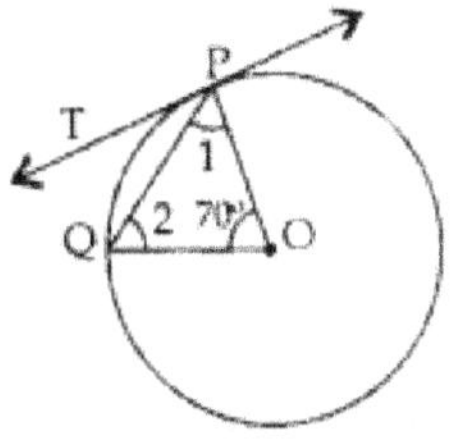

$\angle 1 = \angle 2$

$\angle 1 + \angle 2 + 70° = 180°$

$\angle 1 + \angle 1 = 180° - 70°$ **[1]**

$2\angle 1 = 110°$

$\Rightarrow$ $\angle 1 = 55°$

$\angle 1 + \angle TPQ = 90°$

$55° + \angle TPQ = 90°$

$\Rightarrow$ $\angle TPQ = 90° - 55° = 35°$ **[1]**

4. Volume of a Cylinder of Radius R and height h = $\pi R^2 h$ **[½]**

$\therefore$ Volume of the given ncylinder = $\pi \times R^2 \times 7 = 448\ \pi cm^3$ **[½]**

$R^2 = 64$

$R = 8$ cm

Curved surface are of a cylinder of radius "R" and height "h" = $2\ \pi Rh$ **[½]**

$\therefore$ Curved surface are of the given cylinder = $2 \times \pi \times 8 \times 7 = 112\ \pi cm^2$ **[½]**

5. We have given that

19, 25, 59, 48, 35, 31, 30, 32, 51.

Now, put all the value into order, median is the middle value.

19, 25, 30, 31, 32, 35, 48, 51, 59. **[1]**

median = 32

if 25 is replaced by 52 i.e.

19, 30, 31, 32, 35, 48, 51, 52, 59.

median = 35

Hence, new median is 35. **[1]**

6. Let the number be x

Then,
$$x + \frac{1}{x} = \frac{10}{3}$$
$$3x^2 + 3 = 10x \quad \textbf{[1]}$$
$$3x^2 - 10x + 3 = 0$$
$$3x^2 - 9x - x + 3 = 0$$
$$(3x - 1)(x - 3) = 0$$
$$x = 3, \frac{1}{3} \quad \textbf{[1]}$$

Since, x is a natural number, x = 3

OR

Given,
$$\frac{1}{x+3} - \frac{1}{x-6} = \frac{9}{20}; x \neq -3, 6$$
$$\Rightarrow \frac{(x-6)-(x+3)}{(x+3)(x-6)} = \frac{9}{20}$$
$$\Rightarrow \frac{-9}{(x+3)(x-6)} = \frac{9}{20}$$
$$\Rightarrow (x + 3)(x - 6) \quad \textbf{[1]}$$
$$\Rightarrow -20 \text{ or } x^2 - 3x + 2 = 0$$
$$\Rightarrow x^2 - 2x - x + 2 = 0$$
$$\Rightarrow x(x - 2) - 1(x - 2) = 0$$
$$\Rightarrow (x - 1)(x - 2) = 0$$
$$\Rightarrow x = 1 \text{ or } x = 2 \quad \textbf{[1]}$$

Both x = 1 and x = 2 are satisfying the given equation.

Hence, x = 1, 2 are the solutions of the equation.

Section-B

7. From the given data, n = 60

Median of the given data = 28.5

$$\text{Where, } \frac{n}{2} = 30$$

Median class is 20 – 30 with a cumulative frequency = 25 + x **[½]**

Lower limit of median class = 20,

Cf = 5 + x,

f = 20 and h = 10

$$\text{Median} = l + \left(\frac{\frac{n}{2} - cf}{f}\right) \times h$$ **[½]**

Substitute the values

$$28.5 = 20 + 10\left(\frac{30 - 5 - x}{20}\right)$$

$$8.5 = \frac{(25 - x)}{2}$$ **[1]**

$$17 = 25 - x$$

Therefore, $x = 8$

Now, from cumulative frequency, we can identify the value of $x + y$ as follows:

Since, $60 = 5 + 20 + 15 + 5 + x + y$

Now, substitute the value of x, to find y

$$60 = 5 + 20\ 15 + 5 + 8 + y$$

$$y = 60 - 53$$

$$y = 7$$

Therefore, the value of $x = 8$ and $y = 7$ **[1]**

8. **Step 1 :** Draw a circle with a radius of 3 cm with centre "O".

Step 2 : Draw a diameter of a circle with endpoints P and Q, and it extends 7 cm from the centre.

Step 3 : Draw the perpendicular bisector of the line PO and mark the midpoint as M. **[1]**

Step 4 : Draw a circle with M as centre and MO as the radius

Step 5 : Now join the points PA and PB in which the circle with radius MO intersects the circle at points A and B. **[1]**

Step 6 : Now PA and PB are the required tangents.

Step 7 : Similarly, from point Q, we can draw the tangents.

Step 8 : From that, QC and QD are the required tangents. **[1]**

9. Taking continuous class interval with width = 10

$\therefore$ For "90 – 100" = Below 100 – Below 90 = 85 – 83 = 2 **[½]**

$\therefore$ For "80 – 90"= Below 90 – Below 80 = 83 – 78 = 5 **[½]**

Similarly for other classes also.

Thus our frequency distribution table is

Marks	Students f_i	$x_i = \frac{\text{lower limit + upper limit}}{2}$	$f_i x_i$
0-10	5	5	25
10-20	4	15	60
20-30	8	25	200
30 – 40	12	35	420
40 – 50	16	45	720
50 – 60	15	55	825
60 – 70	10	65	650
70 – 80	8	75	600
80 – 90	5	85	425
90 – 100	2	95	190
	$\Sigma f_i = 85$		$\Sigma f_i x_i = 4115$

[1]

Mean = 48.4 **[1]**

10. **[1]**

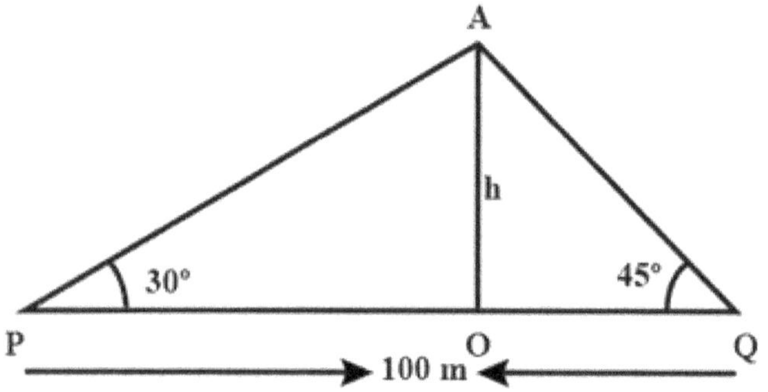

Let OA be the tree of height h metre.

In triangle POA and QOA, we have

$$\tan 30° = \frac{OA}{OP} \text{ and } \tan 45° = \frac{OA}{OQ}$$

$$\Rightarrow \quad \frac{1}{\sqrt{3}} = \frac{h}{OP} \text{ and } 1 = \frac{h}{OQ}$$

$$\Rightarrow \quad OP = \sqrt{3}\,h \text{ and } OQ = h$$

$$\Rightarrow \quad OP + OQ = \sqrt{3}\,h + h$$

$$\Rightarrow \quad PQ = (\sqrt{3} + 1)h$$

$\Rightarrow \quad 100 = (\sqrt{3} + 1)h \qquad [\because PQ = 100 \text{ m}]$

$\Rightarrow \quad h = \dfrac{100}{\sqrt{3}+1} \text{m}$

$\Rightarrow \quad h = \dfrac{100(\sqrt{3}+1)}{2} \text{m}$ **[1]**

$\Rightarrow \quad h = 50(1.732 - 1)\text{m} = 36.6 \text{ m}$ **[1]**

Hence, the height of the tree is 36.6 m.

OR

In the fig let AD is the Flag-Staff or height h (m)

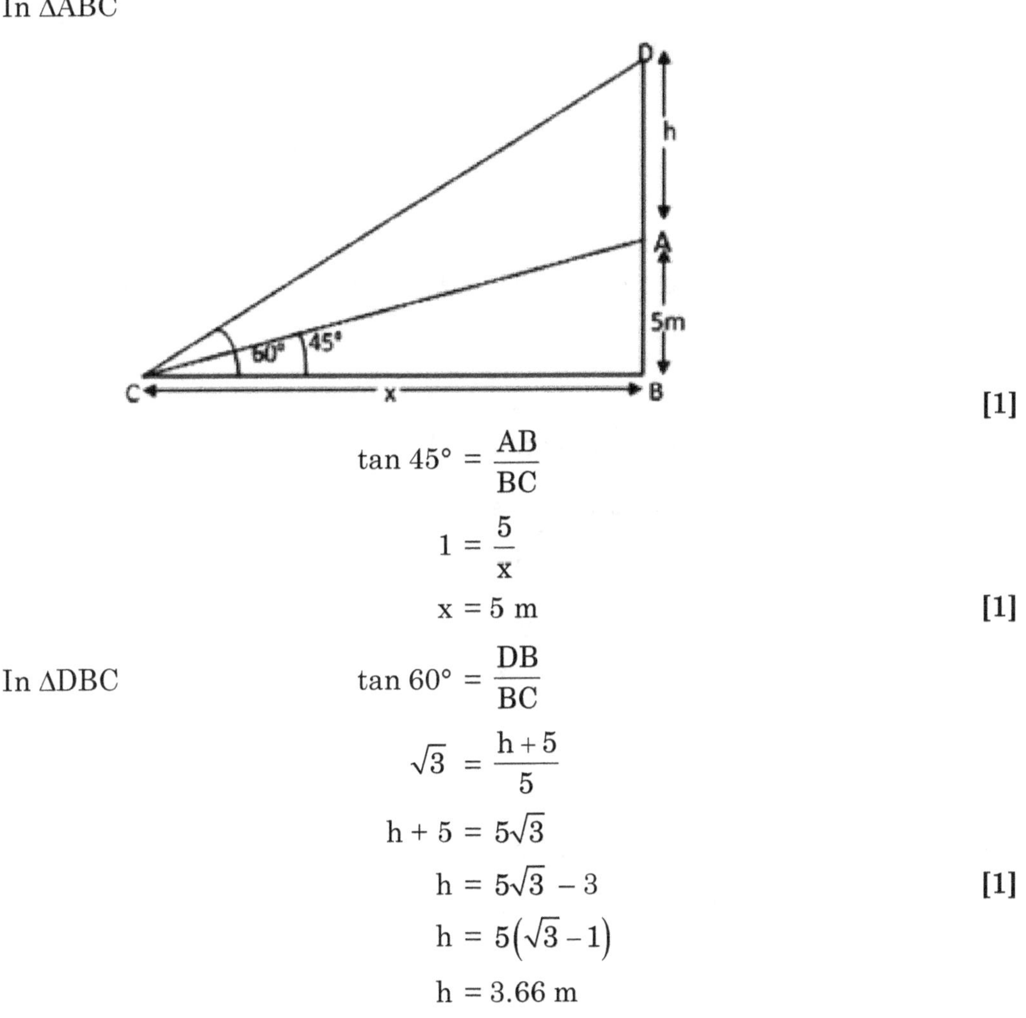

In ΔABC

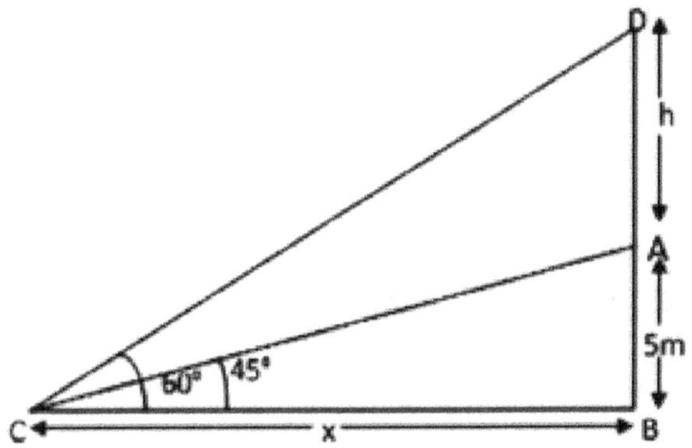

[1]

$$\tan 45° = \frac{AB}{BC}$$

$$1 = \frac{5}{x}$$

$$x = 5 \text{ m}$$ **[1]**

In ΔDBC $\quad \tan 60° = \dfrac{DB}{BC}$

$$\sqrt{3} = \frac{h+5}{5}$$

$$h + 5 = 5\sqrt{3}$$

$$h = 5\sqrt{3} - 3$$ **[1]**

$$h = 5(\sqrt{3}-1)$$

$$h = 3.66 \text{ m}$$

Therefore height of flat-staff is 3.66 m

Section-C

11. The wire is in the shape of a cylinder.

Since the sphere is melted and a cylindrical wire is formed, their volumes are equal

Volume of a sphere = $\frac{4}{3}\pi r^3$ **[½]**

As the diameter of the sphere is 6 cm, its radius r = 3 cm **[½]**

Volume of a Cylinder = $\pi R^2 h$

Length of the wire h = 36 m = 3600 cm

Hence, Volume os sphere = Volume of the wire

$$\frac{4}{3}\pi r^3 = \pi R^2 h$$ **[1½]**

$$R^2 = \frac{1}{100}$$

$$R = \frac{1}{10} = 0.1 \text{ cm}$$ **[1½]**

Hence, radius of the cross-section of the wire = 0.1 cm

12. Given : ABCD is a IIgm.

To prove. ABCD is a rhombus.

Proof. In IIgm, opposite sides are equal

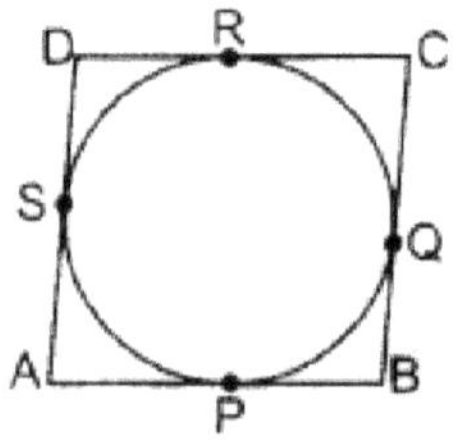

[1]

AB = CD

and AD = BC ...(i) **[1]**

AP = AS ...[Tangents drawn from an external point are equal in length]

PB = BQ

CR = CO

DR = DS

By adding these tangents,

$$(AP + PB) + (CR + DR) = AS + BQ + CQ + DS$$

$$AB + CD = (AS + DS) + (BQ + CQ)$$

$$AB + CD = AD + BC \quad \textbf{[1]}$$

$$AB + AB = BC + BC \quad \text{...[From (i)]}$$

$$2\ AB = 2\ BC$$

$$AB = BC \quad \text{...(ii)}$$

From (i) and (ii), AB = BC = CD = DA

∴ II^{gm} ABCD is a rhombus. **[1]**

OR

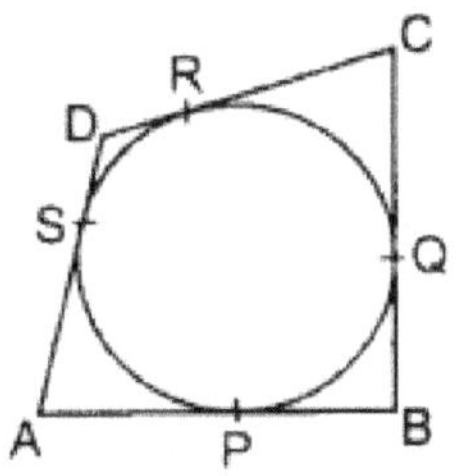

[1]

AP = AS ...(i) (Tangents drawn from an external point are equal in length **[1]**

BP = BO ...(ii)

CR = CQ ...(iii)

DR = DS ...(iv)

By adding (i) to (iv)

(AP + BP) + (CR + DR) = AS + BQ + CQ + DS **[1]**

AB + CD = (BQ + CQ) + (AS + DS)

∴ AB + CD = BC + AD (Hence proved) **[1]**

13. (i) 1139.4 km and 1937 km **[1+1]**

(ii) 1937 km **[2]**

14. (i) Rs 3900 **[1]**

Rs 44500 **[1]**

(ii) 10 : 49 **[2]**

CBSE

Sample Question Paper 3

TERM II

CLASS X

MATHEMATICS- STANDARD

Time Allowed: 2 Hours | *Maximum Marks: 40*

General Instructions

1. *The question paper consists of 14 questions divided into 3 sections A, B, C.*
2. *All questions are compulsory.*
3. *Section A comprises of 6 questions of 2 marks each. Internal choice has been provided in two questions.*
4. *Section B comprises of 4 questions of 3 marks each. Internal choice has been provided in one question.*
5. *Section C comprises of 4 questions of 4 marks each. An internal choice has been provided in one question. It contains two case study based questions.*

Section-A

6 × 2 = 12

1. The 7th term of an A.P. is 20 and its 13th term is 32. Find the A.P.

OR

How many natural numbers are there between 200 and 500, which are divisible by 7?

2. Find the value of p such that quadratic equation $(p - 12)x^2 - 2(p - 12)x + 2 = 0$ has equal roots.

3. In the given figure, PQ R is a tangent at a point C to a circle with centre O. If AB is a diameter and $\angle CAB = 30°$. Find $\angle PCA$.

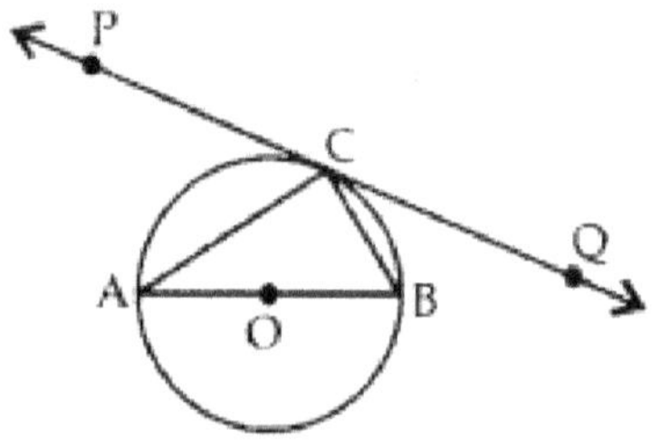

4. The radius of the base and the height of a right circular cone are 7 cm and 24 cm respectively. Find the volume and total surface area of the cone.

5. Find the mean of the first 10 natural numbers.

6. The product of Ramu's age (in yeras) five years ago and his age (in years) nine years later is 15. Find Ramu's present age.

OR

If the equation $(1 + m^2)x^2 + 2mcx + c^2 - a^2 = 0$ has equal roots, show that $c^2 = a^2(1 + m^2)$.

Section-B

4 × 3 = 12

7. If the mean of 4 numbers, 2, 6, 7 and a is 15 and also the mean of other 5 numbers, 6, 18, 1, a, b is 50. What is the value of b?

8. Draw a circle with the help of a compass. Take a point outside the circle. Construct the pair of tangents from this point to the circle.

9. Find the mean age of 100 residents of a town from the following data:

Age equal and above (in years)	0	10	20	30	40	50	60	70
Number of persons	100	90	75	50	25	15	5	0

10. A vertical tower stands on a horizontal plane and is surmounted by a flagstaff of height 7 m. From a point on the plane, the angle of elevation of the bottom of the flag-staff is 30° and that of the top of the flag-staff is 45°. Find the height of the tower.

OR

The length of a string between a kite and a point on the roof of a building 10 m high is 180 m. If the string makes an angle θ with the level ground such that $\tan \theta = \frac{4}{3}$, how high is the kite from the ground?

Section-C

4 × 4 = 16

11. 50 circular discs, each of radius 7 cm and thickness 0.5 cm are placed one above the other. Find the total surface area of the solid so formed. Find how much space will be left in a cubical box of side 25 cm if the solid formed is placed inside it.

12. In the given figure, an isosceles ΔABC, with AB = AC, circumscribes a circle. Prove that the point of contact P bisects the base BC.

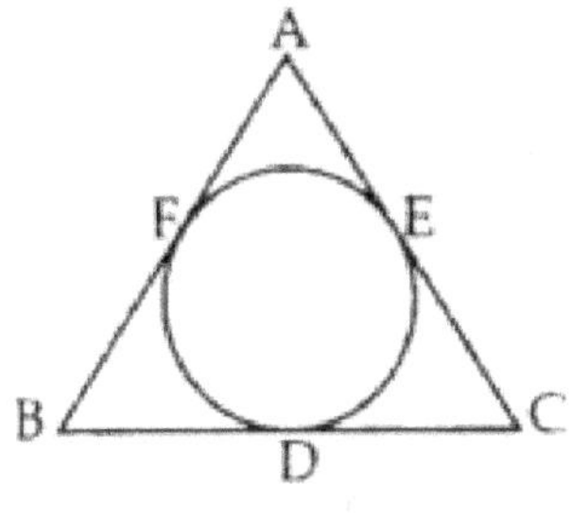

OR

In Figure, a right triangle ABC, circumscribes a circle of radius r. If AB and BC are of lengths 8 cm and 6 cm respectively, find the value of r.

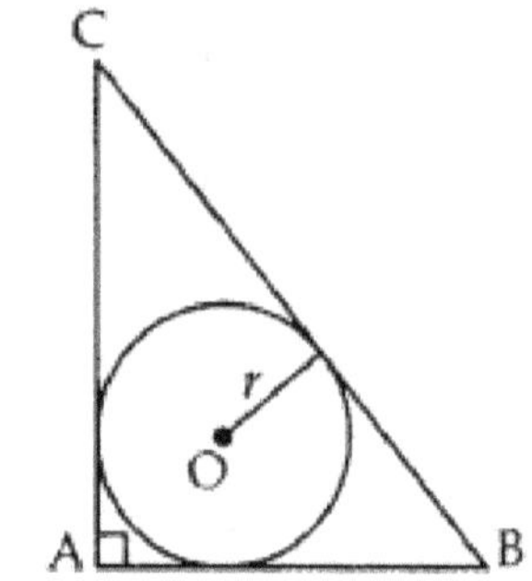

Case study–1

13. India is competitive manufacturing location due to the low cost of manpower and strong technical and engineering capabilities contributing to higher quality production runs. The production of TV sets in a factory increases uniformly by a fixed number every year. It produced 16000 sets in 6th year and 22600 in 9th year.

(i) Find the production in first year and during first three years.

(ii) Find the difference of the production during 7th year and 4th year.

Case study–2

14. An electrician has to repair an electric fault on a pole of height 5 m. He needs to reach a point 1.3 m below the top of the pole to undertake the repair work.

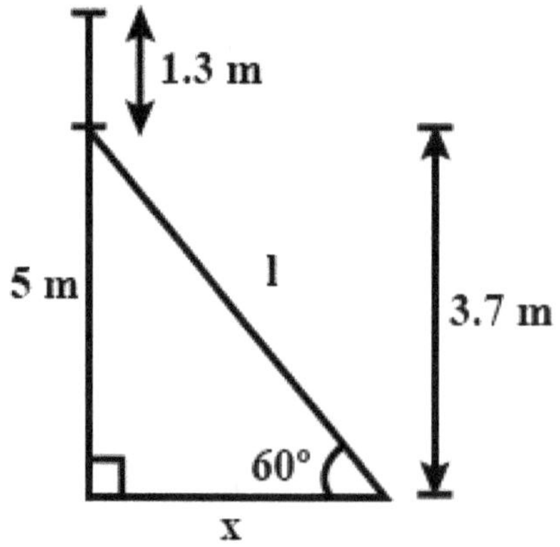

(i) What should be the length of the ladder that he should use which, when inclined at an angle of 60° to the horizontal, would enable him to reach the required position?

(ii) Also, how far the foot of the pole should she place the foot of the ladder?

SOLUTION

Section-A

1. Let a be the 1th term and d be the common difference.

$$a + 6d = 20 \quad ...(i) \quad ...[\because a_7 = 20]$$

$$\pm a \pm 12d = \pm 32 \quad ...(ii) \quad ...[\because a_{13} = 32]$$

$$-6d = -12 \quad \textbf{[1]}$$

$$\Rightarrow \quad d = \frac{12}{6} = 2 \quad ...\text{[by subtracting]}$$

Putting the value of d in (i), we get

$$a + 6(2) = 20$$

$$\Rightarrow \quad a + 12 = 20$$

$$\therefore \quad a = 8$$

$\therefore$ A.P. is a, a + d, a + 2d, a + 3d, ...

= 8; 8 + 2; 8 + 2(2); 8 + 3(2); ... **[1]**

= 8, 10, 12, 14, ...

OR

203, 210, 217, ..., 497

Here a = 203, d = 210 – 203 = 7, a_n = 497

$$\therefore \quad a + (n-1)d = a_n \quad \textbf{[1]}$$

$$203 + (n-1)7 = 497$$

$$(n-1)7 = 497 - 203 = 294$$

$$n - 1 = \frac{294}{7} = 42$$

$$\therefore \quad n = 42 + 1 = 43 \quad \textbf{[1]}$$

$\therefore$ There are 43 natural nos. between 200 and 500 which are divisible by 7.

2. $(p - 12)x^2 - 2(p - 12)x + 2 = 0$

For quadratic equation to has equal roots **[½]**

$$b^2 = 4ac$$

$$4(p-12)^2 = 4(p-12)(2)$$

$$p - 12 = 2 \quad \textbf{[1]}$$

$$p = 2 + 12$$

$$p = 14 \quad \textbf{[½]}$$

3. $\angle ACB = 90°$ ...[Angle in the semi-circle] **[1]**

In ΔABC,

$$\angle CAB + \angle ACB + \angle CBA = 180°$$

$$30 + 90° + \angle CBA = 180°$$

$$\angle CBA = 180° - 30° - 90° = 60°$$

$\angle PCA = \angle CBA$ ...[Angle in the alternate segment]

$\therefore$ $\angle PCA = 60°$ **[1]**

4. Here, r = 7 cm h = 24 cm Volume of the cone = $\frac{1}{3}\pi r^2 h$ **[½]**

$$= \frac{1}{3} \times \frac{22}{7} \times (7)^2 \times 24$$

$= 1232 \text{ cm}^3$ **[½]**

and, total surface area of the cone = $\pi r(l + r)$

$= \pi r\left(\sqrt{r^2 + h^2} + r\right)$ **[½]**

$$= \frac{22}{7} \times 7 \times \left(\sqrt{(7)^2 + (24)^2} + 7\right)$$

$$= 22 \times \left(\sqrt{49 + 576} + 7\right)$$

$$= 22 \times \left(\sqrt{625} + 7\right)$$

$$= 22 \times (25 + 7)$$

$= 22 \times 32 = 704 \text{ cm}^2$. **[½]**

5. The first 10 natural numbers are 1, 2, 3, 4, 5, 6, 7, 8, 9, 10 **[1]**

$$\text{Mean} = \frac{(1 + 2 + 3 + 4 + 5 + 6 + 7 + 8 + 9 + 10)}{10}$$

$= \frac{55}{10} = 5.5$ **[1]**

6. $\Rightarrow$ Let Ramu's present age be x years.

According to the question, **[½]**

$\Rightarrow$ $(x - 5)(x + 9) = 15$

$\Rightarrow$ $x^2 + 9x - 5x - 45 - 15 = 0$

$\Rightarrow$ $x^2 + 4x - 60 = 0$

$\Rightarrow$ $x^2 + 10x - 6x - 60 = 0$

$\Rightarrow$ $x(x + 10) - 6(x + 10) = 0$ **[1]**

$\Rightarrow$ $(x + 10)(x - 6) = 0$

$\Rightarrow \quad x + 10 = 0$ and $x - 6 = 0$

$\Rightarrow \quad x = -10$ and $x = 6$ **[½]**

$\Rightarrow$ Age cannot be negative.

$\therefore$ Ramu's present age is 6 years.

OR

The given equation is $(1 + m^2)x^2 + (2mc)x + (c^2 - a^2) = 0$

Here, $A = 1 + m^2$, $B = 2\ mc$ and $C = c^2 - a^2$

Since the given equation has equal roots, therefore $D = 0 = B^2 - AC = 0$. **[½]**

$\Rightarrow \quad (2\ mc)^2 - 4(1 + m^2)(c^2 - a^2) = 0$

$\Rightarrow \quad 4\ m^2c^2 - 4(c^2 - a^2 + m^2c^2 - m^2a^2) = 0$

$\Rightarrow \quad m^2c^2 - c^2 + a^2 - m^2c^2 + m^2a^2 = 0.$ [Dividing throughout by 4] **[1]**

$\Rightarrow \quad - c^2 + a^2(1 + m^2) = 0$ **[½]**

$\Rightarrow \quad c^2 = a(1 + m^2)$ Hence Proved

Section-B

7. $$\text{Mean} = \frac{\text{sum of observations}}{\text{no. of observations}}$$ **[½]**

$$15 = \frac{(2+6+7+a)}{4}$$

$$15 = \frac{(15+a)}{4}$$

$$15 \times 4 = 15 + a$$

$$60 - 15 = a$$

$$a = 45$$ **[1]**

Similarly, $$\text{Mean} = \frac{\text{Sum of observations}}{\text{no. of observations}}$$ **[½]**

$$50 = \frac{(18+6+1+a+b)}{5}$$

$$50 = \frac{(18+6+1+45+b)}{5}$$

$$50 = \frac{(70+b)}{5}$$ **[1]**

$$250 = 70 + b$$

$$b = 250 - 70 = 180$$

So, the value of $b = 180$.

8. **Step 1 :** Draw a circle with the help of a bangle.

Step 2 : Draw two non-parallel chords such as AB and CD [1]

Step 3 : Draw the perpendicular bisector of AB and CD

Step 4 : Take the centre as O where the perpendicular bisector intersects.

Step 5 : To draw the tangents, take a point P outside the circle.

Step 6 : Join the points O and P. [1]

Step 7 : Now draw the perpendicular bisector of the line PO and the midpoint is taken as M.

Step 8 : Take M as centre and MO as radius, draw a circle.

Step 9 : Let it intersect the circle at the points Q and R. [1]

Step 10 : Now join PQ and PR.

Therefore, PQ and PR are the required tangents.

9. [1+½]

Marks CI	No. of Students	x	f_x
0-10	10	5	50
10-20	15	15	225
20-30	25	25	625
30-40	25	35	875
40-50	10	45	450
50-60	10	55	550
60-70	5	65	325
	Sum = 100		Sum = 3200

$$\bar{x} = \frac{\Sigma fx}{\Sigma f} = \frac{3200}{100} = 32$$ [1+½]

10. [1]

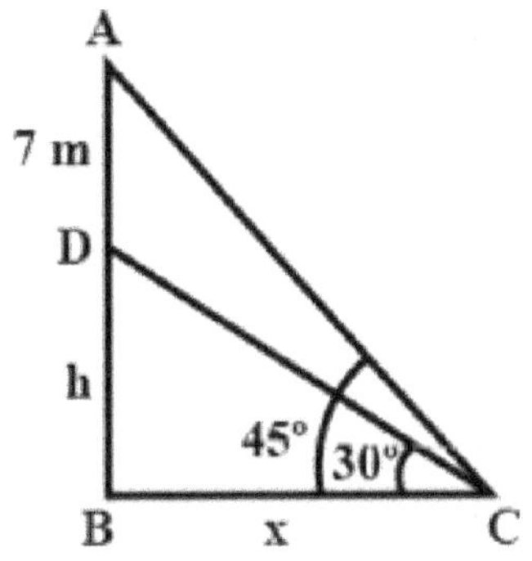

$\Rightarrow$ In ΔCBD, $\tan 30° = \frac{BD}{BC}$

$\Rightarrow$ $\frac{1}{\sqrt{3}} = \frac{h}{x}$ **[½]**

$\Rightarrow$ $x = \sqrt{3}h$ ...(1)

$\Rightarrow$ In ΔABC, $\tan 45° = \frac{AB}{BC}$ **[½]**

$\Rightarrow$ $1 = \frac{7+h}{x}$

$\Rightarrow$ $x = 7 + h$

$\Rightarrow$ $\sqrt{3}h = 7 + h$ [From (1)]

$\Rightarrow$ $\sqrt{3}h - h = 7$

$\Rightarrow$ $(\sqrt{3}h - 1)h = 7$

$\Rightarrow$ $h = \frac{7}{\sqrt{3}-1}$

$\Rightarrow$ $h = \frac{7}{\sqrt{3}-1} \times \frac{\sqrt{3}+1}{\sqrt{3}+1}$

$\therefore$ $h = \frac{7(\sqrt{3}+1)}{3-1} = \frac{7(1.73+1)}{2} = 9.55$ m **[1]**

$\therefore$ Height of the tower is 9.55 m.

OR

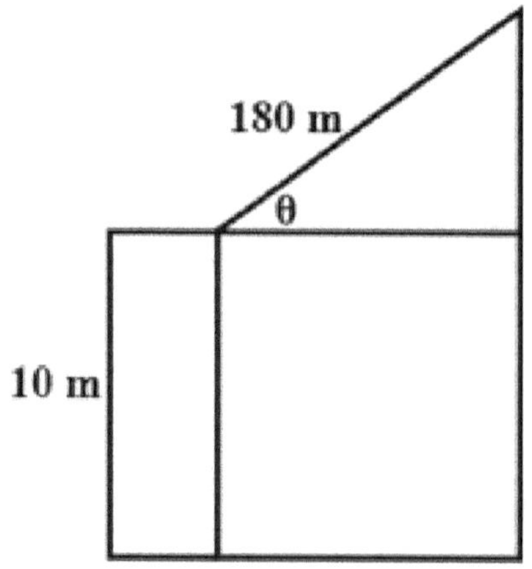

[1]

$$\tan \theta = \frac{4}{3}$$ **[½]**

Hence $\sin \theta = \frac{4}{5}$ and $\cos \theta = \frac{3}{5}$

Hence the perpendicular height of the kite from teh rooftop of the building is

$$= 180 \sin \theta$$

$$= 180.\frac{4}{5}$$

$$= 36(4) = 144 \text{ m}$$ **[½]**

Hence the height of the kite from the ground will be

= Height of the building + height of thekite from the rooftop of the building.

= 144 + 10

= 154 m **[1]**

Section-C

11. r = 7 cm, h = 50 × 0.5 = 25 cm **[½]**

Total Surface Area $= 2\pi r(r + h)$ **[½]**

$$= 2 \times \frac{22}{7} \times 7 \times (7 + 25)$$

$$= 1408 \text{ cm}^2$$ **[1]**

Volume of the box = 25 × 25 × 25

$$= 15625 \text{ cm}^3$$ **[1]**

Volume of the solid formed $= \pi r^2 h$

$$= \frac{22}{7} \times 7 \times 7 \times 25 = 3850 \text{ cm}^3$$ **[1]**

Space left $= 15625 - 3850 = 11775 \text{ cm}^3$

12. Given : The in circle of ΔABC touches the sides BC, CA and AB at D, E and F respectively.

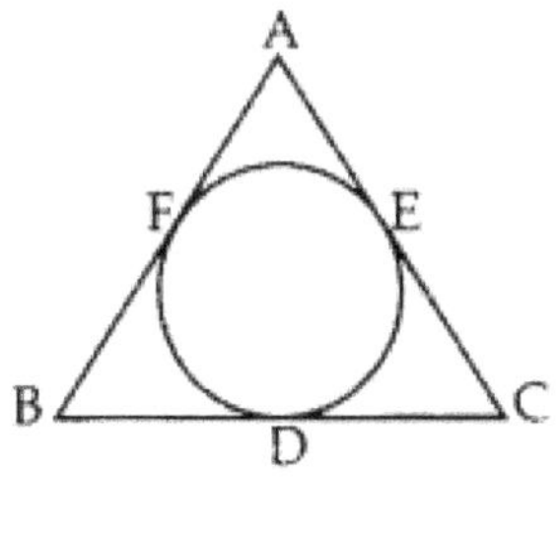

AB = AC

To prove: BD = CD

Proof : Since the lengths of tangents drawn from an external point to a circle are equal **[1]**

∴ AF = AE ...(i)

BF = BD ...(ii)

CD = CE ...(iii) **[1]**

Adding (i), (ii) and (iii), we get

AF + BF + CD = AE + BD + CE

⇒ AB + CD = AC + BD **[1]**

But AB = AC ...[Given]

∴ CD = BD **[1]**

OR

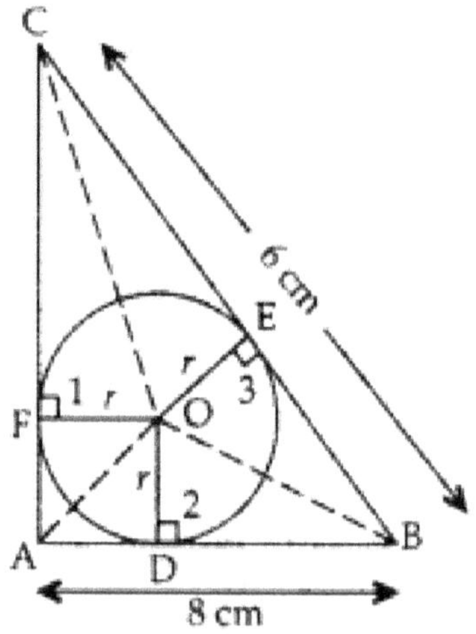

[2]

Const. : Join AO, OB, CO

Proof : area of ΔABC

$$= \frac{1}{2} \times AB \times AC$$

$$= \frac{1}{2} \times 6 \times 8$$

= 24 sq. cm ...(i)

$$\text{Again ar } \Delta ABC = ar(\Delta AOB) + ar(\Delta BOC) + ar(\Delta AOC)$$

$$= \frac{1}{2} \times r \times AB + \frac{1}{2} \times r \times BC + \frac{1}{2} \times r \times AC$$

...[$\because$ OD = OE = OF = r]

$$= \frac{1}{2}r(AB + BC + AC)$$

$$= \frac{1}{2}r[6 + 10 + 8]$$

$$= \frac{1}{2}r \times 24 = 12r \text{ sq. cm} \quad \text{...(ii)}$$

From (i) and (ii), we get 12r = 24 **[2]**

$\therefore$ r = 2 cm

13. (i) First year – Rs. 5000 **[1]**

First three years – Rs. (5000 + 7200 + 9400) = Rs. 21600 **[1]**

(ii) Difference = Rs. (18200 – 11600) = Rs. 6600 **[2]**

14. $\sin 60° = \frac{3.7}{1}$ **[1]**

$$\frac{\sqrt{3}}{2} = \frac{3.7}{1}$$

$1 = 4.277$ m **[1]**

$$\tan 60° = \frac{3.7}{x}$$

$$x = 2.138$$

$x \approx 2.14$ m **[2]**

Length of ladder = 4.27 m

Distance = 2.14 m

CBSE

Sample Question Paper 4

TERM II

CLASS X

MATHEMATICS- STANDARD

Time Allowed: 2 Hours *Maximum Marks: 40*

General Instructions

1. *The question paper consists of 14 questions divided into 3 sections A, B, C.*
2. *All questions are compulsory.*
3. *Section A comprises of 6 questions of 2 marks each. Internal choice has been provided in two questions.*
4. *Section B comprises of 4 questions of 3 marks each. Internal choice has been provided in one question.*
5. *Section C comprises of 4 questions of 4 marks each. An internal choice has been provided in one question. It contains two case study based questions.*

Section-A

6 × 2 = 12

1. Find the middle term of the A.P. 213, 205, 197, ... 37.

OR

How many terms of the A.P. 27, 24, 21, ... should be taken so that their sum is zero?

2. In the given, determine whether the given quadratic equation has real roots and if so, find the roots.

$$2x^2 + 5\sqrt{3}x + 6 = 0$$

3. In the given figure, PA and PB are tangents to the circle with centre O such that ∠APB = 50°. Write the measure of ∠OAB.

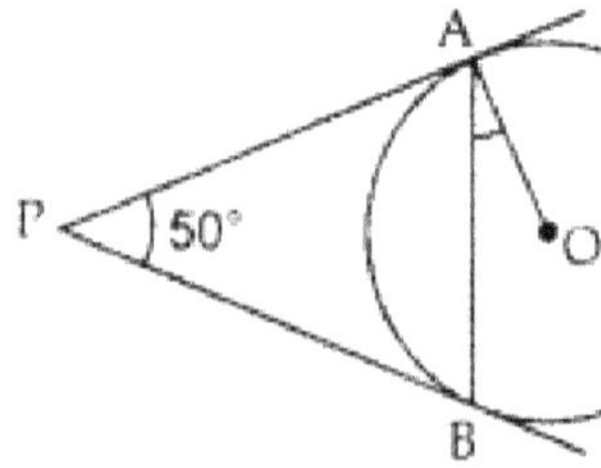

4. The curved surface area of a cone is 12320 cm^2. If the radius of its base is 56 cm, find its height.

5. Find the value of y from the following observations if these are already arranged in ascending order. The Median is 63.

20, 24, 42, y, y + 2, 73, 75, 80, 99

6. One side of a reactangle exceeds its other side by 2 cm. If its area is 195 cm^2, determine the sides of the reactangle.

OR

Solve for x :

$$\left(\frac{2x-1}{x+3}\right) - 3\left(\frac{x+3}{2x-1}\right) = 5;\ x \neq -3, \frac{1}{2}$$

Section-B

4 × 3 = 12

7. A student noted the number of cars passing through a spot on a road for 100 periods each of 3 minutes and summarised it in the table given below. Find the mode of the data:

Number of cars	Frequency
0-10	7
10-20	14
20-30	13
30-40	12
40-50	20
50-60	11
60-70	15
70-80	8

8. Draw two concentric circles of radii 3 cm and 5 cm. Taking a point on the outer circle, construct the pair of tangents to the other.

9. If mean of following data is 21.5, then find K.

Class	0-10	10-20	20-30	30-40	40-50
Frequency	6	4	3	K	2

10. An airplane flying horizontally at a height of $2500\sqrt{3}$ above that ground, is observed to be at an angle of elevation 60° from the ground. After a flight of 25 sec the angle of elevation is 30°. Find the speed of the plane in m/sec.

OR

A balloon is connected to a meteorological ground station by a cable of length 215 m inclined at 60° to the horizontal. Determine the height of the balloon from the ground. Assume that there is no slack in the cable.

Section-C

4 × 4 = 16

11. A vessel is in the form of a hemispherical bowl mounted by a hollow cylinder. The diameter is 14 cm and the height of the vessel is 13 cm. Find the capacity of the vessel.

12. In the given figure, a circle inscribed in ΔABC touches its sides AB, BC and AC at points D, E & F K respectively. If AB = 12 cm, BC = 8 cm and AC = 10 cm, then find the lengths of AD, BE and CF.

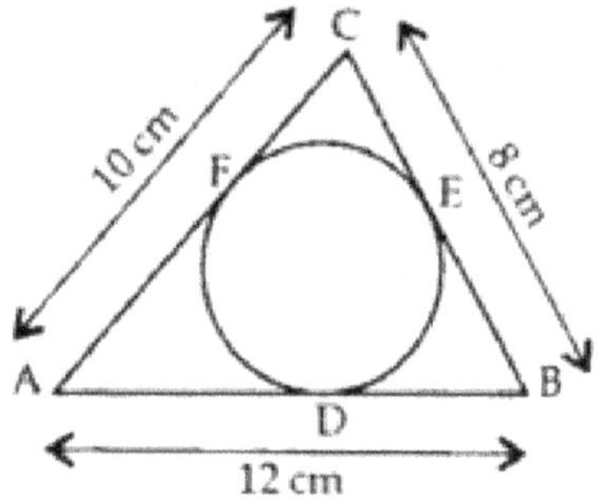

OR

In the figure, a ΔABC is drawn to circumscribe a circle of radius 3 cm, such that the segments BD and DC are respectively 6 cm, 9 cm. If the area of ΔABC is 54 cm^2, then find the lengths of sides AB and AC.

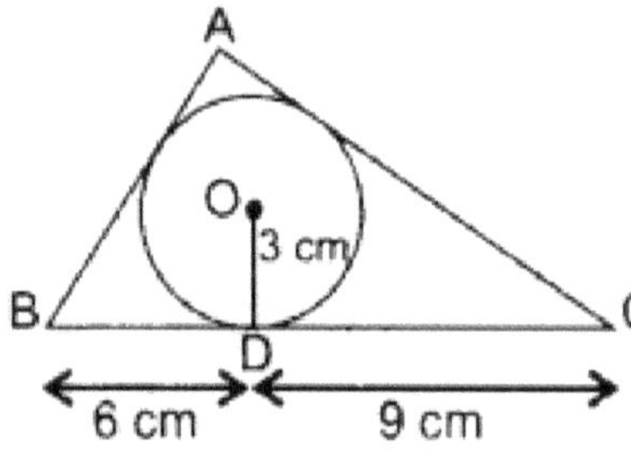

Case study–1

13. Amit was playing a number card game. In the game, some number cards (having both +ve or –ve numbers) are arranged in a row such that they are following an arithmetic progression. On his first turn, Amit picks up 6th and 14th card and finds their sum to be –76. On the second turn he picks up 8th and 16th card and finds their sum to be –96.

(i) What is the difference between the numbers on any two consecutive cards?

(ii) Find the sum of numbers on the first 15 cards.

Case study–2

14. Two hoardings are put on two poles of equal heights standing on either side of the road. From a point between them on the road the angle of elevation of the top of poles are 60° and 30° respectively. Height of the each pole is 20 m.

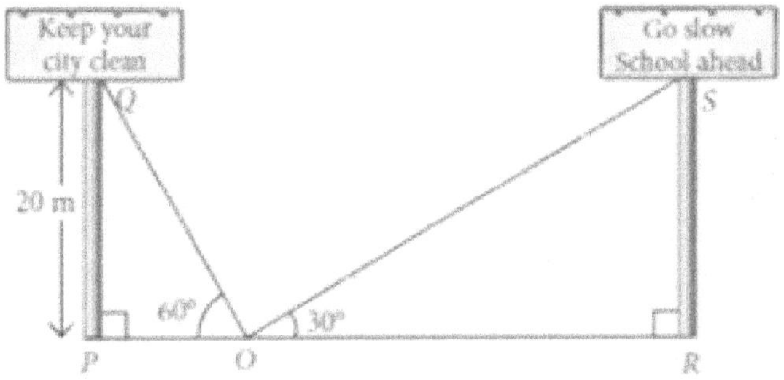

(i) Find the length of the PO and RO.

(ii) If the angle of elevation made by pole PQ is 45°, then the length of the PO.

SOLUTION

Section-A

1. A.P. : 213, 205, 197, ... 37.

Let a and d be the first term and common difference of A.P. respectively,

Here a = 213, d = –8, a_n = 37, where n is the number of terms.

$$a_n = a + (n - 1)d$$ **[1]**

$$\therefore \quad 37 = 213 + (n - 1)(-8)$$

$$\frac{-176}{-8} = n - 1$$

$$\Rightarrow \quad n = 23$$

$$\therefore \quad \text{Middle term} = \left(\frac{n+1}{2}\right)^{th}$$

$$= \left(\frac{23+1}{2}\right)$$ **[1]**

$$= 12^{th} \text{ term}$$

$$\therefore \quad a_{12} = a + 11(d) = 213 + 11(-8) = 125$$

OR

Here, 1st term, a = 27

Common difference, d = 24 – 27 = –3

Given : $S_n = 0$

$$\Rightarrow \quad \frac{n}{2}[2a + (n - 1)d] = 0$$ **[1]**

$$\Rightarrow \quad \frac{n}{2}[2(27) + (n - 1)(-3)] = 0$$

$$\Rightarrow \quad n(54 - 3n + 3) = 0$$

$$\Rightarrow \quad n(57 - 3n) = 0$$

$$\Rightarrow \quad n = 0$$

$$\text{or} \quad (57 - 3n) = 0$$

$$\Rightarrow \quad -3n = -57$$ **[1]**

$$\Rightarrow \quad n = 19$$

Since n, i.e., number of terms cannot be zero.

$\therefore$ Number of terms = 19

2. The given equationis $2x^2 + 5\sqrt{3}x + 6 = 0$

Here $a = 2$, $b = 5\sqrt{3}$, $c = 6$ **[1]**

$\therefore\ D = b^2 - 4ac = (75) - 4 \times 2 \times 6 = 27 > 0$

So, the given equation has real roots givenby

$$\alpha = \frac{-b+\sqrt{D}}{2a} = \frac{-5\sqrt{3}+\sqrt{27}}{2\times 2} = \frac{-\sqrt{3}}{2}$$

$$\beta = \frac{-b-\sqrt{D}}{2a} = \frac{-5\sqrt{3}-\sqrt{27}}{2\times 2} = -2\sqrt{3}$$ **[1]**

3. PA = PB ...[∵ Tangetns drawn from external point are equal]

$\angle OAP = \angle OBP = 90°$

$\angle OAB = \angle OBA$ ...[Angles opposite equal sides]

$\angle OAP + \angle AOB + \angle OBP + \angle APB = 360°$ ...[Quadratic rule]

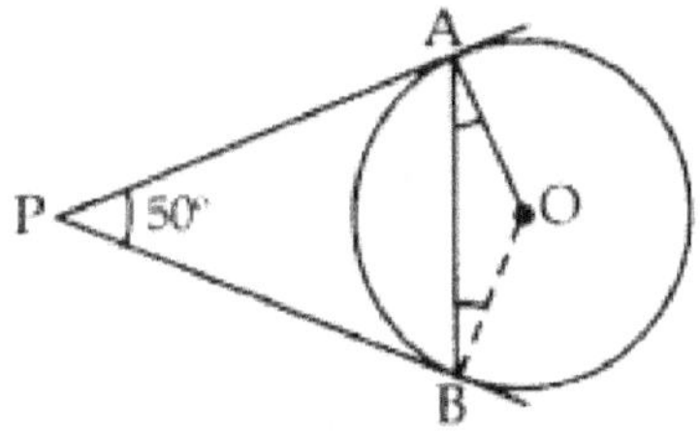

$90° + \angle AOB + 90° + 50° = 360°$ **[1]**

$\angle AOB = 360° - 230° = 130°$

$\angle AOB + \angle OAB + \angle OBA = 180°$ ...[Δ rule]

$130° + 2\angle OAB = 180°$ ...[From (i)]

$2\angle OAB = 50°$

$\Rightarrow\ \angle OAB = 25°$ **[1]**

4. **Given :** radius of the base of the cone = 56 cm

We know that curve d surface area of a cone = πrl. **[½]**

Given that curved surface area of a cone = 12320. **[½]**

$$\pi rl = 12320$$

$$\frac{22}{7} \times 56 \times 1 = 12320$$

$$22 \times 8 \times 1 = 12320$$

$$176 \times 1 = 12320$$

$$1 = \frac{12320}{176} = 70.$$ **[1]**

5. As the number of observations made is odd, so the median will be the middle term, i.e. y + 2.

Therefore, $y + 2 = 63$

$y = 63 - 2 = 61$ **[1]**

We know that height of the cone,

$$h = \sqrt{l^2 - r^2}$$

$$= \sqrt{70^2 - 56^2}$$

$$= \sqrt{4900 - 3136}$$

$$= \sqrt{1764}$$

$$= 42$$ **[1]**

Therefore the height of the cone = 42 m.

6. Let one of the side be x.

Therefore, Other side = x + 2

Area of rectangle = length × breadth **[1]**

$\Rightarrow x(x + 2) = 195$

$\Rightarrow x^2 + 2x = 195$

$\Rightarrow x^2 + 2x - 195 = 0$

$\Rightarrow x^2 + 15x - 13x - 195 = 0$

$\Rightarrow x(x + 15) - 13(x + 15) = 0$

$\Rightarrow (x + 15)(x - 13) = 0$

So, One of the side is 13

And other side = 13 + 2 = 15. **[1]**

OR

$$2\left(\frac{2x-1}{x+3}\right) - 3\left(\frac{x+3}{2x-1}\right) = 5$$

$\Rightarrow \left(\frac{4x-2}{x+3}\right) - 3\left(\frac{3x+9}{2x-1}\right) = 5$ **[1]**

$\Rightarrow (4x - 2)(2x - 1) - (3x + 9)(x + 3) = 5(x + 3)(2x - 1)$

$\Rightarrow (8x^2 - 4x - 4x + 2) - (3x^2 + 9x + 9x + 27) = 5(2x^2 - x + 6x - 3)$

$\Rightarrow 8x^2 - 8x + 2 - 3x^2 - 18x - 27 = 10x^2 + 25x - 15$

$\Rightarrow 5x^2 - 26x - 25 = 10x^2 + 25x - 15$

$\Rightarrow 5x^2 + 51x + 10 = 0$

$\Rightarrow 5x^2 + 50x + x + 10 = 0$

$\Rightarrow \quad 5x(x + 10) + 1(x + 10) = 0$

$\Rightarrow \quad (5x + 1)(x + 10) = 0$

$\Rightarrow \quad 5x + 1 = 0 \text{ or } x + 10 = 0$

$\Rightarrow \quad x = \frac{-1}{5} \text{ or } x = -10$ **[1]**

Section-B

7. From the given data:

Modal class = 40 – 50, l = 40,

class width (h) = 10, $f_m = 20$, $f_1 = 12$ and $f_2 = 11$

$$\text{Mode} = l + \left(\frac{f_m - f_1}{2f_m - f_1 - f_2}\right) \times h$$ **[1+½]**

Substitute the values

$$\text{Mode} = 40 + \left(\frac{20 - 12}{40 - 12 - 11}\right) \times 10$$

$$\text{Mode} = 40 + \left(\frac{80}{17}\right)$$

$$= 40 + 4.7 = 44.7$$ **[1+½]**

Thus, the mode of the given data is 44.7 cars

8. **Step 1 :** Draw a circle with centre O and radius 3 cm.

Step 2 : Draw another circle with centre O and radius 5 cm. **[1]**

Step 3 : Take a point P on the circumference of a larger circle and join OP.

Step 4 : Draw another circle such that it intersects the smallest circle at A and B. **[1]**

Step 5 : Join A to P and B to P.

9. **[1]**

Class	Frequency (f_1)	Mid-value (x_i)	$f_i x_i$
0-10	6	5	30
10-20	4	15	60
20-30	3	25	75
30-40	K	35	35K
50-60	2	45	90
	$\Sigma f_i = 15 + K$		$\Sigma f_i x_i = 255 + 35K$

$\because$ $\text{Arithmetic mean} = \dfrac{\Sigma f_i x_i}{\Sigma f_i}$

$$21.5 = \frac{255 + 35K}{15 + K} \quad \textbf{[1]}$$

$\Rightarrow$ $322.5 + 21.5 = 255 + 35K$

$\Rightarrow$ $322.5 - 255 = 35K - 21.5K$

$\Rightarrow$ $13.5K = 67.5$

$$K = \frac{67.5}{13.5} = 5 \quad \textbf{[1]}$$

$\therefore$ $K = 5$

10. **[1]**

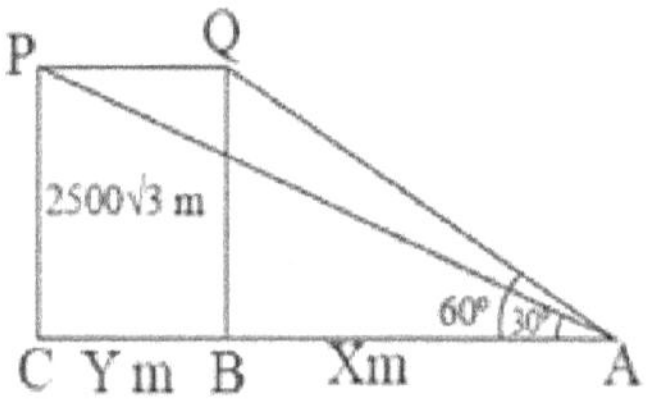

$$QB = 2500\sqrt{3} \text{ m}$$

Let the speed of the aeroplane be x m/sec.

In ΔABQ, $\tan 60° = \dfrac{QB}{AB}$

$$\sqrt{3} = \frac{2500\sqrt{3}}{x}$$

$$x = 2500 \text{ m} \quad \textbf{[1]}$$

In ΔAPC, $\tan 30° = \dfrac{2500\sqrt{3}}{x + y}$

$$\frac{1}{\sqrt{3}} = \frac{2500\sqrt{3}}{x + y}$$

$$x + y = 3 \times 2500$$

$$2500 + y = 7500$$

$$y = 5000 \text{ m} \quad \textbf{[1]}$$

So, the speed of the plane will be,

$$\frac{5000}{25} = 200 \text{ m/sec}$$

OR

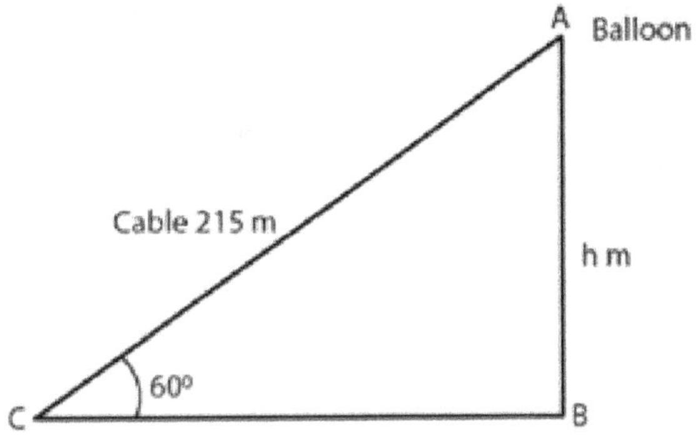

[1]

Let the height of the balloon from the ground = hm

Given, the length of the cable = 215 m and the inclination of the cable is 60°.

In ΔABC

$$\sin 60° = \frac{AB}{AC}$$

$$\frac{\sqrt{3}}{2} = \frac{h}{215}$$

$$h = \frac{215\sqrt{3}}{2} = 185.9$$ **[2]**

Hence, the height of the balloon from the ground is 186 m (approx).

Section-C

11. **[1]**

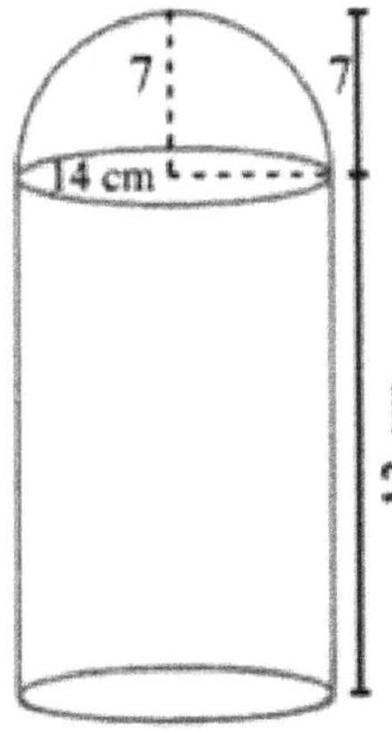

$$\text{Diameter} = 14 \text{ cm}$$

$$\text{Radius} = 7 \text{ cm}$$

$$\text{Total height} = 13 \text{ cm}$$

Height of the cylindrical part = 13 – 7 = 6 cm **[1]**

$\therefore$ Capacity of the vessel = Capacity of the cylinder + Capacity of the hemisphere.

$$\text{Volume of the cylinder} = \pi r^2 h = \frac{22}{7} \times 7 \times 7 \times 6 = 924$$

$$\text{Volume of the hemisphere} = \frac{2}{3}\pi r^3$$

$$= \frac{2}{3} \times \frac{22}{7} \times 7 \times 7 \times 7$$

$$= \frac{2156}{3} = 718.67$$ **[2]**

$\therefore$ The total volume = 924 + 718.67

The capacity of the vessel = 1672.67 cm^3.

12 . **[1]**

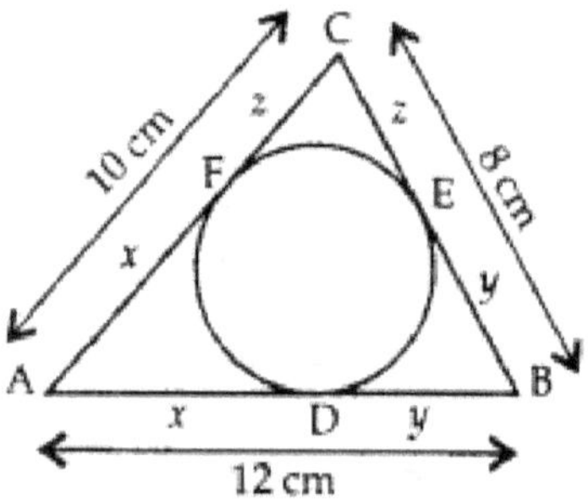

Let AD = AF = x

BD = BE = y ...[Two tangents drawn from and an external point are equal]

CE = CF = z

AB = 12 cm ...[Given]

$\therefore$ x + y = 12 cm ...(i)

Similarly,

y + z = 8 cm ...(ii)

and x + z = 10 cm ...(iii)

By adding (i), (ii) and (iii)

2(x + y + z) = 30

x + y + z = 15 ...[$\because$ x + y = 12]

z = 15 – 12 = 3 **[1]**

Putting the value of z in (ii) and (iii),

$$y + 3 = 8$$

$$y = 8 - 3 = 5$$

$$x + 3 = 10$$ **[2]**

$$x = 10 - 3 = 7$$

$\therefore$ AD = 7 cm, BE = 5 cm, CF = 3 cm

OR

Given : OD = 3 cm; OE = 3 cm; OF = 3 cm ar (ΔABC) = 54 cm^2

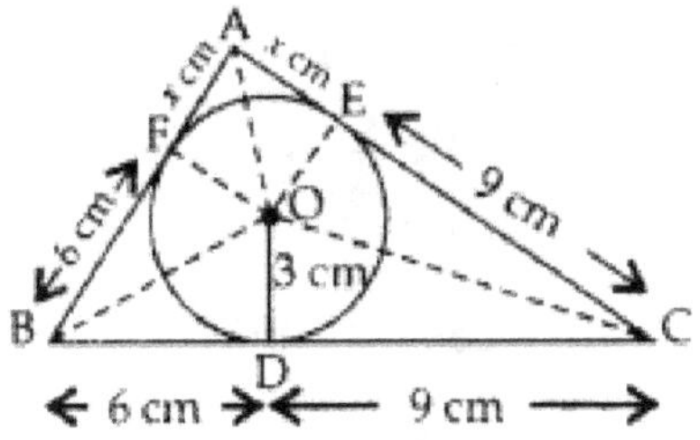

[1]

Joint : OA, OF, OE, OB and OC **[1]**

Let AF = AE = x

BD = BF = 6 cm

CD = CE = 9 cm

$\therefore$ AB = AF + BF = x + 6 ...(i)

AC = AE + CE = x + 9 ...(ii)

BC = DB + CD = 6 + 9 = 15 cm ...(iii)

In ΔABC,

Area of ΔABC = 54 cm^2 ...[Given]

ar(ΔABC) = ar(ΔBOC) + ar(ΔAOC) + ar(ΔAOB)

$\Rightarrow$ $\frac{1}{2} \times BC \times OD + \frac{1}{2} \times AC \times OD + \frac{1}{2} \times AB \times OD$

...[Area of $\Delta = \frac{1}{2} \times$ Base $\times$ Height]

$\Rightarrow$ $\frac{1}{2}[AB + AC + BC] \times OD = 54$

$\Rightarrow$ $\frac{1}{2}[x + 6 + x + 9 + 15] \times 3 = 54$ ...[From (i), (ii) and (iii)]

$\Rightarrow \quad \frac{1}{2}[2x + 30] \times 3 = 54$

$\Rightarrow \quad 6x + 90 = 108$

$\Rightarrow \quad 6x = 18$

$\Rightarrow \quad x = 3$

$\Rightarrow \quad AB = x + 6 = 3 + 6 = 9$ cm **[2]**

$\Rightarrow \quad AC = x + 9 = 3 + 9 = 12$ cm

$\therefore \quad AB = 9$ cm, $AC = 12$ cm

13. Let the numbers on the cards be a, a + d, a = 2d, ...

According to question we have $(a + 5d) + (a + 13d) = -76$

$\Rightarrow \quad 2a + 18d = -76$

$\Rightarrow \quad a + 9d = -38$ ...(1)

and $\quad (a + 7d) + (a + 15d) = -96$

$\Rightarrow \quad 2a + 22d = -96$

$\Rightarrow \quad a + 11d = -48$ ...(2)

From (1) and (2), we get

$2d = -10$

$\Rightarrow \quad d = -5$

From (1), $\quad a + 9(-5) = -38 \Rightarrow a = 7$

(i) The difference between the numbers on any two consecutive cards

= common difference of the A.P. = – 5 **[2]**

(ii) $S_{15} = \frac{15}{2}[2(7) + 14(-5)] = -420$ **[2]**

14. (i) In ΔOPQ, we have

$$\tan 60° = \frac{PQ}{PO}$$

$$\Rightarrow \quad \sqrt{3} = \frac{20}{PO}$$

$$\Rightarrow \quad PO = \frac{20}{\sqrt{3}} \text{ m}$$ **[2]**

Also, In ΔORS, we have

$$\tan 30° = \frac{RS}{OR}$$

$$\Rightarrow \qquad \frac{1}{\sqrt{3}} = \frac{20}{OR}$$

$$\Rightarrow \qquad OR = 20\sqrt{3}\text{m}$$

(ii) In ΔIPQ, if ∠POQ = 45°, then

$$\tan 45° = \frac{PQ}{PO}$$

$$\Rightarrow \qquad 1 = \frac{20}{PO}$$

$$\Rightarrow \qquad PO = 20 \text{ m}$$

$$= 20\left(\frac{4}{\sqrt{3}}\right)\text{m}$$

$$= \frac{80}{\sqrt{3}}\text{m} = 46.24 \text{ m}$$

[2]

CBSE

Sample Question Paper 5

TERM II

CLASS X

MATHEMATICS- STANDARD

Time Allowed: 2 Hours *Maximum Marks: 40*

General Instructions

1. *The question paper consists of 14 questions divided into 3 sections A, B, C.*
2. *All questions are compulsory.*
3. *Section A comprises of 6 questions of 2 marks each. Internal choice has been provided in two questions.*
4. *Section B comprises of 4 questions of 3 marks each. Internal choice has been provided in one question.*
5. *Section C comprises of 4 questions of 4 marks each. An internal choice has been provided in one question. It contains two case study based questions.*

Section-A

6 × 2 = 12

1. Find the sum of the first 25 terms of an A.P. whose nth term is given by $t_n = 2 - 3n$.

OR

The first and the last terms of an AP are 5 and 45 respectively. If the sum of all its terms is 400, find its common difference.

2. In the given, determine whether the given quadratic equation has real roots and if so, find the roots.

$$\sqrt{2}x^2 + 7x + 5\sqrt{2} = 0$$

3. In the given figure, PQ is a chord of a circle with centre O and PT is a tangent. If $\angle QPT = 60°$, find $\angle PRQ$.

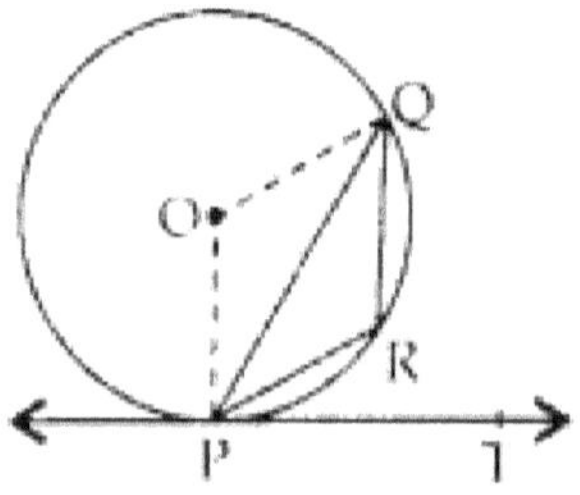

4. Find the volume and curved surface area of a sphere-shaped metallic shotput having a diameter of 8.4 cm.

$$\left(\text{Take } \pi = \frac{22}{7}\right)$$

5. The following table shows the age distribution of COVID cases admitted during a day in the hospital:

Age (in years)	5-15	15-25	25-35	35-45	45-55	55-65
No. of cases	8	16	10	42	24	12

Find the mode and upper limit of the modal class.

6. A passenger train takes 2 hours less for a journey of 300 km if its speed is increased by 5km/hr from its usual speed. Find its usual speed of the train.

OR

Solve for x : $+5x - (a^2 + a - 6) = 0$

Section-B

4 × 3 = 12

7. The following data gives the distribution of the total monthly household expenditure of 200 families of a village. Find the modal monthly expenditure of the families.

Expenditure	Number of families
1000-1500	24
1500-2000	40
2000-2500	33
2500-3000	28
3000-3500	30
3500-4000	22
4000-4500	16
4500-5000	7

8. Draw a line segment AB of length 7 cm. Taking A as the centre, draw a circle of radius 3 cm and taking B as centre, draw another circle of radius 2 cm. Construct tangents to each circle from the centre of the other circle.

9. Find the missing frequencies f_1 and f_2 in the following frequency distribution if it is known that the mean of the distribution is 50 and the total frequency is 150:

x	10	30	50	70	90
f	17	f_1	32	f_2	19

10. The angles of elevation of the top of a tower from two points at a distance of 4 m and 9 m from the base of the tower and in the same straight line with it are complementary. Prove that the height of the tower is 6 m.

OR

The shadow of a tower standing on a level ground is found to be 40 m longer when the Sun's altitude is 30° than when it is 60°. Find the height of the tower.

Section-C

4 × 4 = 16

11. The barrel of a fountain-pen, cylindrical in shape, is 7 cm long and 5 mm in diameter. A full barrel of ink in the pen will be used up on writing 330 words on an average. How many words would use up a bottle of ink containing one fifth of a litre?

12. In the figure, a circle is inscribed in a ΔABC, such that it touches the sides AB, BC and CA at points D, E and F respectively. If the lengths of sides AB, BC, and CA are 12 cm, 8 cm and 10 cm respectively, find the lengths of AD, BE and CF.

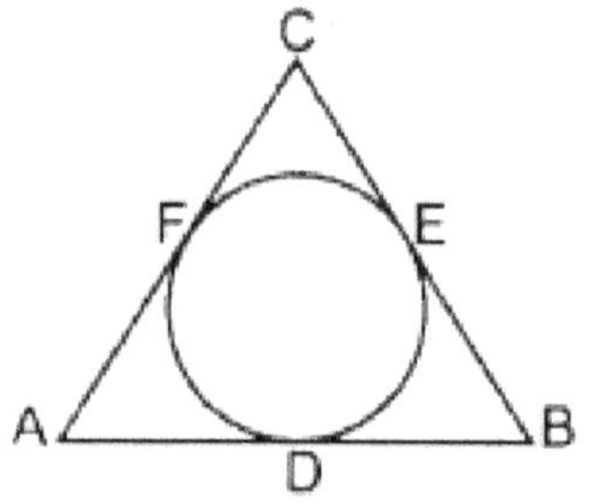

OR

From a point T outside a circle of centre O, tangents TP and TQ aredrawn to the circle. Prove that OT is the right bisector of line segment PQ.

Case study–1

13. Do you know, we can find A.P. in many situations in our day-today life. One such example is a tisse paper roll, in which the first term is the diameter of the core of the roll and twice the thickness of the paper is the common difference. If the sum of first n rolls of tissue on a roll is $S_n = 0.1 n^2 + 7.9n$, then answer the following questions.

(i) What is the diameter of roll when one tissue sheet is rolled over it?

(ii) Find the thickness of each tissue sheet.

Case study–2

14. Flying Pigeon

A boy 4 m tall spots a pigeon sitting on the top of a pole of height 54 m from the ground. The angle of elevation of the pigeon from the eyes of boy at any instant is 60°. The pigeon flies away horizontally in such a way that it remained at a constant height from the ground. After 8 seconds, the angle of elevation of the pigeon from the same point is 45°.

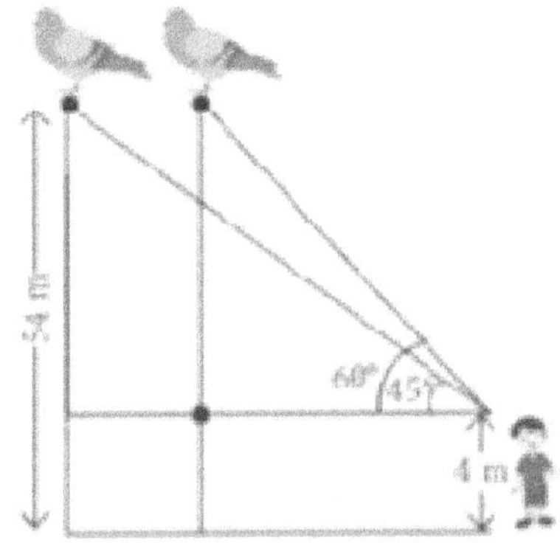

(i) Find the distance of first position of the pigeon from the eyes of the boy.

(ii) How much distance the pigeon covers in 8 seconds? Also find its speed.

SOLUTION

Section-A

1. Given : $t_n = 2 - 3n$

When $n = 1$, $t_1 = 2 - 3(1) = -1$ ...(i)

When $n = 25$, $t_{25} = 2 - 3(25) = -73$ ...(ii) **[1]**

As $S_n = \frac{n}{2}[t_1 + t_n]$, $n = 25$

$$S_{25} = \frac{25}{2}[-1 + (-73)] \quad \text{...[From (i) and (ii)]}$$

$$= \frac{25 \times (-74)}{2}$$

$$= 25 \times (-37) = -925$$ **[1]**

OR

Here, $a_n = 45$, $S_n = 400$, $a = 5$, $n = ?$, $d = ?$

Now, $\frac{n}{2}[a_1 + a_n] = S_n$

$$\frac{n}{2}(5 + 45) = 400$$

$$\frac{n}{2}[50] = 400$$

$$n = \frac{400}{25} = 16$$ ...(i) **[1]**

$$a + (n - 1)d = a_n$$

$$5 + (n - 1)d = 45$$

$$(n - 1)d = 40$$

$$(16 - 1)d = 40 \quad \text{...[From (i)]}$$

$\therefore$ $d = \frac{40}{15} = \frac{8}{3}$ **[1]**

2. The given quadratic equation is

$$\sqrt{2}x^2 + 7x + 5\sqrt{2} = 0$$

To determine the nature of roots, we need to find the discriminant

$$D = b^2 - 4ac = 49 - 4\left(\sqrt{2}\right)\left(5\sqrt{2}\right)$$

$$= 49 - 40 > 0$$

So, the equationhas real roots

$$\sqrt{2}x^2 + 7x + 5\sqrt{2} = 0$$ **[1]**

$$\sqrt{2}x^2 + 5x + 2x + 5\sqrt{2} = 0$$

$$\sqrt{2}x^2 + 2x + 5x + 5\sqrt{2} = 0$$

$$\sqrt{2}x(x + \sqrt{2}) + 5(x + \sqrt{2}) = 0$$

$$(x + \sqrt{2})(\sqrt{2}x + 5) = 0$$

$$x = -\sqrt{2}, -\frac{5}{\sqrt{2}}$$ **[1]**

3. PQ is the chord of the circle and PT is tangent.

$\therefore$ $\angle OPT = 90°$ ...[Tangent is I to the radius through the point of contact] **[½]**

Now $\angle QPT = 60°$ ...[Given]

$\angle OPQ = \angle OPT - \angle QPT$

$\Rightarrow$ $\angle IPQ = 90° - 60° = 30°$

In ΔOPQ, OP = OQ **[½]**

$\angle OQP = \angle OPQ = 30°$ ...[In a Δ, equal sides have equal $\angle$s opp. them]

Now, $\angle OQP + \angle OPQ + \angle POQ = 180°$

$\therefore$ $\angle POQ = 120°$ ...[$\angle POQ = 180° - (30° + 30°)$]

$\Rightarrow$ Reflex $\angle POQ = 360° - 120° = 240°$

...[We know that the angle subtended by an arc at the centre of a circle is twice the angle subtended by it at any point on the remaining part of the circle]

$\therefore$ Reflex $\angle POQ = 2\angle PRO$ **[1]**

$\Rightarrow$ $240° = 2\angle PRQ$

$\Rightarrow$ $\angle PRQ = \frac{240°}{2} = 120°$

4. Diameter = 8.4 cm

Therefore, radius = 4.2 cm

Volume of the sphere $= \frac{4}{3}\pi r^3$ **[½]**

$= \frac{4}{3} \times \frac{22}{7} \times 4.2 \times 4.2 \times 4.2$

= 310.464 cu.cm **[1]**

Now, Surface area of the sphere $= 4\pi r^2$

$= 221.76 \text{ cm}^2$ **[½]**

5. The mode of the given data is 41.4 **[1]**

The upper limit of the modal class is 45. **[1]**

6. Let the usual speed of the train is x km/h.

$$D = 300 \text{ km (Given)}$$

$$\text{Speed} = \frac{\text{Distance}}{\text{Time}}$$

$$\text{Time} = \frac{300}{x}$$

After increasing the speed of the train;

New speed is (x + 5) km/h

$$\text{Time} = \frac{300}{x+5}$$

Now, difference between the time taken by usual speed and after increasing speed of the train is two hours. Therefore,

$$\frac{300}{x} - \frac{300}{x+5} = 2$$

$$\Rightarrow \quad 300\left(\frac{1}{x} - \frac{1}{x+5}\right) = 2$$

$$\Rightarrow \quad \left(\frac{x+5-x}{x^2+5x}\right) = \frac{2}{300}$$

$$\Rightarrow \quad \frac{5}{x^2+5x} = \frac{1}{150}$$

$$\Rightarrow \quad x^2 + 5x - 750 = 0$$

$$\Rightarrow \quad x^2 + 30x - 25x - 750 = 0$$

$$\Rightarrow \quad x(x + 30) - 25(x + 30) = 0$$

$$\Rightarrow \quad (x + 30)(x - 25) = 0$$

$$\Rightarrow \quad x = 25, -30$$ **[2]**

Ignore the negative value of the speed.

Hence, the usual speed of the train is 25 km/hr.

OR

$$x^2 + 5x - (a^2 + a - 6) = 0$$

$$\therefore \quad x = \frac{-5 \pm \sqrt{5^2 - 4 \times 1 \times \left[-(a^2 + a - 6)\right]}}{2 \times 1}$$

$$= \frac{-5 \pm \sqrt{25 + 4a^2 + 4a - 24}}{2}$$

$$= \frac{-5 \pm \sqrt{4a^2 + 4a - 24}}{2}$$

$$= \frac{-5 \pm \sqrt{(2a)^2 + 2.(2a).1 + 1^2}}{2}$$

$$= \frac{-5 \pm \sqrt{(2a+1)^2}}{2}$$

$$= \frac{-5 \pm (2a+1)}{2}$$

$$= \frac{-5 + 2a + 1}{2}, \frac{-5 - 2a - 1}{2}$$

$$= \frac{2a - 4}{2}, \frac{-2a - 6}{2}$$

$= (a - 2), -(a + 3)$ **[2]**

Section-B

7. From the given data:

Modal class $= 1500 - 2000$ **[½]**

$I = 1500$

Frequencies : $f_m = 40$

$f_1 = 24$, $f_2 = 33$ and $h = 500$

Mode formula: $\text{Mode} = l + \left(\frac{f_m - f_1}{2f_m - f_1 - f_2}\right) \times h$ **[½]**

Substitute the values in the formula, we get,

$$\text{Mode} = 1500 + \left(\frac{40 - 24}{80 - 24 - 33}\right) \times 500$$

$$\text{Mode} = 1500 + \left[\frac{(16 \times 500)}{23}\right]$$

$$\text{Mode} = 1500 + \left(\frac{8000}{23}\right)$$

$$= 1500 + 347.83$$

Therefore, the modal monthly expenditure of the families = Rupees 1847.83

[2]

8. **Step 1 :** Draw a line segment AB of 7 cm.

Step 2 : Taking A and B as centres, draw two circles of 3 cm and 2 cm radius respectively. **[1]**

Step 3 : Bisect line AB. Let the midpoint of AB be C.

Step 4 : Taking C as the centre, draw a circle of radius AC that intersects the two circles at points P, Q, R and S. **[1]**

Step 5 : Join BP, BQ, AS and AR. **[1]**

9. **[1]**

x_i	f_i	$f_i x_i$
10	17	170
30	f_1	$30f_1$
50	32	1600
70	f_2	$70f_2$
90	19	1710
	$\Sigma f_i = 68 + f_1 + f_2$	$\Sigma f_i x_i = 3480 + 30f_1 + 70f_2$

$$\Sigma f_i = 150 \quad \textbf{[1]}$$

$$= 68 + f_1 + f_2 \quad (\text{Given } \Sigma f_i = 150)$$

$$\Rightarrow \quad f_1 + f_2 = 82 \quad \ldots\text{(i)}$$

$$\bar{x} = \frac{\Sigma f_i x_i}{\Sigma f_i}$$

$$\Rightarrow \quad 50 = \frac{3480 + 30f_1 + 70f_2}{150} \quad (\bar{x} = 50 \text{ and } \Sigma f_i = 150)$$

$$\Rightarrow \quad 50 = \frac{348 + 3f_1 + 7f_2}{15}$$

$$\Rightarrow \quad 750 = 348 + 3f_1 + 7f_2 \quad \textbf{[1]}$$

$$\Rightarrow \quad 3f_1 + 7f_2 = 402 \quad \ldots\text{(ii)}$$

Multiplying (i) by 3 and subtracting (ii)

$$3f_1 + 3f_2 = 246$$

$$3f_1 + 7f_2 = 402$$

$$-4f_2 = -156$$

$$\Rightarrow \quad f_2 = 39$$

$$\therefore \quad f_1 = 82 - 39 = 43 \quad \{\text{substituting } f_2 \text{ in (i)}\}$$

Hence, $f_1 = 43$ and $f_2 = 39$ **[1]**

10.

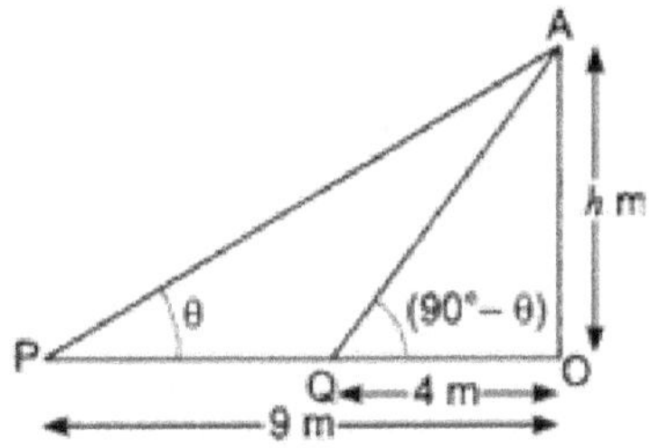

$$\tan\theta = \frac{OA}{OP} = \frac{h}{9}$$

$$\Rightarrow \qquad \tan\theta = \frac{h}{9} \qquad ...(i)$$

Again, in ΔAQO we have

$$\tan(90° - \theta) = \frac{OA}{OQ} = \frac{h}{4}$$

$$\Rightarrow \qquad \tan\theta = \frac{h}{4} \qquad ...(ii)$$

Multiplying (i) and (ii), we have

Let OA be the tower of height h metre and P, I be the two points at distance of 9 m and 4 m respectively from the base of the tower.

Now, we have OP = 9 m, OQ = 4m,

Let ∠APO = θ, ∠AQO = (90° – θ)

and OA = h metre

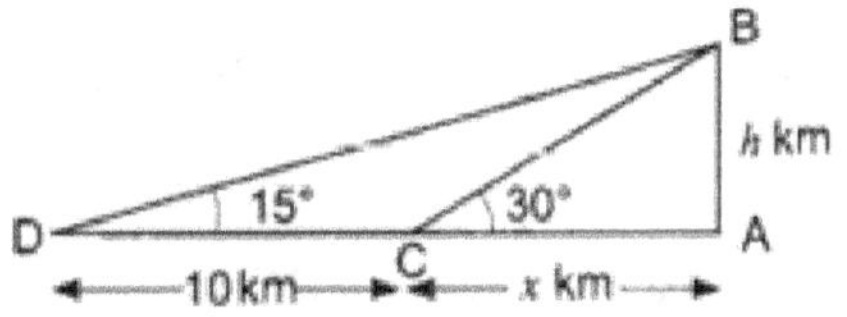

Now, in ΔPOQ, we have

$$\tan\theta \times \cot\theta = \frac{h}{9} \times \frac{h}{4}$$

$$\Rightarrow \qquad 1 = \frac{h^2}{36}$$

$$\Rightarrow \qquad h^2 = 36$$

$$h = \pm 6$$

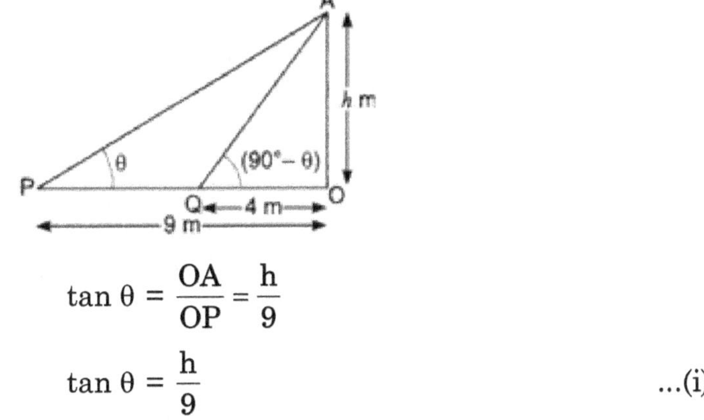

$$\tan 30° = \frac{AB}{AC}$$

$$\Rightarrow \qquad \frac{1}{\sqrt{3}} = \frac{h}{x}$$

$$\Rightarrow \qquad x = \sqrt{3}h$$

In ΔADB, we have $\qquad \tan 15° = \frac{AB}{AD}$

$$\Rightarrow \qquad 0.27 = \frac{h}{x+10}$$

$$\Rightarrow \qquad 0.27(x + 10) = h$$ **[3]**

Height cannot be negative.

Hence, the height of the tower is 6 metre.

OR

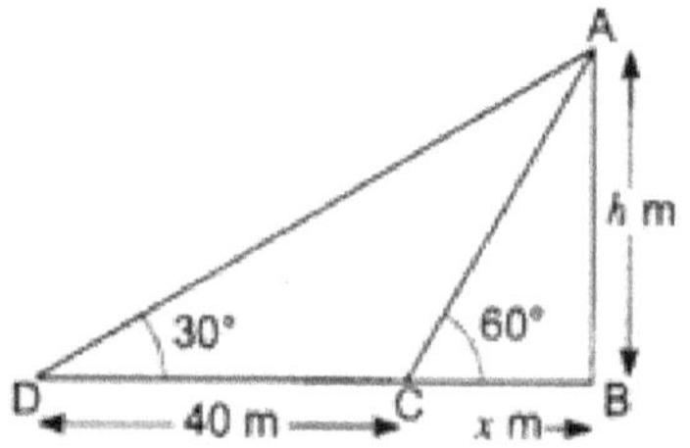

AB is the tower and BC is the length of the shadow when the Sun's altitude is 60°, i.e., the angle of elevation of the top of the tower from the tip of the shadow is 60° and DB is the length of the shadow, when the angle of elevation is 30°.

Now, let AB be h m and BC be x m.

According to the question, DB is 40 m longer than BC.

So, $\qquad BD = (40 + x)m$

Now, we have two right triangles ABC and ABD.

Now, we have two right triangles ABC and ABD.

In ΔABC, $\qquad \tan 60° = \frac{AB}{BC}$

or $\qquad \sqrt{3} = \frac{h}{x}$

$$\Rightarrow \qquad x\sqrt{3} = h \qquad ...(i)$$

In ΔABD, $\qquad \tan 30° = \frac{AB}{BD}$

i.e., $\qquad \frac{1}{\sqrt{3}} = \frac{h}{x+40} \qquad ...(ii)$

Using (i) in (ii), we get $(x\sqrt{3})\sqrt{3} = x + 40$, i.e., $3x = x + 40$

i.e., $x = 20$

So, $h = 20\sqrt{3}$ [From (i)]

Therefore, the height of the tower is $20\sqrt{3}$ m. **[3]**

Section-C

11. Volume of a barrel $= \frac{22}{7} \times 0.25 \times 0.25 \times 7 = 1.375 \text{ cm}^3$ **[1]**

Volume of ink in the bottle $= \frac{1}{5}$ litre $= \frac{1000}{5} = 200 \text{ cm}^3$ **[1]**

Therefore, total number of barrels that can be filled from the given volume of in k

$$= \frac{200}{1.375}$$ **[1]**

So, required number of words $= \frac{200}{1.375} \times 330 = 48000$ **[1]**

12. **[1]**

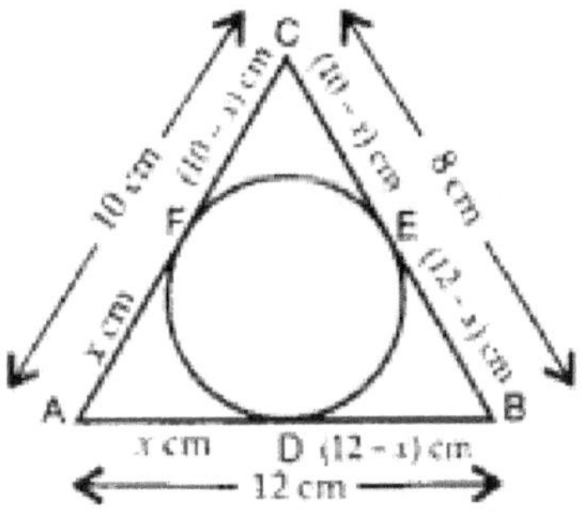

AB = 12 cm, BC = 8 cm, CA = 10 cm

As we know,

AF = AD

CF = CE

BD = BE

Let AD = AF = x cm

then, DB = AB – AD = (12 – x) cm

∴ BE = (12 – x) cm...[Tangents drawn from an external point are equal

[1]

Similarly,

CF = CE = AC – AF = (10 – x) cm

BC = 8 cm ...[Given]

$\Rightarrow$ BE + CE = 8

$\Rightarrow$ 12 – x + 10 – x = 8

$\Rightarrow$ 22 – 8 = 2x

$\Rightarrow$ 2x = 14

$\therefore$ x = 7 **[1]**

$\therefore$ AD = x = 7 cm

BE = 12 – x = 12 – 7 = 5 cm

CF = 10 – x = 10 – 7 = 3 cm **[1]**

OR

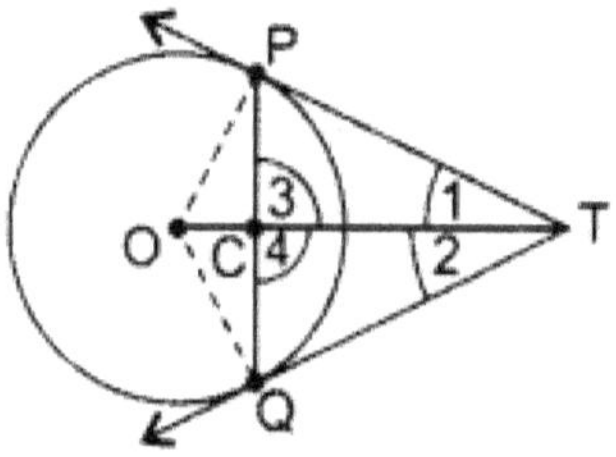

[1]

In Δs' TPC and TQC ...[Tangents drawn from an external point are equal]

TP = TQ

TC = TC ...[Common]

$\angle 1 = \angle 2$ ...[TP and TQ are equally inclined to OT]

$\therefore$ ΔTPC ≅ ΔTQC ...[SAS]

$\therefore$ PC = QC ...[CPCT] **[1]**

$\angle 3 = \angle 4$ ...(i)

$\Rightarrow$ $\angle 3 + 24 = 180°$ ...[Linear pair]

$\Rightarrow$ $\angle 3 + \angle 3 = 180°$ ...[From (i)]

$\Rightarrow$ $2\angle 3 = 180°$

$\Rightarrow$ $\angle 3 = 90°$

$\therefore$ $\angle 3 = \angle 4 = 90°$ **[1]**

$\therefore$ OT is the right bisector of PQ. **[1]**

13. (i) Required diameter = $t_2 = S_2 - S_1 = 16.2 - 8 = 8.2$ cm **[2]**

(ii) As $d = t_2 - t_1 = 8.2 - 8 = 0.2$ cm

So, thickness of tissue = $0.2 \div 2 = 0.1$ cm = 1 mm **[2]**

14.

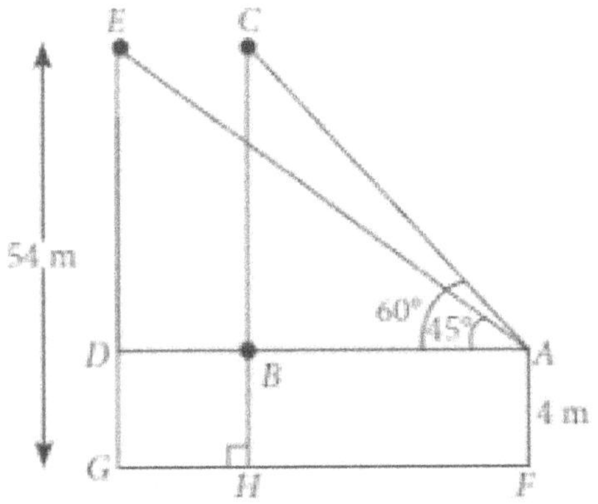

(i) Distance of first position of pigeon from the eyes of boy = AC

In ΔABC, $\sin 60° = \frac{BC}{AC}$

$\Rightarrow$ $AC = \frac{CH - BH}{\sin 60°}$ **[2]**

$$= \frac{54 - 4}{\frac{\sqrt{3}}{2}} = \frac{100}{\sqrt{3}} \text{ m}$$

(ii) In ΔAED, $\tan 45° = \frac{ED}{AD}$

$\Rightarrow$ $AD = BC = 50$ m ($\because$ ED = BC)

Now, distance between two positions of pigeon = EC

$$= BD = AD - AB$$

$$= \left(50 - \frac{50}{\sqrt{3}}\right) \text{ m}$$ **[2]**

$$= \frac{50(1.73 - 1)}{1.73} = 21.09 \text{ m}$$

$$\text{Speed of pigeon} = \frac{\text{Distance covered}}{\text{Time taken}}$$

$$= \left(\frac{21.09}{8}\right) \text{m/sec} = 2.63 \text{ m/sec}$$

Science

CBSE

Sample Question Paper 1

TERM II

Class X

Science

Time Allowed: 2 Hours **Maximum Marks: 40**

General Instructions

i. *All questions are compulsory.*

ii. *The question paper has three sections and 15 questions. All questions are compulsory.*

iii. *Section–A has 7 questions of 2 marks each; Section–B has 6 questions of 3 marks each; and Section–C has 2 case based questions of 4 marks each.*

iv. *Internal choices have been provided in some questions. A student has to attempt only one of the alternatives in such questions.*

Section – A

(7 × 2 Marks)

1. The following table shows melting and boiling points of some compounds:

Compound	Melting point (K)	Boiling point (K)
A	1074	1686
B	90	111
C	1045	1900
D	156	351

Use the table to answer the following questions:

(a) Identify the two covalent compounds.

(b) Are these compounds good conductors of electricity? Give reason.

2. Consider the following diagram and answer the questions:

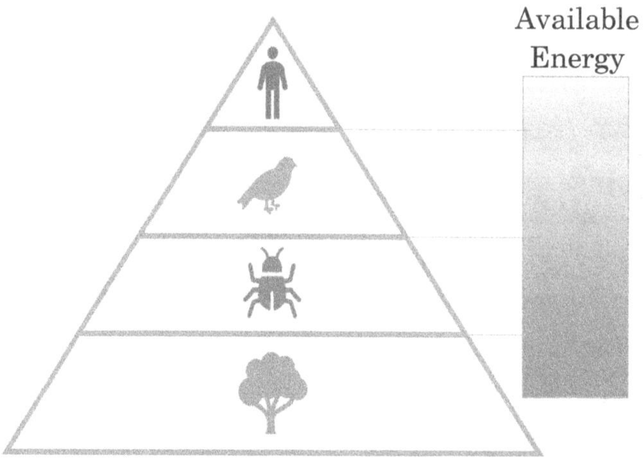

(a) State one reason to justify the position of man at the apex of food pyramid.

(b) Why energy of herbivores never come back to autotrophs?

OR

The number of malarial patients in a village increases tremendously when a large number of frogs were exported from the village. What could be the cause for it? Illustrate with the help of a food chain.

3. a. Why is regeneration considered a method of reproduction?

(b) Why does asexual mode of reproduction has limitations in evolution of species?

OR

Look at the given diagram:

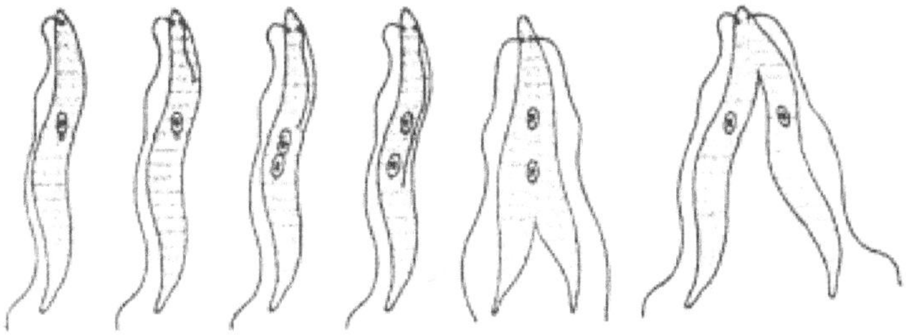

(a) Identify the unicellular organism.

(b) Name one disease caused by this organism.

(c) Which method of asexual reproduction is being performed here?

(d) What is the advantage of a whip-like structure at one end of its cell?

4. The atomic numbers of elements of a period are given below:

Elements	Li	Be	B	C	N
Atomic numbers	3	4	5	6	7

(a) Predict the valencies of given elements from their atomic numbers.

(b) State a reason how valency of an element is determined.

5. Magnetic field is a quantity that has both direction and magnitude. The direction of the magnetic field is taken to be the direction in which a north pole of the compass needle moves inside it. Therefore, it is taken by convention that the field lines emerge from north pole and merge at the south pole. Inside the magnet, the direction of field lines is from its south pole to its north pole. Thus the magnetic field lines are closed curves.

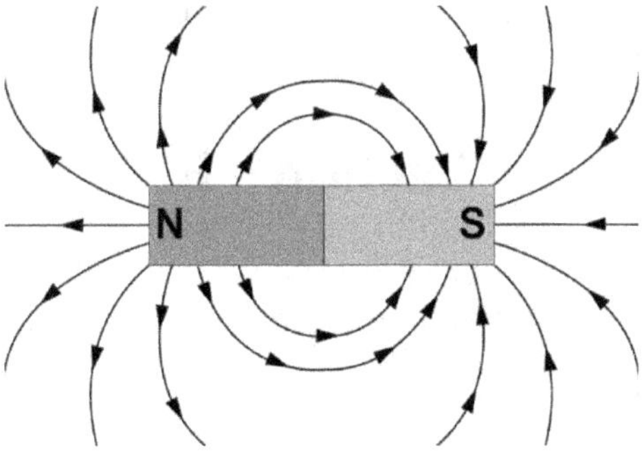

The relative strength of the magnetic field is:

(a) the degree of closeness of the field lines

(b) the degree of farness of the field lines.

(c) Proportional to the number of lines per unit area perpendicular to the lines.

Choose the correct option:

(i). Only A

(ii). A and B both

(iii). A,B and C

(iv). A and C both

OR

AB is a current carrying conductor in the plane of the paper as shown in Figure. What are the directions of magnetic fileds produced by it at points P and Q?

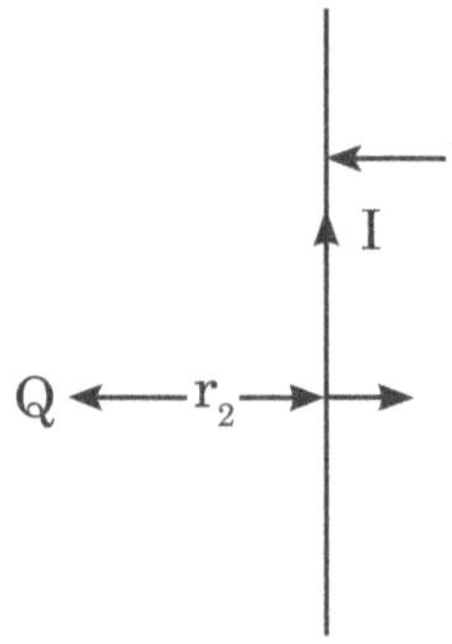

6. (a) Give symbol of:

(i) an electric cell (ii) battery of cells.

(b) What will be the amount of heat (H) produced in a resistor (R) carrying a current (I) and having a potential difference (V) across it in time (t)?

7. (a) In humans if gene B gives brown eyes and gene b gives Blue Eyes. What will be the colour of the persons having the following combination of genes:

i. Bb ii. Bb iii. BB

(b) Explain which characteristic trait is inherited in the above question?

Section – B

(6 × 3 Marks)

8. The position of three elements A,B and C in the periodic table is shown below:

Group XVI	Group XVII
-------	-------
-------	A
-------	-------
B	C

(a) State whether A is a metal or non-metal.

(b) Which type of ion, cation or anion will be formed by A?

(c) State whether C is more reactive or less reactive than B? Give reason.

9. (a) Why the homologous series of carbon compounds are called so?

(b) Write chemical formula of two consecutive members of homologous series and state the part that determines their i) physical properties and ii) chemical properties.

OR

(a) Identify which two of the following organic compounds belong to the same homologous:

(b) $CH_{3,}$ C_2H_6, C_2H_6O, $C_2H_6O_2$, CH_4O

(c) Write the name and formula of the first member of the series of alkenes.

10. A circuit is shown in the diagram given below:

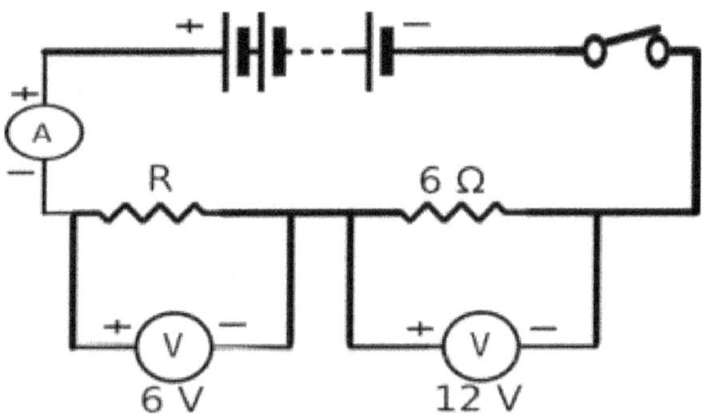

(a) Find the value of R.

(b) Find the potential difference across the terminals of the battery.

11. Magnetic field lines of two magnets are shown in fig. A and fig. B:

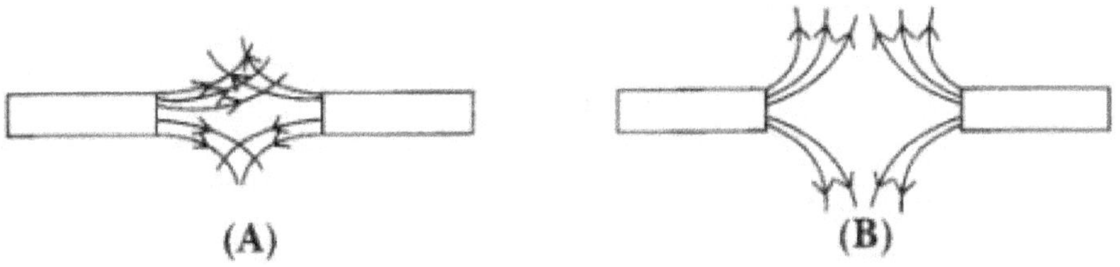

(a) Select the figure that represents the correct pattern of field lines.

(b) Give reasons for your answer.

(c) Name the poles of the magnets facing each other.

12. In a biology class, the students were being taught about a phenomenon whose diagrammatic representation has been shown below:

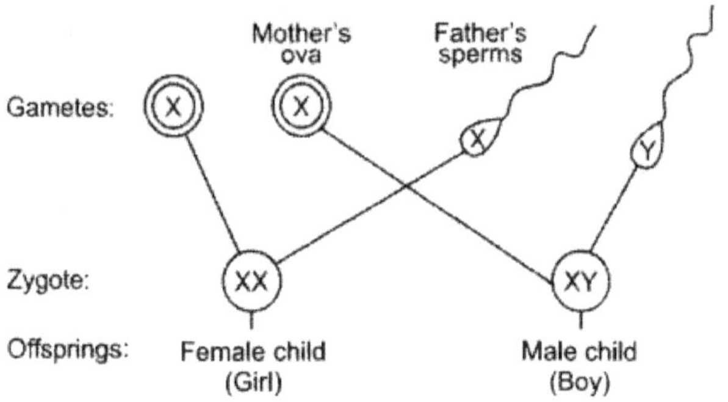

(a) A student wants to know why a father is responsible for determination of the sex of the child. Can you explain the reason?

(b) Identify the male and female sex chromosomes.

(c) At what stage of human reproduction do this determination take place?

OR

(a) In a bisexual flower inspite of the young stamens being removed artificially, the flower produces fruit. Provide a suitable explanation for this situation.

(b) Colonies of yeast fail to multiply in water, but multiply in sugar solution. Give reason.

(c) Why does bread mould grow profusely on a moist slice of bread rather than on a dry slice of bread?

13. Shivani goes to her village with her parents. In the village she saw farmers using DDT as pesticide. Shivani with her parents goes and educates the farmer about ill-effects of DDT.

(a) Why is using the pesticide considered harmful for the crops?

(b) Explain biological magnification of DDT in a food chain.

Section – C

(2 × 4 Marks)

This section has 02 case-based questions (14 and 15). Each case is followed by 03 sub-questions (a, b and c). Parts a and b are compulsory. However, an internal choice has been provided in part c.

14. Sir Gregor Mendel used a number of contrasting visible characters of garden peas – round/wrinkled, tall/short plants, white/violet flowers and so on. He produced progeny by crossing them and also calculated the percentages of resulting progeny.

Refer to the given table regarding results of F_2 generation of Mendelian cross:

Plants with round and yellow coloured seeds (P)	315
Plants with round and green coloured seeds (Q)	108
Plants with wrinkled and yellow coloured seeds (R)	101
Plants with wrinkled and green coloured seeds (S)	32

(a) What will be the percentage of yR gamete produced by YyRR parent?

(b) Which of the following will result when plant YyRr is self-pollinated?

(i) 9:3:3:1 ratio of phenotypes only

(ii) 9:3:3:1 ratio of genotypes only

(iii) 1:1:1:1 ratio of phenotypes only

(iv) 1:1:1:1 ratio of phenotypes and genotypes

(c) What would be the phenotype of F_1 generation regarding given data of F_2 generation? Also predict the genotype of parental generation regarding given result of F_2 generation.

OR

Why did Mendel choose pea plant for his experiments? Write two reasons.

15. An insulated copper wire wound on a cylindrical cardboard tube such that its length is greater than its diameter is called a solenoid. When an electric current is passed through the solenoid, it produces a magnetic field around it. The magnetic field produced by a current-carrying solenoid is similar to the magnetic field produced by a bar magnet. The field lines inside the solenoid are in the form of parallel straight lines. The strong magnetic field produced inside a current-carrying solenoid can be used to magnetise a piece of magnetic material like soft iron, when placed inside the solenoid. The strength of magnetic field produced by a current carrying solenoid is directly proportional to the number of turns and strength of current in the solenoid.

Answer the following questions:

(a) A soft iron bar is enclosed by a coil of insulated copper wire as shown in figure. When the plug of the key is closed, the face B of the iron bar marked as:

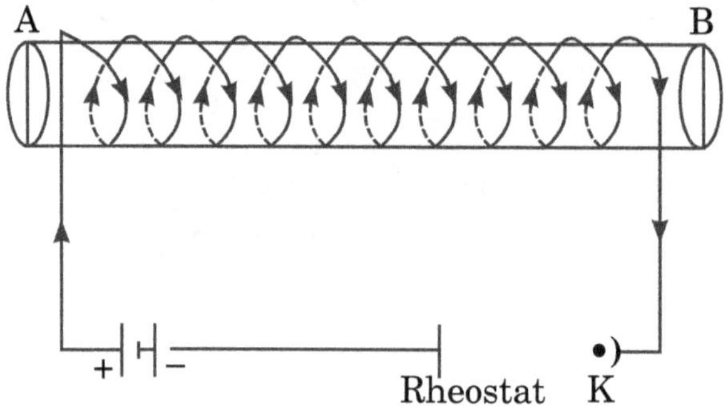

(i) N-pole

(ii) S-pole

(iii) N-pole if current is large

(iv) S-pole if current is small

(b) A long solenoid carrying a current produces a magnetic field B along its axis. If the current is doubled and the number of turns per cm is halved, then new value of magnetic field is:

(i) B (ii) 2B

(iii)4B (iv) B/2

(c) An electric fuse of rating 3 A is connected in a circuit in which an electric iron of power 1 kilo watt is connected which operates at 220 V. What would happen? Explain.

OR

Two circular coils A and B are placed close to each other. If the current in the coil A is changed, will some current be induced in coil B? Give reason.

SOLUTIONS

Section A

1. (a) B and D (½ + ½)

(b) No, the covalent compounds are mainly non-conductors of electricity as the bonding in these compounds does not give rise to any ions. (1)

2. (a) The position of man is at the apex of most food chains as the mankind has adapted itself to consume any form of food and is an omnivore. Therefore, it is not trophic level specific or restricted to a particular level. (1)

(b) Energy of herbivores never comes back to autotrophs as flow of energy is always unidirectional. So, once it passes the trophic level it is no longer available to the previous level. (1)

OR

The number of malaria patients in the village increased because frogs feed upon the insects that cause the disease malaria. Due to the export of frogs, there is a drastic increase in the population of insects that cause the disease of malaria.

Food chain:

Grass	→	Insect	→	Frog	(2)
(Producer)		(Consumer)		(Secondary consumer)	

3. (a) Regeneration is a method of asexual reproduction in which specialised cells of an organism proliferate and make whole individual out of their body parts. (1)

(b) Asexual reproduction involves no genetic diversity which leads to lower adaptability to changing environments. Hence, it has limitations in evolution of species. (1)

OR

(a) The organism is Leishmania. (½)

(b) Kala-azar (½)

(c) Binary fission (½)

(d) The whip-like structure is the agella which helps in its locomotion. (½)

4. (a)The valencies are as follows:

Li – 1 Be – 2 B – 3 C – 4 N – 3 (1)

(b) An element's valency is determined by the number of electrons in its outer shell i.e. the number of electrons lost, gained or shared by the element to attain the noble gas configuration. (1)

5. (iv) A and C both (1 + 1)

OR

Applying the right hand thumb rule, the direction of magnetic field would be anti-clockwise as shown in diagram around the direction of current. So, the magnetic field at point P would be into the plane of paper.

At point Q, the direction of magnetic current would be out from the plane of paper. (2)

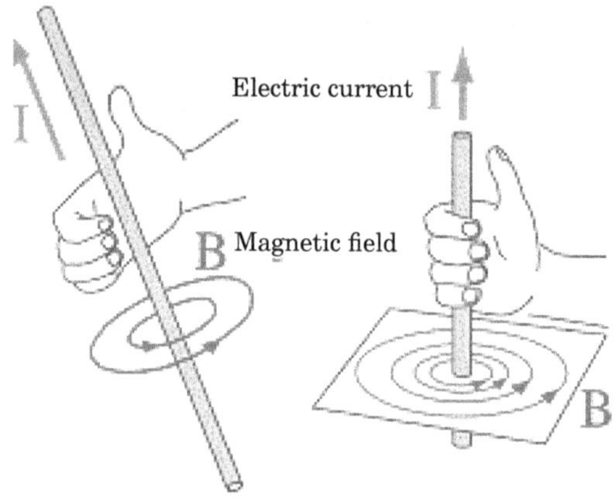

6. (a) i) Symbol of an electric cell:

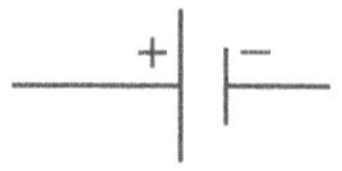

(½)

(ii) symbol of battery of cells:

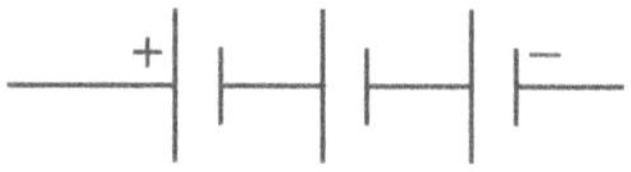

(½)

(b) H = V.I.t (1)

7. (a) (i) Brown

(ii) Blue

(iii) Brown (1)

(b) The colour of the eye is an example of multiple genes. These genes are present on the DNA and expressed in the phenotype. (1)

Section – B

8. (a) A is a non-metal (1)

(b) A non-metal forms anion. (1)

(c) Along a period in non-metals, the reactivity increases on moving from left to right. Hence, C is more reactive than B as it has higher electronegativity. (1)

9. (a) The series consists of members of same family with similar physical and chemical properties. Therefore, homologous series are called so. (1½)

(b) CH_3OH and CH_3CH_2OH are two consecutive members. The alkyl group - CH_3 and - CH_3CH_2 determines physical properties and the functional group –OH determines its chemical properties. (1½)

OR

(a) C_2H_6O and CH_4O belong to the same homologous. (1½)

(b) C_2H_4 or $CH_2{=}CH_2$ or Ethene is the first member of alkene series. (1½)

10. (a) The potential difference across 6 Ω = 12 V (1½)

Reading across ammeter = I = V/R = 12/6 = 2A

both R and 6 Ω are connected in series

according to Ohm's law: R = V/I = 6/2 = 3 Ω

(b) $V = V_1 + V_2 = (6 + 12)V = 18\ V$ (1½)

11. (a) Figure B (1)

(b) In figure A, all the magnetic field lines intersect each other which is not possible. In figure B, the magnetic field lines are emerging from both the poles separately. (1)

(c) The poles facing each other will be North poles and the poles opposite to them will be South poles. (1)

12. (a) In human beings, the sex of thc individual is genetically determined. Human beings have 1 unpaired sex chromosome. Sex chromosome of male is XY. Thus, father is responsible for the determination of the sex of a child. (1)

(b) Male sex chromosome – XY (½ + ½)

Female sex chromosome – XX

(c) Fertilisation (1)

OR

(a) When stamens of a bisexual flower are removed. Cross pollination can take place which results in fertilization and production of fruit. (1)

(b) Sugar provides energy for sustaining all life activities in yeasts. Yeasts can metabolize sugars as they ferment sugar resulting in the formation of ethanol. (1)

(c) Bread mould grows profusely on a moist slice of bread rather than on a dry slice of bread because microorganisms need optimum temperature and moisture to grow and if there is no moisture they will not grow profusely. (1)

13. (a) Pesticides are used to protect crops against insects, weeds, fungi and other pests. Pesticides are potentially toxic to humans and can have both acute and chronic health effects, depending on the quantity and ways in which a person is exposed. (1½)

(b) Biomagnification is the increase in the concentration of a toxin at successive trophic levels. The toxin gets accumulated because a toxic substance cannot be metabolised or excreted, and is thus passed on the next higher trophic level. In aquatic ecosystem the concentration of DDT increases at successive trophic levels. It is present in low amount in water and reaches a high concentration in fish-eating birds through biomagnification. Very high concentrations of DDT disturb calcium metabolism in birds, which causes thinning of eggshell and their premature breaking, eventually causing decline in bird populations. (1½)

Section - C

14. (a) Gametes produced by YyRR parent would be 50% YR and 50% yR. (1)

(b) i) 9:3:3:1 ratio of phenotypes only. (1)

(c) The phenotype of F_1 generation will be plants with round and yellow coloured seeds. YYRR and yyrr will be the genotype of the parental generation. (1+1)

OR

The reason for the selection of pea plants for the genetic experiments are:

(i) They have easily identifiable traits (1)

(ii) The generation time of pea plants is less. (1)

15. (a) i) North pole (1)

(b) i) The magnetic field of a solenoid depends directly on the current flowing through the solenoid and the number of turns. So, the answer will be B i.e. no change in the magnetic field. (1)

(c) P = VI

or I = P/V = 1000/220 = 4.54 (1)

As the current 4.54 A is greater than 3 A(current of fuse), the circuit will break. The fuse will also melt. (1)

OR

When the current in coil A is changed, the magnetic field associated with it also changes. As a result, the magnetic field around coil B also changes. This change in magnetic field lines around coil B induces an electric current in it. This happens due to electromagnetic induction. **(2)**

CBSE

Sample Question Paper 2

TERM II

Class X

Science

Time Allowed: 2 Hours **Maximum Marks: 40**

General Instructions

i *All questions are compulsory.*

ii. *The question paper has three sections and 15 questions. All questions are compulsory.*

iii. *Section–A has 7 questions of 2 marks each; Section–B has 6 questions of 3 marks each; and Section–C has 2 case based questions of 4 marks each.*

iv. *Internal choices have been provided in some questions. A student has to attempt only one of the alternatives in such questions.*

Section – A

(7 × 2 Marks)

1. Give reason why two carbon atoms cannot be linked to each other by more than three covalent bonds.

2. In upright pyramid (e.g., grassland & cropland ecosystem), biomass or number of organisms or amount of energy decreases on moving to upper trophic levels. The pyramid of energy is always upright.

   Consider the diagram to answer the following questions:

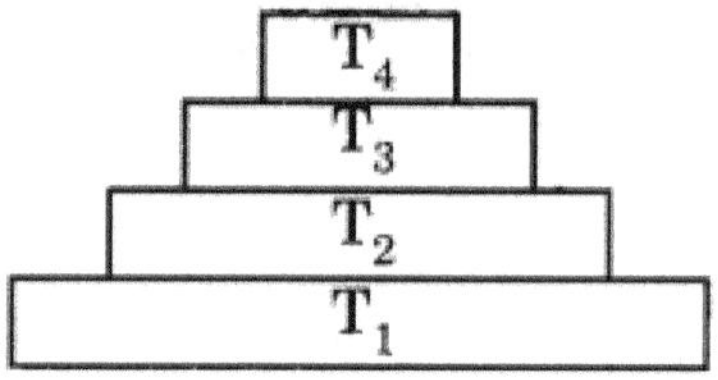

   (a) Name the different trophic levels in the given diagram of upright pyramid.

   (b) Give examples of grassland organisms for these different trophic levels of an ecosystem.

OR

In the given food chain, suppose the amount of energy at fourth trophic level is 5 kJ, what will be the energy available at the producer leverl?

Grass → Grasshopper → Frog → Snake → Hawk

3. The values of current I flowing in a given resistor for the corresponding values of potential difference V across the resistor are as given below:

I (ampere)	0.5	1.0	2.0	3.0	4.0
V (Volts)	1.6	3.4	6.7	10.2	13.2

   (a) Plot a graph between V and I.

   (b) Calculate the resistance of the resistor.

4. The following figure shows the reproductive system of human female

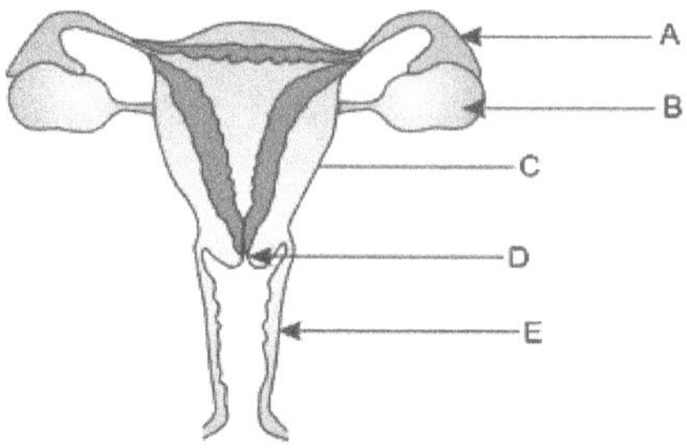

Among the reproductive parts A,B,C,D and E where do the following functions occur:

(a) Production of an egg

(b) Fertilisation

(c) Implantation of zygote

(d) Development of foetus

OR

Give reason:

i. Placenta is extremely essential for foetal development.

ii. Blocking of Vas deferens prevents pregnancy.

5. The given magnet is divided into three parts A, B, and C.

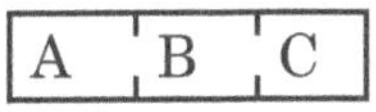

(a) Name the parts where the strength of the magnetic field is:

(i) maximum

(ii) minimum.

(b) State the rule to determine the direction of a magnetic field produced around a straight conductor carrying current.

6. The three elements A, B and C with similar properties have atomic masses X, Y and Z respectively. The mass of Y is approximately equal to the average mass of X and Z. what is such an arrangement of elements called as? give one example of such a set of elements.

7. Three resistors of 3Ω each are connected to a battery of 3V .Calculate the current drawn from the the battery as shown in the given figure:

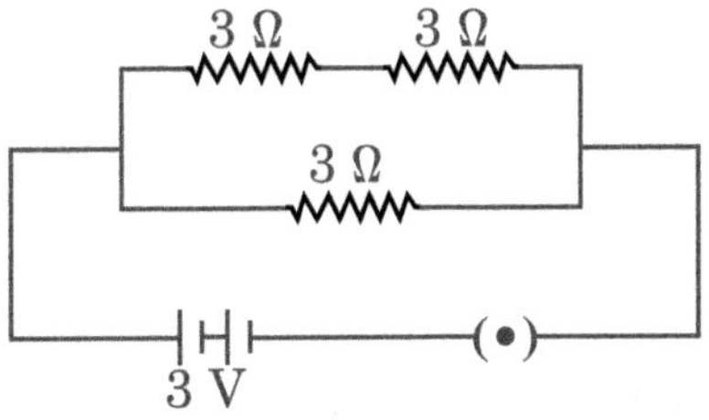

OR

Find the highest and the lowest value of resistance that can be obtained by the combination of four resistors of 4Ω , 8Ω, 12Ω and 24Ω.

Section – B

(6 × 3 Marks)

8. The following table shows the formulae of three organic compounds that belong to the same homologous series:

$CH_3 - O - CH_3$
$CH_3CH_2 - O - CH_3$
$CH_3CH_2CH_2 - O - CH_3$

- First member of the homologous series

- Second member of the homologous series

- Third member of the homologous series

(a) Write the general formula of this series.

(b) What is the general formula of all the members of homologous series of alkynes?

(c) Identify the incorrect statement about the characteristics of homologous series:

(i) They possess varying chemical properties

(ii) Their physical properties vary in regular and predictable manner

(iii) Their formulae fit the general molecular formula

(iv) Adjacent members differ by one carbon and two hydrogen atoms

OR

Identify and name the functional groups present in the following compounds.

(a) 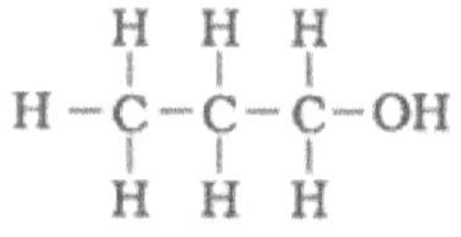

(b) 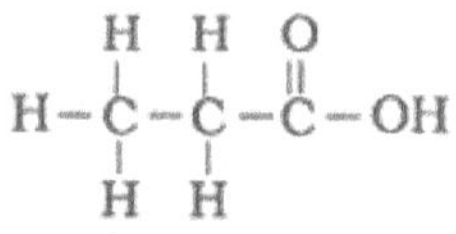

(c) 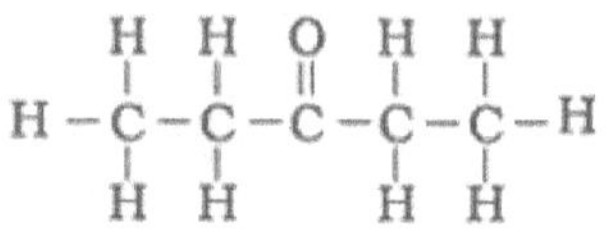

9. (a) Why and when does a current carrying conductor kept in a magnetic field experience force?

(b) List the factors on which direction of this force depends?

(c) How is the strength of magnetic field near a straight current-conductor

(i) related to the strength of current in the conductor?

(ii) is affected by changing the direction of flow of current in the conductor?

10. Atoms of seven elements A, B, C, D, E, F and G have a different number of electronic shells but have the same number of electrons in their outermost shells. The elements A and C combine with chlorine to form an acid and common salt respectively. The oxide of element A is liquid at room temperature and is a neutral substance, while the oxides of the remaining six elements are basic in nature. Based on the above information, answer the following questions:

(i) What could the element A be?

(ii) Will elements A to G belong to the same period or same group of the periodic table?

(iii)Write the formula of the compound formed by the reaction of the element A with oxygen,

(iv) Show the formation of the compound by a combination of element C with chlorine with the help of electronic structure.

(v) What would be the ratio of number of combining atoms in a compound formed by the combination of element A with carbon?

(vi) Which one of the given elements is likely to have the smallest atomic radius?

11. A blue colour flower plant denoted by BB is crossbred with that of white colour flower plant denoted by bb.

(a) State the colour of flowers you would expect in their F1 generation plants.

(b) What must be the percentage of white flower plants in F2 generation if flowers of F1 plants are self-pollinated?

(c) State the expected ratio of the genotypes BB and Bb in the F2 progeny

12. Consider the circuit diagram shown below:

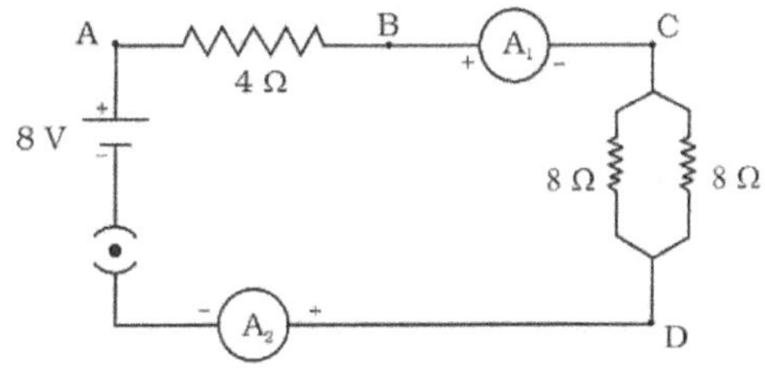

(a) Find the effective resistance of two 8Ω resistors in the combination

(b) Power dissipated in 4Ω resistor

(c) Difference in ammeter readings

13. We already know that a food chain contains different organisms at different trophic levels in a typical ecosystem. In the diagram of energy flow in an ecosystem given below, identify the secondary consumers and explain why did you choose it:

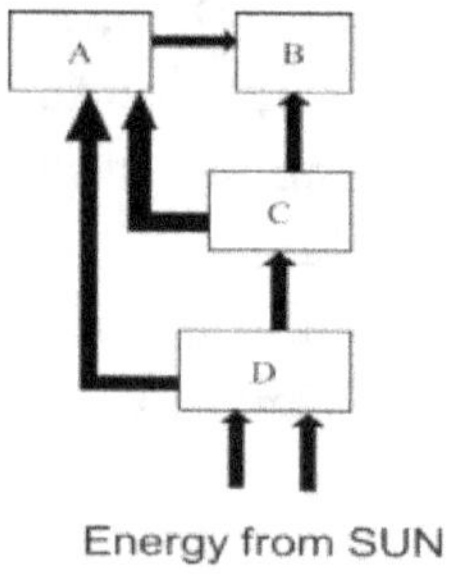

OR

Diya always puts vegetable and fruit peels in composting pits and makes compost out of it. She uses this compost in her kitchen garden. Nikita uses fertilizers for plants in her garden.

(a) Compare the effect of Diya's and Nikita's action on environment.

(b) How is the compost important for the soil?

Section – C

(2 × 4 Marks)

This section has 02 case-based questions (14 and 15). Each case is followed by 03 sub-questions (a, b and c). Parts a and b are compulsory. However, an internal choice has been provided in part c.

14. The relationship between potential difference and current was first established by George Simon Ohm called Ohm's law. According to this law, the current through a metallic conductor is proportional to the potential difference applied between its ends, provided the temperature remain constant i.e.

$$I \propto V \qquad V = IR$$

Where R is a constant for the conductor and is called resistance of the conductor.

Although Ohm's law has been found valid over a large class of materials, there do exist materials and devices used in electric circuits where the proportionality of V and I does not hold.

Using the above information, answer the following questions:

(a) If both the potential difference and the resistance in a circuit are doubled, then what happens to the current?

(b) For a conductor, which graph between V and I is correct?

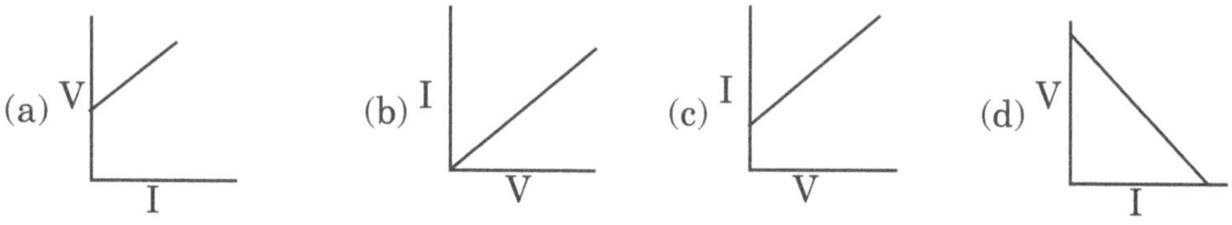

(c) The slope of V-I graph (V on x-axis and I on y-axis) gives:

(i) Resistance

(ii) Reciprocal of resistance

(iii) Charge

(iv) Reciprocal of charge

State reason for your choice.

OR

A battery of 9V is connected across a conductor and the current which flows through it is 0.1 A. Find its resistance.

15. There are two organisms X and Y that produce new offspring from single parent only. Organism X when reaches its maximum growth, divides its body into two new organisms. The parent organism does not exist any more and two new daughter organisms grow fully and divide again.

Organism Y forms a small outgrowth on its body called bud which detaches and develops into new organism.

Refer to the above paragraph and answer the following questions:

(a) Idenify the organisms X and Y.

(b) Write the mode of reproduction in both organisms X and Y.

(c) Which of the following statements are incorrect?

(i) Plasmodium reproduces by the same method as is adopted by organism X.

(ii) Organism X could be any multicellular plant like Riccia, Sphagnum etc.

(iii) If organism Y is Hydra, then it may also reproduce through regeneration.

(iv) Both (i) and (ii)

OR

Name the process and orientation of plane through which organism Euglena reproduces by the method shown in the given figure:

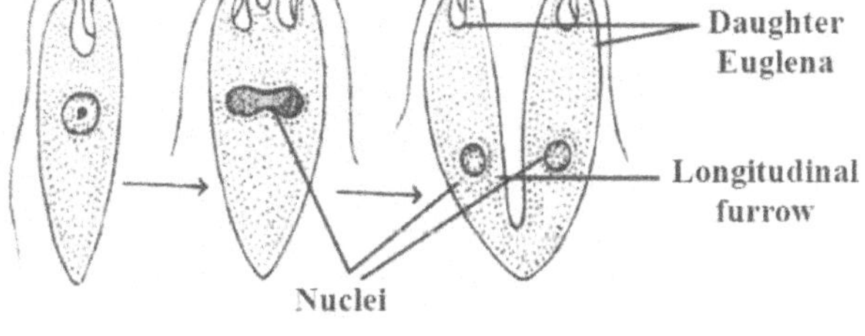

SOLUTIONS

Section A

1. The following statements are the reason behind carbon not having more than three covalent bonds:

(i) There is a single bond between the two carbon atoms.

(ii) Both share their one atom therefore for completing its shell it needs to combine with three atoms of carbon or other element.

(iii) The shell of the carbon will be incomplete to become stable if it forms more than three covalent bonds. (2)

2. The following diagram shows the various levels of grassland upright pyramid with examples:

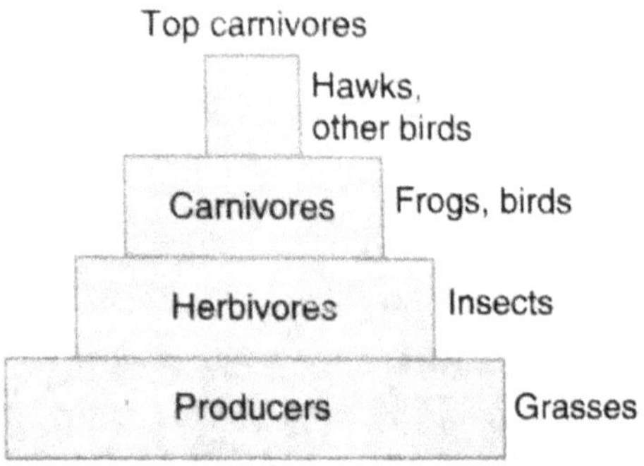

(2)

OR

In the given food chain if the amount of energy at fourth trophic level is 5 KJ, then 5000 KJ will be the energy available at the producer level. As only 10% of energy is trasferred to next higher trophic level, above producers, 500 KJ energy will be stored in body of grasshopper and 50 KJ in frog. 5 KJ energy will be present in the body of snake and 0.5 KJ in hawk. (2)

3. (a) The following plot shows the V-I graph:

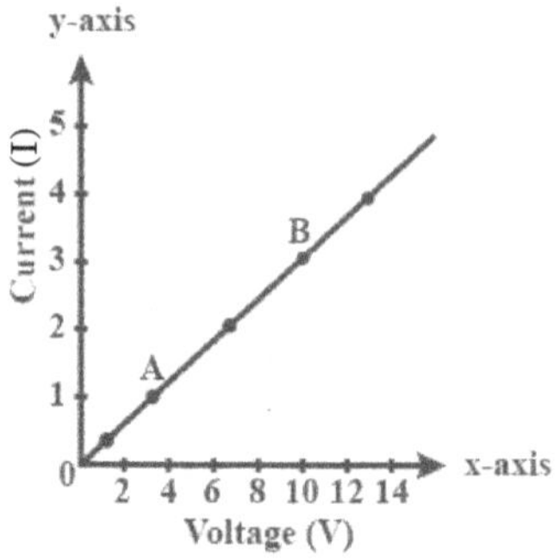

(1)

(b) Resistance = 1/Slope

From the graph, Slope = (1 – 0.5)/(3.4 – 1.6) = 0.278 Ω^{-1}

Therefore, the resistance will be 1/0.278 = 3.6 Ω (1)

4. (a) B – Ovary (½)

(b) A – Fallopian tube (½)

(c) C – Uterus (½)

(d) C – Uterus (½)

OR

(i) Placenta is extremely essential for foetal development because it helps in nutrition, respiration, excretion, etc., of the foetus through the maternal supply. (1)

(ii) Blocking of vas deferens prevents passage of sperms, hence, there is no fertilisation thus preventing pregnancy. (1)

5. (a) (i) Maximum magnetic field is in the region A and C. (½)

(ii) Minimum magnetic field is in the region B. (½)

(b) Right hand thumb rule is used to determine the direction of magnetic field around the straight conductor carrying current. (1)

6. The arrangement of these elements is known as Dobereiner triad. Example: lithium, sodium and potassium. (1 + 1)

7. Consider the following circuit diagram:

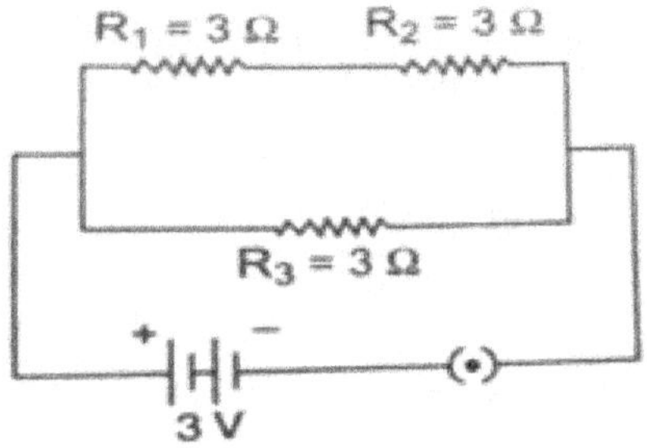

(1 + 1)

$$\frac{1}{R} = \frac{1}{R_1 + R_2} + \frac{1}{R_3} = \frac{1}{3+3} + \frac{1}{3} = \frac{1}{6} + \frac{1}{3} = \frac{1}{2}$$

R = 2Ω

$$I = \frac{V}{R} = \frac{3}{2} = 1.5\text{ A}$$

OR

$R_s = 4 + 8 + 12 + 24 = 48\Omega$

$$\frac{1}{R} = \frac{1}{4} + \frac{1}{8} + \frac{1}{12} + \frac{1}{24} = \frac{6+3+2+1}{24}$$ (1 + 1)

$$\frac{1}{R} = \frac{2}{24} = \frac{1}{2}$$

$R = 2\Omega$

Section – B

8. (a) The general formula of the given series is $C_nH_{2n+2}O$. (1)

(b) The general formula of alkynes is $C_nH_{2n-2.}$ (1)

(c) (i) The chemical properties of a homologous series are similar. (1)

OR

(a) alcohol (1)

(b) carboxylic acid (1)

(c) Ketone (1)

9. (a) The drifting of free electrons of a conductor in a definite direction causes the current to flow through it. When such conductor is placed in a uniform magnetic field, each drifted electron of a conductor experience a magnetic force. This force is collectively experience by a conductor as a whole. Hence a current carrying conductor kept in a magnetic field experience a force. (1)

(b) The direction of magnetic force depends on: (½ + ½)

(i) direction of current through the conductor

(ii) direction of magnetic field.

(c) (i) The strength of magnetic field around a straight current conductor increases on increasing the strength of current in the conductor or vice versa. (½)

(ii) The direction of magnetic field around a straight current carrying conductor gets reversed if the direction of current through that conductor is reversed. (½)

10. (i) 'A' is hydrogen because its oxide H_2O is liquid at room temperature. (½)

(ii) A to G belong to same group of the periodic table as these have same number of valence electrons. (½)

(iii) A_2O (½)

(iv) (C•) (Cl:) → $(C)^{+}(Cl)^{-}$ (½)

(v) A_1 C_4 A_4C, i.e., 4 : 1 (½)

A_4C

(vi) 'A' has smallest atomic size. (½)

11. (a)

Parents: Blue flower × white flower

BB bb

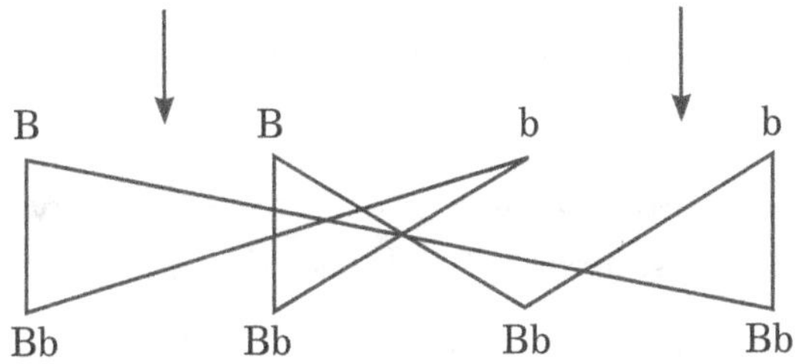

F_1 generation: Blue flower Blue flower Blue flower Blue flower

Bb × Bb

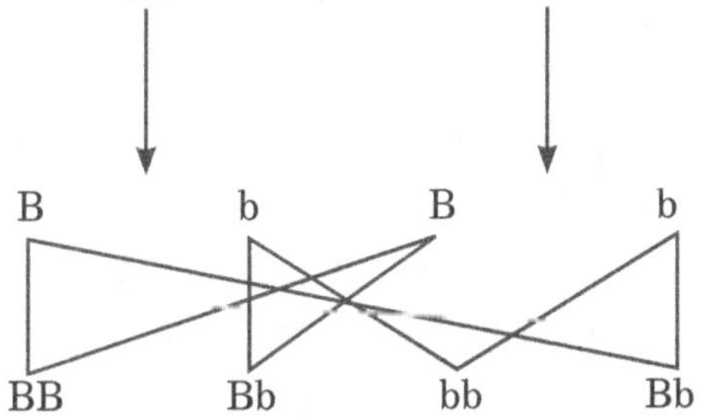

F_2 generation: Blue flower Blue flower White flower Blue flower (1)

The blue colour flowers in F_1 generation.

(b) 25 (1)

(c) 1:2 (1)

12. (a) $\frac{1}{R} = \frac{1}{R_1} + \frac{1}{R_2}$

$\frac{1}{R} = \frac{1}{8} + \frac{1}{8}$ (½ + ½)

$\frac{1}{R} = \frac{2}{8}$ $\frac{1}{R} = \frac{1}{4}$

R = 4Ω

Equivalent resistance is 8Ω

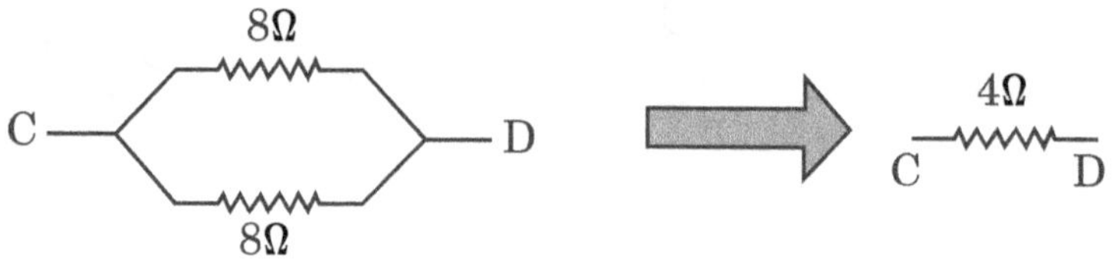

(b) Power dissipated = VI

Putting $V = IR = (IR)I = I^2R$ (1)

$= (1)^2 \times 4 = 4$ W

(c) There will be no difference in ammeter readings as they are connected in series and current flowing through them will be equal. (1)

13. In the given diagram,

- D is the primary producer which utilises the energy of sun for production of plants. This is consumed by C. Hence, C is the primary consumer. (1)
- B is the secondary consumer as it feeds on C. (1)
- A falls under the category of decomposers which decompose B, C or D. (1)

OR

(a) Effect of Diya's action – The natural decomposition of vegetable and fruit peels produces compost. It naturally increases soil organic matter. It can be used as a natural fertilizer for the soil. (1 + 1)

Effect of Nikita's action – Fertilizers are chemicals which cause an increase in pests and kills the beneficial microbes present in the soil.

(b) In several ways, compost is important for the soil as a natural fertilizer, manure, and a natural soil pesticide. (1)

Section - C

14. (a) Here, V becomes 2V and R becomes 2R

According to Ohm's law,

$V = IR$ Or $I = V/R = 2V/2R$ (1)

So, the value of the current will not vary even if potential difference and resistance is doubled.

(b) The graph (b) is the correct option as it is a straight line and passing through the origin. (1)

(c) ii) Reciprocal of resistance (1)

Reason : Slope of the graph will be $I/V = 1/R$ (1)

OR

Given,

$V = 9V$

$I = 0.1\ A$

$R = V/I = 9/0.1 = 90\ \Omega$ (2)

15. (a) X – Amoeba, Paramecium or Leishmania (1)

Y – Hydra, Yeast or Sycon (1)

(b) Both organisms reproduce asexually. X reproduces by binary fission while Y reproduces by budding.

(c) iv) both (i) and (ii) statements are incorrect. Plasmodium reproduces by multiple fission and multicellular plants do not reproduce through binary fission. (1 + 1)

OR

Euglena reproduces by binary fission and the plane of orientation is longitudinal. (2)

CBSE

Sample Question Paper 3

TERM II

Class X

Science

Time Allowed: 2 Hours | **Maximum Marks: 40**

General Instructions

i. All questions are compulsory.

ii. The question paper has three sections and 15 questions. All questions are compulsory.

iii. Section–A has 7 questions of 2 marks each; Section–B has 6 questions of 3 marks each; and Section–C has 2 case based questions of 4 marks each.

iv. Internal choices have been provided in some questions. A student has to attempt only one of the alternatives in such questions.

Section – A

(7 × 2 Marks)

1. (a) Give reason why covalent compounds generally have low melting and boiling points?

(b) Identify them:

(i) It is the hardest substance known.

(ii) Carbon atoms arranged in the shape of a football.

2. In the given figure, What is the ratio of current in A_1 and A_2?

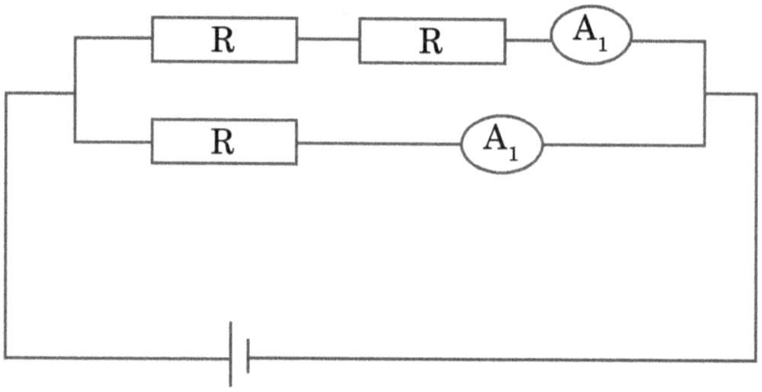

OR

How will the magnetic field produced at a point due to a current-carrying circular coil change if we:

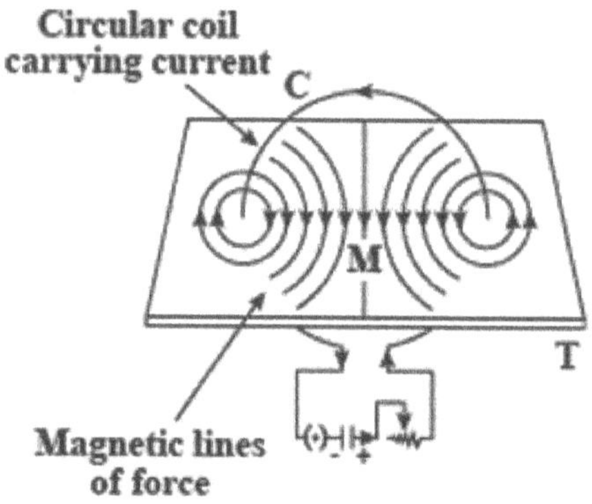

Magnetic Field Pattern Around a Circular Loop

(i) increase the current flowing through the coil?

(ii) reverse direction of current through the coil?

3. (a) What is the effect of DNA copying which is not perfectly accurate on the reproduction process?

(b) State the method used for growing rose plants.

4. (a) How does carbon attain noble gas configuration?

(b) Why are carbon and its compounds used as fuels in most cases?

OR

Name the functional groups present in the following compounds.

(i) $CH_2 - CO - CH_2 - CH_2 - CH_2 - CH_3$

(ii) $CH_3 - CH_2 - CH_2 - COOH$

(iii) $CH_3 - CH_2 - CH_2 - CH_2 - CHO$

(iv) $CH_3 - CH_2 - OH$

5. The elements of the third period of the Periodic Table are given below:

Group	I	II	III	IV	V	VI	VII
Period 3	Na	Mg	Al	Si	P	S	Cl

(a) Which atom is bigger, Na or Mg? Why?

(b) Identify the most (i) metallic and (ii) non-metallic element in Period 3.

OR

Elements have been arranged in the following sequence on the basis of their increasing atomic masses.

F, Na, Mg, Al, Si, P, S, Cl, Ar, K

(a) Pick two sets of elements which have similar properties.

(b) The given sequence represents which law of classification of elements?

6. a. Out of the two wires X and Y shown below, which one has greater resistance? Justify your answer:

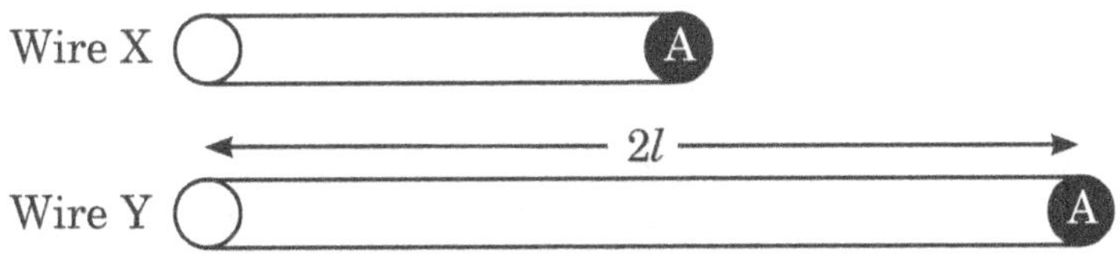

(b) The charge possessed by an electron is 1.6×10^{-19} coulombs. Find the number of electrons that will flow per second to constitute a current of 1 ampere.

7. (a) A conducting rod AB moves across two magnets as shown in figure and the needle in the galvanometer deflects momentarily. What is the name of this physical phenomenon?

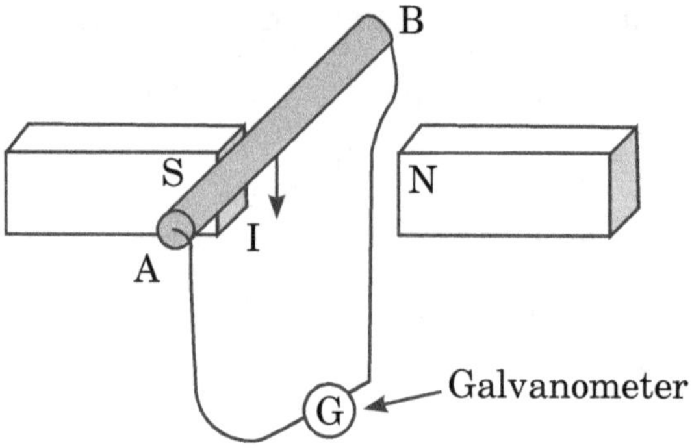

(b) A bar magnet is pushed steadily into a long solenoid connected to a sensitive meter.

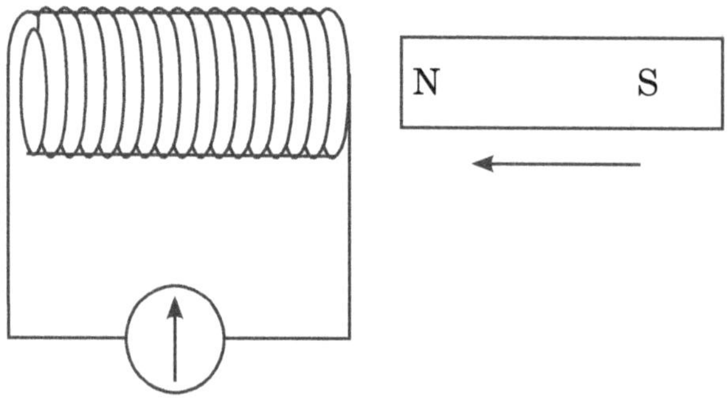

Which of the following would affect the magnitude of the deflection of the meter?

i) How fast the magnet is pushed into the coil.

ii) The direction in which the coil is wound.

iii) The end of the solenoid the magnet enters.

iv) The pole of the magnet enters the coil first.

Section – B

(6 × 3 Marks)

8. The population of a village was 10,000 in the year 2010. It has surprisingly increased to 15,000 in a year. As a village Panchayat doctor what measures would you suggest to the people of that village to control population? Explain. (Any 3)

OR

Imagine that you are a doctor who is specialized in Gynaecology. A married lady walked into your clinic for terminating her foetus which is 24 weeks old since the foetus is a female. You as a doctor advised her not to do so.

(a) How is the sex of female child genetically determined?

(b) What is meant by medical termination of pregnancy?

9. How much current will an electric bulb draw from 220 V source if the resistance of the bulb is 1200Ω? If in place of bulb, a heater of resistance 100 Ω is connected to the sources, calculate the current drawn by it.

10. In the formation of a compound XY_2, atom X donates one electron to each Y atom.

(a) Show the electron dot structure of X and Y and the formation of XY_2.

(b) Write any three properties of compound XY_2.

11. Two wires A and B are of equal length and have equal resistance. If the resistivity of A is more than that of B which wire is thicker and why? For the electric circuit given below calculate:

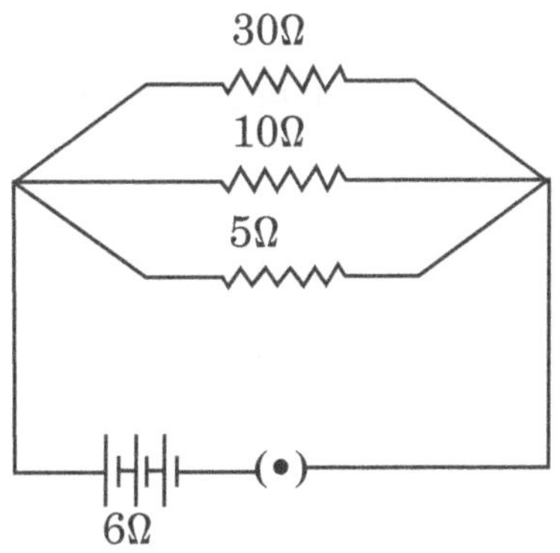

(i) Current in each resistor

(ii) Total current drawn from the battery

(iii)Equivalent resistance of the Circuit

12. In the following crosses, write the characteristics of the progeny:

(a) RrYy x RrYy

(b) rryy x rryy

(c) RRYY x rryy

OR

What do you understand by the term Monohybrid cross? Explain it with an example.

13. (a) In a food chain comprising lion, deer and grass, which will transfer the maximum amount of energy and which will receive minimum amount of energy?

(b) If a harmful chemical enters a food chain comprising snakes, peacocks ,rats and plants. Which of the organisms is likely to have maximum concentration of the harmful chemical in the body?

Section – C

(4 × 2 Marks)

This section has 02 case-based questions (14 and 15). Each case is followed by 03 sub-questions (a, b and c). Parts a and b are compulsory. However, an internal choice has been provided in part c.

14. Advancement of the technology has resulted in improvement of our lifestyle and has also changed our attitude. When the human population was low and technology was in its infancy, the various kinds of solid wastes generated due to human activities were easily degraded by decomposers present in nature and it did not create any significant harmful effect on the environment. In the recent times, however human population has increased tremendously and the technology has become greatly advanced. These two factors have contributed significantly in the deterioration of our environment due to addition of number of wastes.

Based on the information given above, answer the following questions:

(a) Rohan took three types of solid wastes P,Q, R and buried them under the soil in a pot, as he wanted to study their rate of decomposition. His findings are shown in the graph:

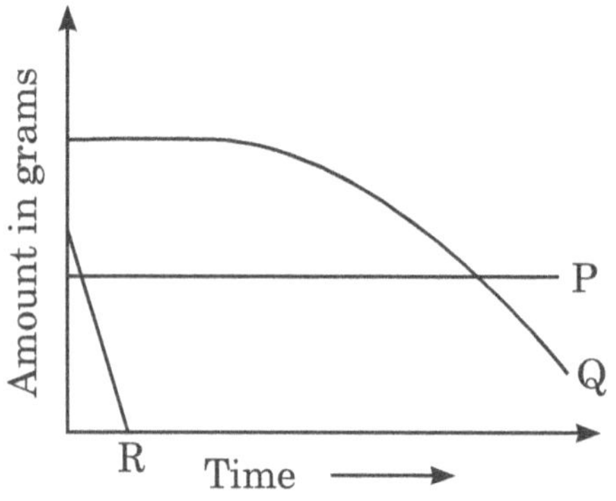

Select the option that correctly identifies P,Q and R:

	P	Q	R
i)	Polythene bag	Leather bag	Fruit peel
ii)	Used syringes	Broken glass	Leather purse
iii)	Cardboard	Cow dung	Rubber mat
iv)	Human excreta	Paper cup	Cow dung

(b) Select the incorrect option which mismatches the type of solid waste with its correct disposal system:

(i) Plastic bottle – send for recycling

(ii) Used tea and kitchen waste – collect in a pot to form compost

(iii) Used syringes and needles – wash and reuse

(iv) Municipal solid waste and fecal sludge – buried in low lying areas to level uneven surface of land

(c) Why is the correct waste disposal considered beneficial for our environment?

OR

Name two methods which can reduce the problem of waste disposal.

15. After the discovery of large number of elements it became necessary to classify them and arrange them in a regular manner in order of their periodic properties. In 1817, Johann Wolfgang Dobereiner tried to arrange the elements with similar properties into groups. He identified some groups of three elements having similar physical and chemical properties, known as Dobereiner's triads.

In 1865, John Netherlands arranged all known elements in the order of increasing atomic masses and found that the properties of every eighth element are similar to the properties of first elements.

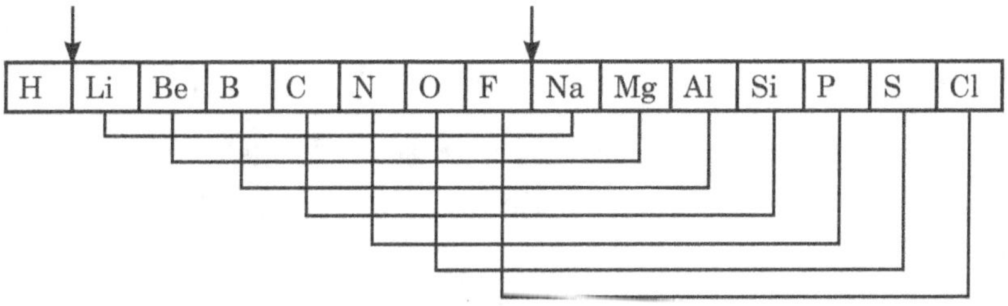

Based on the given information, answer the following questions:

(a) If Cl, Br and I is a Dobereiner's triad and the atomic masses of Cl and I are 35.5 and 127 respectively, then find the atomic mass of Br.

(b) Give another example of elements of Dobereiner's triad.

(c) (i) A and B are two elements having similar properties which obey Newland's law of octaves. How many elements are there in between A and B?

(ii) State Mendeleev's law.

OR

(i) According to the Newlands' law of octaves, the properties of magnesium are similar to which element?

(ii) Write one limitation of Dobereiner's triad.

SOLUTIONS

Section A

1. (a) Covalent compounds generally have low melting and boiling points because the forces of attraction between the molecules are not very strong. (1)

(b) (i) Diamond

(ii) Fullerenes (½ + ½)

2. We know that

V = IR

So, I α 1/R ......(V = constant)

$\Rightarrow A_1/A_2 = R/2R$

$\Rightarrow A_1/A_2 = ½$ (1 + 1)

OR

(i) B α I i.e. The magnitude of the magnetic field will also increase. (1)

(ii) The direction of the magnetic field will also get reversed. (1)

3. (a) When the DNA copying is inaccurate, it leads to variation in the gene expression and hence the individual may have the genetic defects and variations. (1)

(b) Cutting is used for growing rose plants. (1)

4. (a) Carbon has four electrons in its valence shell. So, it can neither accept nor gain four-electrons. One way to complete octet is by sharing of electrons. So, carbon forms a covalent bond to complete its octet. (1)

(b) The carbon and its compounds burn in oxygen to produce a large amount of energy.

$C + O_2 \rightarrow CO_2$ + Energy (huge amount)

This is the reason that these compounds are used as a fuel. (½ + ½)

OR

(i) $CH_2 - CO - CH_2 - CH_2 - CH_2 - CH_3$ – Ketone (½)

(ii) $CH_3 - CH_2 - CH_2 - COOH$– Carboxilic acid (½)

(iii) $CH_3 - CH_2 - CH_2 - CH_2 - CHO$– Aldehycle (½)

(iv) $CH_3 - CH_2 - OH$– Alcohol (½)

5 (a) Na atom is bigger than the atom of Mg.

Reason - atomic number of magnesium is more than sodium but the numbers of shells are same, the nuclear pull is more in case of Mg atom. Hence its size is smaller than sodium. (½ + ½)

(b) (i) Na is the most metallic in nature. It is bigger in size and more likely to lose its outermost electron.

(ii) Cl is the most non-metallic in nature. Being small in size and most likely to accept an electron. (½ + ½)

OR

(a) (i) F and Cl (ii) Na and K (1)

(b) Newland's law of octaves (1)

6. (a) Wire Y (½ + ½)

Reason – Greater resistance is offered by wire with more length Or $l \propto R$

(b) Given: $q = 1.6 \times 10^{-19}$ C, $I = 1$ A, $n = ?$, $t = 1$ s

We know, $q = It$ and $q = ne$

$$ne = It$$

$$n = \frac{It}{e} = \frac{1 \times 1}{1.6 \times 10^{-19}} = 6.25 \times 10^{18} \text{ electrons}$$ (½ + ½)

7. (a) Electromagnetism (1)

(b) i) If the magnet is pushed too quickly, there will a large change in flux. Due to this, a large current is induced in the coil and the galvanometer shows a large deflection in one direction. (1)

Section – B

8. As a doctor we should:

(i) Spread awareness about challenges with the growing population and suggestion that the couple should bear not more than two children. (1)

(ii) Use of physical barriers should be encouraged among the village couples. (1)

(iii) Couples who have already planned their families should be promoted for tubectomy or vasectomy so that they do not face unwanted pregnancy in future. (1)

OR

(a) The sex of female child is genetically determined by the father. The male sex chromosomes bear XY. If the egg is fertilized with X chromosome from both male and female, then the sex is determined to be of a girl. (1½)

(b) The medical termination of pregnancy refers to abortion of pregnancy with the use of combination of hormones or surgically by the help of a medical professional. (1½)

9. (a) R = 12000 Ω, V = 220 Volt

$$I = \frac{220}{1200} = \frac{11}{60} A$$

$\Rightarrow$ I = 0.183 A (1½)

(b) R = 100 Ω, V = 220 Volt

$$I = \frac{220}{100} = 2.2 \text{ A}$$ (1½)

10. (a) X = 2, 8, 2 Y = 2, 7

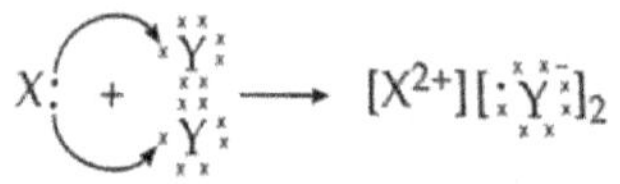

(1½)

(b) i) It is soluble in water

ii) Soluble in petrol or kerosene

iii) Flow of electric current is possible due to presence of ions. (1½)

11. (i)

$$I_1 = \frac{V}{R_1} = \frac{6}{5} = 1.2A$$

$$I_2 = \frac{V}{R_2} = \frac{6}{10} = 0.6A$$

$$I_3 = \frac{V}{R_3} = \frac{6}{30} = 0.2A$$

(1)

(ii) $I = I_1 + I_2 + I_3 = 1.2 + 0.6 + 0.2 = 2.0$ A (1)

(iii) $$\frac{1}{R} = \frac{1}{R_1} = \frac{1}{R_2} = \frac{1}{R_3}$$

$$= \frac{1}{5} + \frac{1}{10} + \frac{1}{30} = \frac{1}{3}$$

R = 3 Ω (1)

12. (a) (i) Round and yellow (ii) Round and green

(iii) Wrinkled and yellow (iv) Wrinkled and green (½ + ½)

(b) Wrinkled and green (1)

(c) Round and yellow (1)

OR

(a) monohybrid cross is the hybrid of two individuals with homozygous genotypes which result in the opposite phenotype for a certain genetic trait. (1)

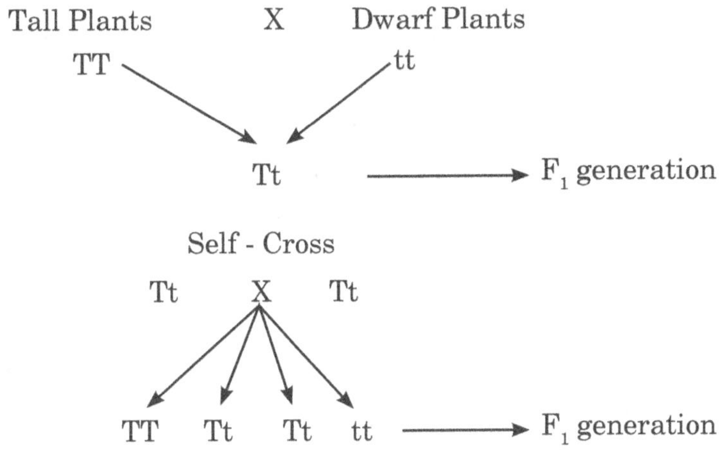

Phenotype - 3 : 1

Genotype - 1 : 2 : 1 (1 + 1)

13. (a) Grass – Maximum

Lion – Minimum (1 + 1)

(b) Peacock (1)

Section – C

14. (a) (i) P – Polythene bag

Q – Leather bag

R – Fruit peel (1)

(b) iii) The used syringes should not be washed and reused. (1)

(c) i) Transmission of diseases due to accumulation of wastes is a major threat to people and environment. (1)

(ii) Due to waste accumulation on land and water bodies, diseases are spread through flies, mosquitoes, rodents and pet animals. (1)

OR

(i) We can reuse the waste product i.e. using the empty jars to plant household plants. (1)

(ii) We can also recycle the waste products. (1)

15. (a) Atomic mass of Bromine = (35.5 + 127)/2 = 81.25 (1)

(b) Li, Na and K is an example of Dobereiner's triad. (1)

(c) (i) There are 5 elements between A and B. (1)

(ii) The Mendeleev's law states that the properties of elements are the periodic functions of their atomic masses. (1)

OR

(i) Properties of Magnesium are similar to those of Beryllium. (1)

(ii) Newly discovered elements did not fit into the triads. (1)

CBSE

Sample Question Paper 4

TERM II

Class X

Science

Time Allowed: 2 Hours **Maximum Marks: 40**

General Instructions

i. All questions are compulsory.

ii. The question paper has three sections and 15 questions. All questions are compulsory.

iii. Section–A has 7 questions of 2 marks each; Section–B has 6 questions of 3 marks each; and Section–C has 2 case based questions of 4 marks each.

iv. Internal choices have been provided in some questions. A student has to attempt only one of the alternatives in such questions.

Section – A

(7 × 2 Marks)

1. The following table gives the value of electrical resistivity of some samples :

Sample	A	B	C
Resistivity	1.6×10^{-3}	7.5×10^{17}	44×10^{-6}

Which one is the best conductor and insulator?

OR

Should the resistance of an ammeter be low or high? Give reason.

2. Rina went to her friend's house for vacation and she admired the beauty of the rose garden there. She planned to gift a rose garden to her parents for their anniversary next month.

(a) What technique should she follow to get more number of plants before the anniversary?

(b) Is the technique used by her is an example of sexual or asexual reproduction? Justify.

3. Jitu drops his father's old mobile and charger in e-waste bins of one of the thirteen Nokia priority centres of Chennai. In return for old mobile phones and chargers Nokia provided him with pen stand and eco-friendly pencils. When Jitu's friends came to know about this they too were inspired to drop their old, unwanted mobile phones in Nokia e-waste bins.

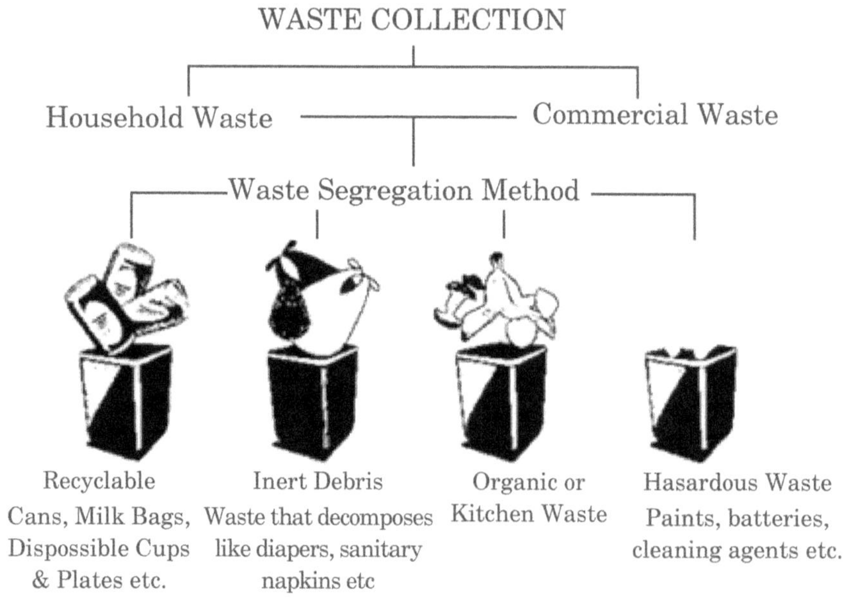

(a) Why is there a need to segregate e-waste?

(b) How does waste accumulation affect the environment?

4. (a) If a women is using a copper-T, will it help in protecting her from sexually transmitted diseases?

(b) Can you think of reasons why more complex organisms cannot give rise to new individuals through regeneration?

5. If we cross pure-bred tall (dominant) pea plant with pure-bred dwarf (recessive) pea plant we will get pea plants of F_1 generation. If we now self-cross the pea plant of F_2 generation, then we obtain pea plants of F_2 generation.

(a) What do the plants of F_2 generation look like?

(b) State the ratio of tall plants to dwarf plants in F_2 generation.

OR

In the following crosses write the characteristics of the progeny

	Cross	Progeny
(a)	RR YY × RR YY Round, yellow round, yellow	....
(b)	Rr Yy × Rr Yy Round, yellow round, yellow	....
(c)	TT yy × rr yy wrinkled, green wrinkled, green	....
(d)	RR yy × rr yy Round, yellow wrinkled green	....

6. (a) State Joule's law of heating.

(b) Find the expression for amount of heat produced.

OR

Define 1 volt. Express it in terms of SI unit of work and charge calculate the amount of energy consumed in carrying a charge of 1 coulomb through a battery of 3 V.

7. A solenoid is a coil of large number of circular turns of thick wire wrapped in the shape of a hollow cylinder. On passing electric current, a magnetic field is developed. The field is along the axis of solenoid such that one end of solenoid behaves as a north pole and other as south pole. Thus, the field of a solenoid is similar to that of a bar magnet.

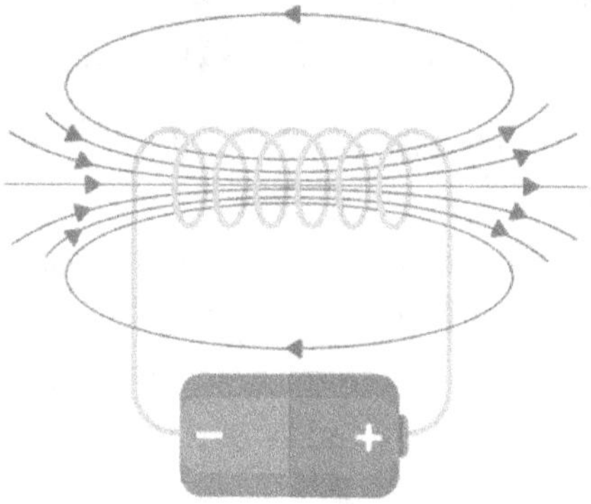

Solenoid

(a) What type of core should be put inside a current-carrying solenoid to make an electromagnet?

(b) Distinguish between a solenoid and a bar magnet.

Section – B

(6 × 3 Marks)

8. The given graph shows the time taken by different types of materials to decompose.

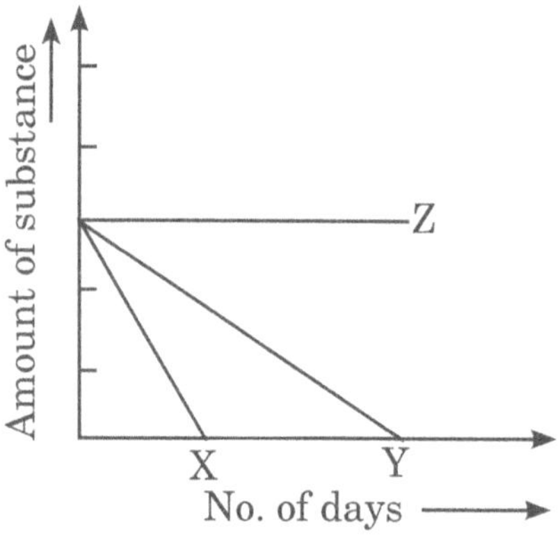

(a) Which of the substances X,Y and Z could be a non-biodegradable material?

(b) A teacher kept few solid waste in her class as given below:

Jute bag (I), Tube light (II), Aluminium foil (III), Paper cup (IV), Fruits (V), Glass tumbler (VI), Hedge trimming (VII), Plastic bag (VIII), Metal keys (IX), DDT (X)

She asked students to arrange them in two groups i.e. group A(Biodegradable) and group B(Non-biodegradable). Select the student that has completed the given task accurately:

(a) Tarun - Group A : I, IV, V, VII Group B : II, III, VI, VIII, IX, X

(b) Shivani - Group A : I, III, V, VIII, X Group B : II, IV, VI, VIII, IX

(c) Neha - Group A : II, III, IV, V, IX Group B : I, VI, VII, VIII, X

(a) Advait - Group A : I, III, IV, V, X Group B : II, VI, VII, VIII, IX

9. (a) State the modern periodic law.

(b) How many groups and periods are there in the modern periodic table?

(c) Write two drawbacks of the Newland's law of octaves.

10. Draw a closed circuit diagram consisting of a 0.5 m long nichrome wire XY, an ammeter, a voltmeter, four cells of 1.5 V each and a plug key.

OR

Following graph was plotted between V and I values :

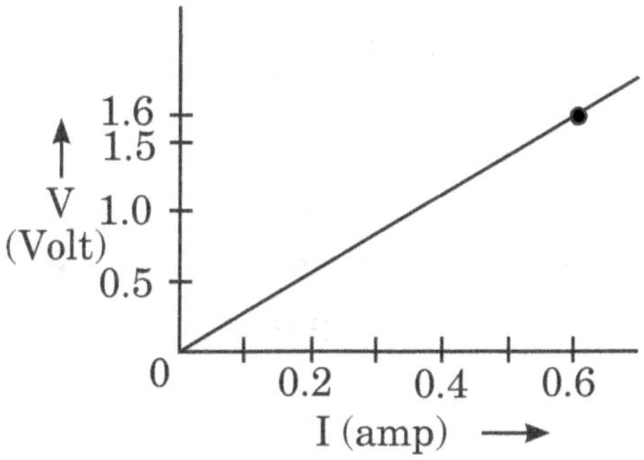

What would be the values of V /I ratios when the potential difference is 0.8 V, 1.2 V and 1.6 V respectively? What conclusion do you draw from these values?

11. (a) Explain depletion of ozone layer.

(b) Name the chemical which is responsible for this?

(c) Write its harmful effects also.

12. In the following table, are given eight elements A, B, C, D, E, F, G and H (here letters are not the usual symbols of the elements) of the Modern Periodic Table with the atomic numbers of the elements in parenthesis.

Period	Group 1	Group 2
2	A (3)	E (4)
3	B (11)	F (12)
4	C (19)	G (20)
5	D (37)	H (38)

(a) What is the electronic configuration of F?

(b) What is the number of valence electrons in the atom of F?

(c) Write the size of the atoms of E, F, G and H in decreasing order.

OR

(a) Hydrogen occupies a unique position in the modern periodic table. Give reason.

(b) Write the formulae of chlorides of Eka-silicon and Eka-aluminium, the elements predicted by Mendeleev's.

13. (a) Define pollination

(b) List two agents of pollination.

(c) How does suitable pollination lead to fertilization?

Section – C

(2 × 4 Marks)

This section has 02 case-based questions (14 and 15). Each case is followed by 03 sub-questions (a, b and c). Parts a and b are compulsory. However, an internal choice has been provided in part c.

14. A hydrocarbon (P) has the molecular formula $C_{10}H_{22}$. A hydrocarbon (Q) has two carbon atoms less than (P) and belong to the same homologous series. A hydrocarbon (R) has two carbon atoms more than (P) and belong to the same homologous series.

(a) What should be the molecular formula of (Q)?

(b) Write the general formula of homologous series of P and R.

(c) Write the molecular formula of (R) and define homologous series.

OR

(i) Give reason why graphite is a good conductor of electricity.

(ii) Which of the following types of binding forces is present in the structure of diamond?

Ionic, Van der Waals' or Covalent

15. Refer to the following figure of contrasting traits in pea plants studied by Mendel:

Character	**Dominant trait**	**Recessive trait**
(i) Seed Colour	 Yellow	 Green
(ii) Flower colour	 Violet	 White
(iii) Pod shape	 Full	 Constricted
(iv) Flower position	 Axial	 Terminal

(a) Identify which of the traits are correctly placed in the figure?

(b) How many colour based contrasting traits were studied by Mendel?

(c) Name some of the dominant traits studied by Mendel other than the traits given in the figure.

OR

Among the seven pairs of contrasting traits in pea plant as studied by Mendel, how many number of traits are related to flower, pod and seed respectively?

SOLUTIONS

Section A

1. Sample A is a conductor as the value of resistivity is the lowest. (1)

   Sample B is an insulator as the value of resistivity is the highest. (1)

OR

The resistance of an ammeter should be low. (1)

Reason - An ammeter has to be connected in series with the circuit to measure current. In case, its resistance is not very low, its inclusion in the circuit will reduce the current to be measured. (1)

2. (a) Rina should employ the technique of cutting to get more number of plants before the anniversary. (1)

   (b) The technique used by her is an example of asexual reproduction. The asexual reproduction in rose plants can occur through the stem cuttings. The new rose plant formed from the cutting is similar to the parent plant, thus rose plants are commonly grown by this method. (1)

3. (a) There is a need to segregate the two types of wastes because both the biodegradable wastes and non-biodegradable wastes require different methods of disposal. E-waste can be recycled. (1)

   (b) Waste accumulation affects the environment in many ways. Accumulation of wastes results in land pollution, landscape degeneration, soil contamination, air pollution, water and soil pollution, health problems, and loss of terrestrial and aquatic life. (1)

4. (a) No, Copper-T which is placed in the uterus prevents pregnancy. It cannot prevent sexually-transmitted diseases. (1)

   (b) Simple organisms are capable of producing new organisms through the process of regeneration. This is possible in simple organisms because the entire body is made up of similar kind of cells in which any part of their body can be formed by growth and development. (1)

In case of the complex organisms have organ system level organization. all the organ systems of their body work together as an interconnected unit.

The tissues in complex organisms cannot regenerate a new individual as they are highly differentiated to perform specialized functions. For example, human skin cannot regenerate into a new individual as it is a highly differentiated tissue performing a designed function.

5 (a) All the plants of F_1 generation will be tall plants.(b) 3:1 (1 + 1)

OR

(a) RRYY (Round yellow) (½)

(b) Round yellow, Round green, Wrinkled yellow, Wrinkled green (½)

(c) rryy (wrinkled green) (½)

(d) RrYy (Round yellow) (½)

6. (a) Joule's law of heating states that, when a current 'i ' passes through a conductor of resistance 'r' for time 't' then the heat developed in the conductor is equal to the product of the square of the current, the resistance and time. (1)

(b) W= QV = ItV or VIt = (IR)It = I^2Rt (1)

OR

$$V = \frac{W}{Q}$$ (1)

W = Q × V = 1 × 3 = 3 J (1)

7. (a) A soft iron core is placed inside a solenoid to make an electromagnet. When a soft iron core is placed inside a solenoid, then the strength of the magnetic field becomes very large because the iron core gets magnetized by induction. This combination of a solenoid and a soft iron core is called an electromagnet. (1)

(b) Bar magnet

It is a permanent magnet.

The strength of a bar magnet cannot be changed.

The polarity (North – South) of a bar magnet cannot be changed.

Solenoid

It is a temporary magnet. It acts as a magnet only as long as the current passes through it.

The strength of a solenoid can be changed by changing the number of turns in its coil or by changing the current passing through it.

The polarity of a solenoid can be changed by changing the direction of current in its coil. (1)

Section - B

8. (a) The substance Z is non-biodegradable as it does not decompose at all. (1½)

(b) A) The student named Tarun has completed the task accurately. (1½)

9. (a) Properties of elements are the periodic function of their atomic numbers. (1)

(b) There are 18 groups(vertical columns) and 7 periods (horizontal lines) in the modern periodic table. (1)

(c) The limitations of Newlands's law of octaves are:

(i) It was applicable to only lighter elements having atomic masses upto 40 u, i.e., upto calcium. (½)

(ii) It was assumed that only 63 elements existed in nature and no new elements would be discovered in the future. (½)

10. The required circuit diagram has been shown below:

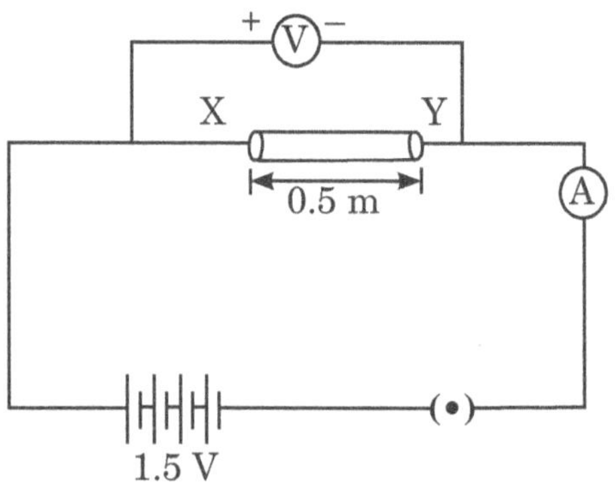

(1 + 1 + 1)

OR

From the graph, when p.d is 1.6 volt and 0.6 A current.

$$\frac{V}{I} = \frac{1.6}{0.6} = 2.67\,\Omega$$

(1)

There for, value of $\frac{V}{I}$ ratio for all potential difference of 0.8 V. 1.2 V and 1.6 volt will be equal to 2.67 Ω (1)

We conclude that at the given temperature, the resistance of wire is constant and is equal to 2.67 Ω (1)

11. (a) Ozone layer depletion is the thinning of the ozone layer present in the upper atmosphere. This happens when the chlorine and bromine atoms in the atmosphere come in contact with ozone and destroy the ozone molecules. (1)

(b) The chemical reactions are as follows:

$$O_{2(g)} \xrightarrow{UV} O_{(g)} + O_{(g)}$$

$$O_{2(g)} + O_{(g)} \xrightarrow{UV} O_{3(g)}$$

$$CF_2Cl_{2(g)} \xrightarrow{UV} Cl_{(g)} + CF_2Cl$$

(1)

$$Cl_{(g)} + O_{3(g)} \longrightarrow ClO_{(g)} + O_{2(g)}$$

$$ClO_{(g)} + O_{(g)} \longrightarrow Cl_{(g)} + O_{2(g)}$$

(c) Harmful effects include increases in certain types of skin cancers, eye cataracts and immune deficiency disorders. (1)

12. (a) 2, 8, 2. (b) 2 (c) H> G> F> E (1 + 1 + 1)

OR

(a) Hydrogen has electron configuration of 1.To become stable, it can either accept to get helium configuration that is a stable configuration or it can even donate one electron. So, it is very confusing where to place either in the metals group as it donates or in non-metal group as it accepts an electron. Hence, it occupies a unique position in the periodic table. (1)

(b) Germanium is called Eka-silicon and Gallium is known as Eka-aluminium. (1 + 1)

13. (a) Transfer of pollen grains from anther to stigma is termed as Pollination. (1)

(b) This transfer of pollen grains occurs with the help of pollinating agents like wind, water, insects, birds etc. (1)

(c) By the process of pollination, pollens grain reaches to the stigma of flower. After that pollen tube develops from pollen grain. Pollen tube develops from pollen grain. Pollen tube contains two male gametes. One male gamete fuses with the egg to form diploid zygote and other male gametes fuses with polar nuclei to form triploid nucleus, which develops into endosperm. Thus, suitable pollination leads to fertilization. (1)

Section - C

14. (a) Molecular formula of Q is C_8H_{18} as it has two carbon atoms less than P. (1)

(b) Compounds P,Q and R are alkanes having general formula $C_nH_{2n+2.}$ (1)

(c) Molecular formula of R is $C_{12}H_{26}$ as it has two carbon atoms more than P.

Homologous series - A series of carbon compounds in which same functional group substitutes the hydrogen atom is called a homologous series. These compounds have similar chemical properties due to the addition of same kind of functional group throughout the chain. (1 + 1)

OR

(i) Graphite is a good conductor of electricity because in graphite, each carbon is bonded to three other carbon atoms hence leaving behind a free electron. Due to the presence of this one delocalised electron. (1)

(ii) In the structure of diamond, there are covalent bonds. (1)

15. (a)

	Trait studied	Dominant	Recessive
1	Plant height	Tall (T)	Dwarf (t)
2	Flower position	Axial (A)	Terminal (a)
3	Flower colour	Violet (V) or (W)	White (v) or (w)
4	Pod shapte	Full or Inflated (I) or (C)	Constricted (i) or (c)
5	Pod colour	Green (G) or (Y)	Yellow (g) or (y)
6	Seed shape	Round (R) or (W)	Wrinkled (r) or (w)
7	Seed colour	Yellow (Y) or (G)	Green (y) or (g)

(1)

Hence all the traits are correctly placed.

(b) Three colour based traits were studied by Mendel. (1)

(c) Violet flower colour, green pod colour and round seed shape are the other dominant characters. (1 + 1)

OR

Flower - Two

Pod - Two

Seed – Two (1 + 1)

CBSE

Sample Question Paper 5

TERM II

Class X

Science

Time Allowed: 2 Hours **Maximum Marks: 40**

General Instructions

i. All questions are compulsory.

ii. The question paper has three sections and 15 questions. All questions are compulsory.

iii. Section–A has 7 questions of 2 marks each; Section–B has 6 questions of 3 marks each; and Section–C has 2 case based questions of 4 marks each.

iv. Internal choices have been provided in some questions. A student has to attempt only one of the alternatives in such questions.

Section – A

(7 × 2 Marks)

1. Write the name and formula of the 2nd member of homologous series having general formula of C_nH_{2n} .

2. In the figure, identify the poles marked P and Q as north or south pole.

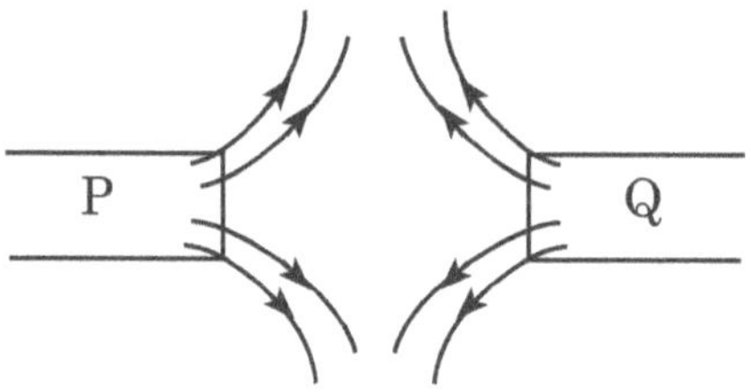

OR

A magnetic compass needle is placed in the plane of paper near point A as shown in Figure. In which plane should a straight current carrying conductor be placed so that it passes through A and there is not change in the deflection of the compass? Under what condition is the deflection maximum?

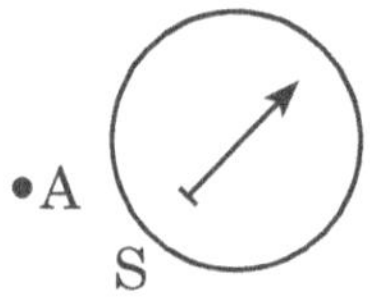

3. Explain why pollination may occur without fertilisation but fertilisation will not take place without pollination?

4. (a) The 2C charge is flowing through a conductor in 100 ms, find the current in the circuit.

(b) What will be the potential difference between two terminals of a battery, if 100 joules of work is required to transfer 20 coulombs of charge from one terminal of the battery to other?

5. (a) Electronic configuration of an element 'X' is 2,1. What will be the number of elements present in the period to which X belongs?

(b) Among the elements A,B,C,D and E with atomic numbers 2,3,7,10 and 30 respectively. Which of these given elements belong to the same period?

OR

An element X (atomic number 17) reacts with an element Y (atomic number 20) to form a divalent halide.

(a) Where in the periodic table are elements X and Y placed?

(b) Classify X and Y as metal, non – metal or metalloid.

(c) What will be the nature of oxide of element Y? Identify the nature of bonding in the compound formed.

6. In fruitflies, the gene for wing shape has two alleles, an unusual allele for curled wings (c) and the normal allele for straight wings (C). The given phenotypes are observed for each genotype:

Genotype	**Phenotype**
CC	Normal, straight wings
Cc	Wings curled up at the ends, has difficulty flying
cc	Unable to hatch from egg

(a) Two curly winged flies are crossed and they produce 150 eggs. What is the proportion of straight-winged flies expected among the live offspring?

(b) Which of the following crosses would be able to produce offspring that has curled wings only?

(i) CC × Cc (ii) CC × cc

(iii) Cc × Cc (iv) Cc × cc

7. (a) Find the current in each resistance:

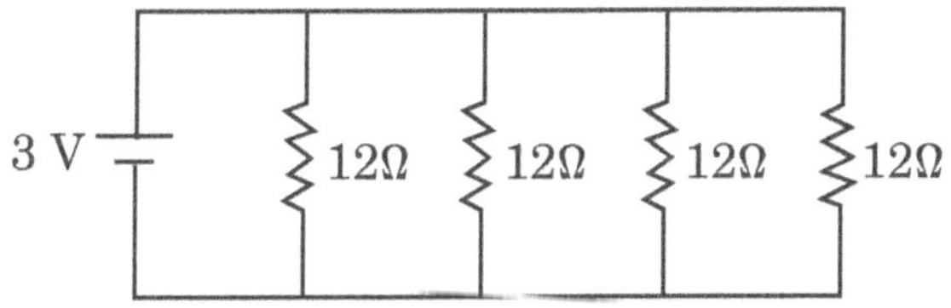

(b) In the following circuit, find the equivalent resistance between A and B is (R = 2Ω)

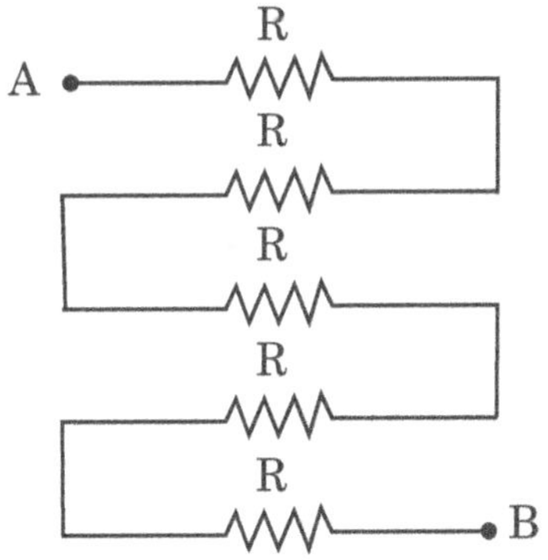

OR

(a) How does use of a fuse wire protect electrical appliances?

(b) What is the commercial unit of electrical energy? Represent it in terms of joules.

Section – B

(6 × 3 Marks)

8. (a) Why do all the gametes formed in human females have an X-chromosome?

(b) In human beings, the statistical probability of getting either a male or a female child is 50 : 50. Give a suitable explanation.

(c) Explain how offspring and parents of organisms formed by asexual reproduction exhibit remarkable similarity?

OR

(a) Give two reasons for the appearance of variations among the progeny formed by sexual reproduction.

(b) In tobacco plant, the male gametes have twenty four chromosomes. What is the number of chromosomes in the female gamete? What is the number of chromosomes in the zygote?

9. (a) Write the structural formula of all the isomers of hexane.

(b) Give the structural differences between saturated and unsaturated hydrocarbons with two examples each.

(c) Write the formula and draw electron dot structure of Carbon tetrachloride.

OR

(a) Carbon Group (14) element in the periodic table, is known to form compounds with many elements.

Write the example of a compound formed with:

(i) Chlorine (Group 17 of periodic table)

(ii) Oxygen (Group 16 of periodic table)

(b) Draw the electron dot structure of chlorine molecule.

(c) Write the names of the following compounds:

(a) 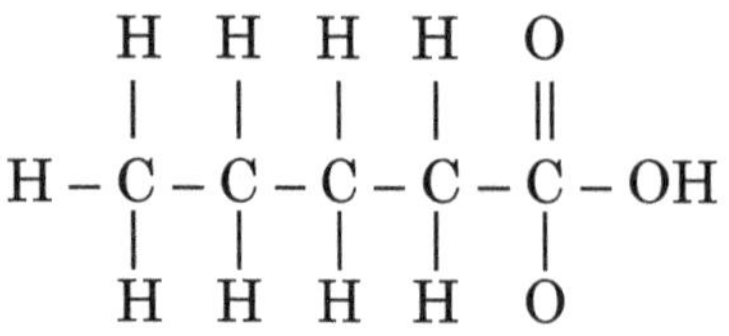

(b) 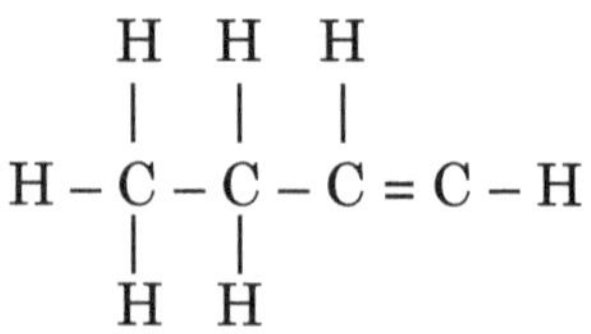

(c) 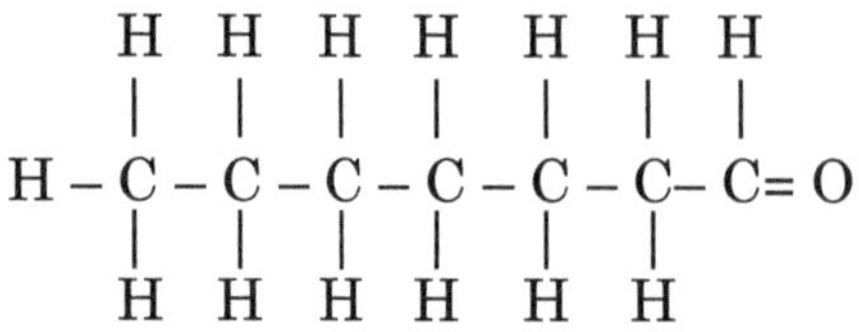

(d) 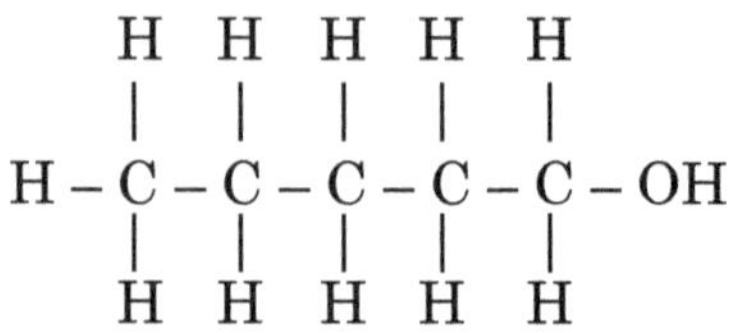

10. B_1, B_2 and B_3 are three identical bulbs connected as shown in Figure. When all the three bulbs glow, a current of 3A is recorded by the ammeter A.

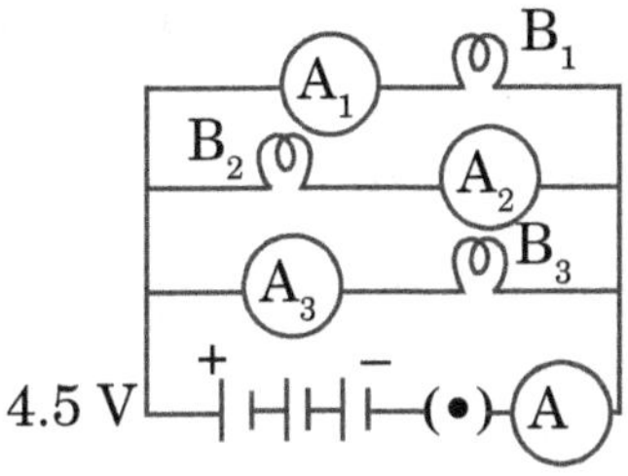

(i) What happens to the glow of the other two bulbs when the bulb B_1 gets fused?

(ii) What happens to the reading of A_1, A_2, A_3 and A. when the bulb B_2 gets fused?

(iii) How much power is dissipated in the circuit when all the three bulbs glow together?

11. (a) What is the difference between a direct current and an alternating current? How many times does AC used in India change direction in one second?

(b) Name four appliances wherein an electric motor, a rotating device that converts electrical energy to mechanical energy, is used as an important component.

(c) Under what conditions permanent electromagnet is obtained if a current carrying solenoid is used?

12. (a) What are Sexually Transmitted Diseases (STD)?

(b) List two bacterial and two viral STDs.

(c) Which of the following is not a Sexually Transmitted Disease?

(a) Wart

(b) Syphilis

(c) Gonorrhoea

(d) Covid -19

13. "Atomic number of an element is considered to be more appropriate parameter than its atomic mass for a chemist." Take the example of the element X (atomic number 13) to justify this statement.

OR

(a) Name the element which has twice as many electrons in its second shell as in the first shell. Write its electronic configuration also.

(b) Calcium, Magnesium and Strontium are kept in the same group of periodic table on the basis of its chemical properties, Write those characteristics. Write which element has the biggest size and why?

Section – C

(4 × 2 Marks)

This section has 02 case-based questions (14 and 15). Each case is followed by 03 sub-questions (a, b and c). Parts a and b are compulsory. However, an internal choice has been provided in part c.

14. Spore formation, a method of asexual reproduction is used by unicellular as well as multicellular organisms. Spores are microscopic units which could be air borne or present in soil etc.

Observe the given figure showing spore formation:

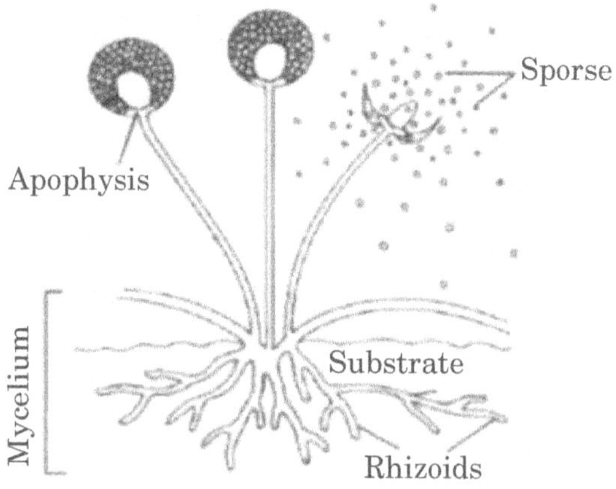

(a) Name two organisms which use it to reproduce. (1)

(b) What is the function of cell wall in a spore? (1)

(c) Explain why spore formation is a method of asexual reproduction. (2)

OR

Give examples of any three contraceptive methods.

15. Andre Marie Ampere suggested that a magnet must exert an equal and opposite force on a current carrying conductor, which was experimentally found to be true. But we know that current is due to charges in motion.

Thus, it is clear that a charge moving in a magnetic field experience a force, except when it is moving in a direction parallel to it. If the direction of motion is perpendicular to the direction of magnetic field, the magnitude of force experienced depends on the charge, velocity(v), strength of magnetic field(B) and sine of the angle between v and B. Direction of magnetic force is given by Fleming's left hand rule:

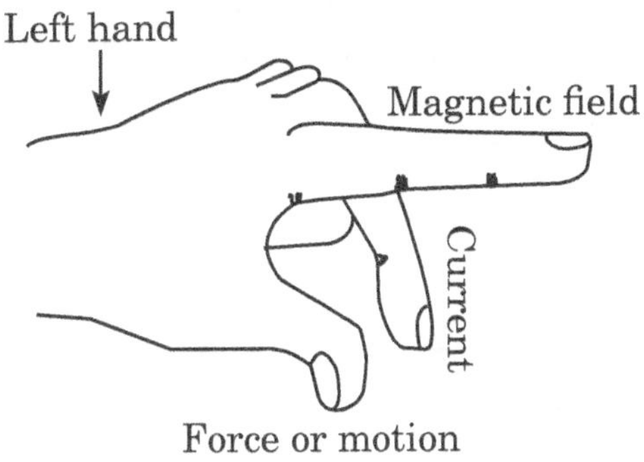

(i)

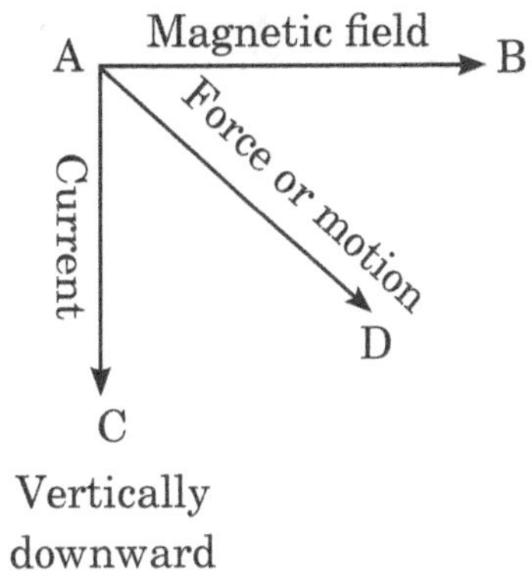

(ii)

(a) If an electron is travelling horizontally towards east and magnetic field has vertically downward direction, in which direction it will exert a force on the electron?

(b) An electron beam enters a magnetic field at right angles to it as shown in the figure. What will be the direction of force acting on the electron?

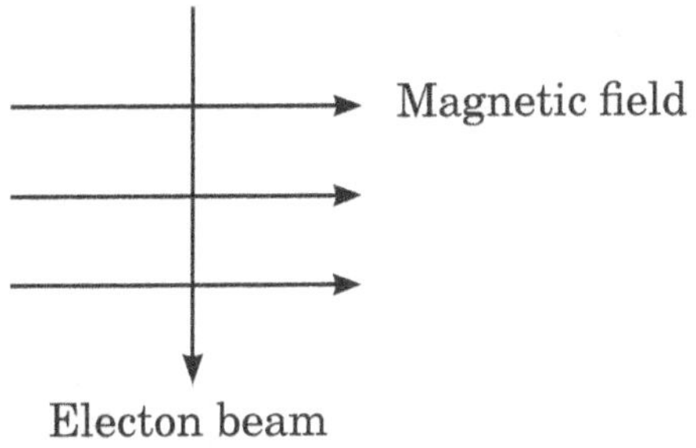

(c) If a charged particle is moving along a magnetic field line, the magnetic force on the particle is?

(i) Along its velocity

(ii) Opposite to its velocity

(iii) Perpendicular to its velocity

(iv) Zero

Give reason for your choice.

OR

State the Fleming's left hand rule.

SOLUTIONS

Section – A

1. The homologous series for n = 1 will be CH_2. (½ + ½)

Its first member will be C_2H_4

The name of the second member will be Propene and its formula is C_3H_6.

2. P – North-pole Q – South-pole (½ + ½)

OR

The deflection will be maximum when the magnetic field due to the compass is perpendicular to the direction of the current. So, if we place the conductor on the plane of the paper the deflection of the compass will be minimum. On the other hand, if the current carrying conductor is perpendicular to the magnetic field, the deflection of the magnetic field will be maximum. (1 + 1)

3. Pollination may occur without fertilization but fertilization will not take place without pollination because pollination does not depend on fertilization but fertilization cannot take place without pollination because for fertilization to occur, it requires both male and female gametes. (1 + 1)

4. (a) q = 2 C, t = 100 ms = 0.1 s

$$I = \frac{q}{t} = \frac{2}{0.1} = 20 \text{ A.}$$ (1)

(b) W = 100 j, q = 20 C

$$V = \frac{W}{q} = \frac{100}{20} = 5 \text{ V}$$ (1)

5 (a) Element 'X' is Li. It belongs to second period.

No. of elements = $2n^2 = 2 \times (2)^2 = 8$ (1)

(b) B, C and D all belong to the same period. (1)

OR

(a) X belongs to Group 17 and 3rd period

Y belongs to Group 2 and 4th period (½ + ½)

(b) X-Non-metal and Y metal (½)

(c) Basic oxide; Ionic bonding (½)

6. (a) 25% of the total number of eggs will not hatch (genotype cc). 50% of the offspring will be curly winged (Cc) and 25% of the offspring are straight winged (CC). (1)

(b) (ii) CC × cc (1)

7. (a) All are in parallel.

$$\frac{1}{R_p} = \frac{1}{12} \times 4 = \frac{1}{3} \Rightarrow R_p = 3\ \Omega$$

$$I = \frac{3}{3} = 1A \qquad (1)$$

So, current in each resistor $I' = \frac{3}{12} = \frac{1}{4}A$

(b) All are in series, $R_s = 5R = 5 \times 2 = 10\ \Omega$ (1)

OR

(a) An electrical fuse works by breaking the circuit when there is a fault in an appliance that causes too much current to flow. The wire within the circuit melts due to the heat generated when the current going through the circuit is too great. In this way, fuse wire protect electrical appliances. (1)

(b) The commercial unit of electrical energy is kilowatt-hour(kWh).

$1\text{ kWh} = 1\text{ kW} \times 1\text{ h}$

$= 1000\text{ W} \times 1\text{ h} = 1000\text{ Js}^{-1} \times 3600\text{ s}$ (1)

$1\text{ kWh} = 3600000\text{ J} = 3.6 \times 10^6\text{ J}$

Section – B

8. (a) Human females have the two X chromosomes called sex chromosomes as the 23rd pair of chromosomes. During meiosis at the time of gamete formation, one X chromosome enters each gamete. Hence all the female gametes possess an X chromosome. (1)

(b) The sex of an infant is determined by the type of sex chromosome contributed by the male gamete. Since the ratio of male gametes containing X chromosome and those containing Y chromosome is 50:50, the statistical probability of male or a female infant is also 50 : 50. (1)

(c) In the case of asexual reproduction, genes are contributed by a single parent. Due to this, offspring produced by asexual reproduction are clones of their parent. (1)

OR

(a) The two major reasons for the appearance of variation among the progeny formed by sexual reproduction are: (1 + 1)

1) Crossing over is the process in which DNA is exchanged between the homologous chromosomes during meiosis, This causes variation in the progeny.

2) The progeny formed due to sexual reproduction has characteristics from the mother as well as the father. Hence because of this the characteristics differ and result in variation.

(b) The number of chromosome in the female gamete would be same as that in the male gamete, i.e., it will have 24 chromosomes. The number of chromosome in the zygote would be double the number present in the gamete and hence, it would be 48. (1)

9. (a) Hexane has five isomers:

(i) Hexane, $CH_3CH_2CH_2CH_2CH_2CH_3$

(ii) Isohexane,$CH_3CH(CH_3)CH_2CH_2CH_3$

(iii) 3-Methylpentane, $CH_3CH_2CH(CH_3)CH_2CH_3$

(iv) 2,3-Dimethylbutane, $CH_3CH(CH_3)CH(CH_3)CH_3$

(v) Neohexane, $CH_3C(CH_3)_2CH_2CH_3$ (1)

(b) Saturated hydrocarbons contain carbon-carbon single bonds. Unsaturated hydrocarbons contain at least one carbon-carbon double or triple bond.

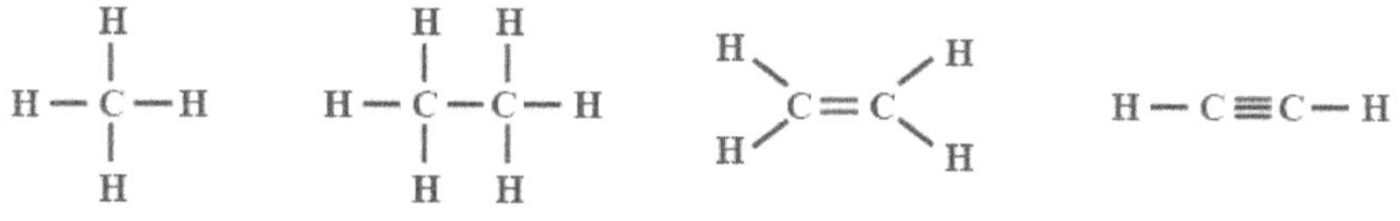

Methane Ethane Ethene Ethyne

Saturated hydrocarbons Unsaturated hydrocarbons (1)

(c) The formula of Carbon tetrachloride is CCl_4. The electron dot structure is shown below:

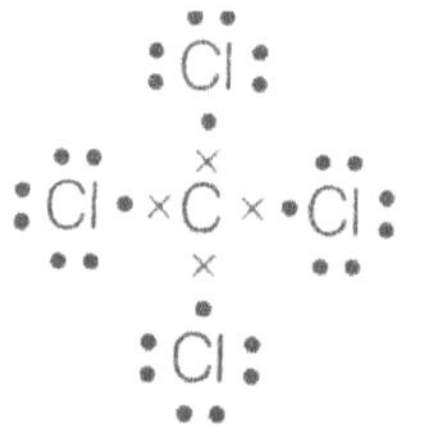

(1)

OR

(a) (i) Carbon tetrachloride

(ii) Carbon dioxide (½ + ½)

(b) 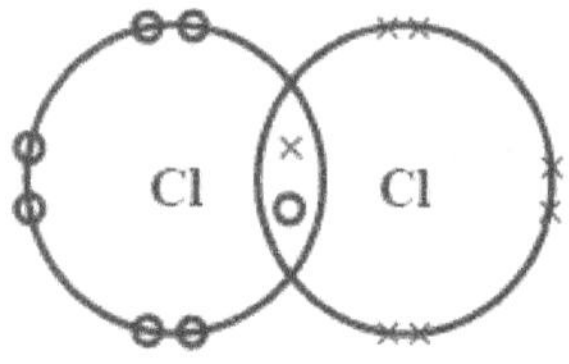

(1)

(c) (a) Pentanoic acid

(b) Butyne (1)

(c) Heptanal

(d) Pentanol

10. (i) When B_1 is fused, there will be no influence on the glow of the other two bulbs, which will remain the same since bulb glowing is dependent on power, and the potential difference and resistance of the other two bulbs remain the same. (1)

(ii) When there are parallel connections

Net resistance will be

$1/R = 1/R_1 + 1/R_2 + 1/R_3$

Since resistance is the same so, R' = R/3

As per ohm's law

V = IR (1)

R = 4.5Ω

Since B_2 gets fused, so now only two bulbs B_1 and B_3 are in parallel

Net resistance in parallel 1/R' =2/R

R' = 4.5/2 Ω

I = V/R' = 2×4.5/4.5 = 2A

Current will be distributed in both the bulbs as 1 A each.

(iii) Power dissipated when all three bulbs glow together

P = V × I

P= 4.5 × 3 = 13.5 W (1)

11. (a) In case of AC; the direction of current keeps on changing at fixed intervals or periodically, while the direction of current always remains the same in case of DC.

The AC in India changes its direction at the rate of 100 times in a second, which is equal to 50 Hz and in each cycle it alters direction twice, hence 100 times a second. (1)

(b) Vacuum cleaners,Washing Machines, Air conditioners, Grinders and mixers **are a few home appliances that use electric motors.** (1)

(c) The conditions to obtain permanent electromagnet as following if a current carrying solenoid is used are (i) The current through the solenoid should be direct current. (ii) The rod inside is made of a magnetic material such as steel.

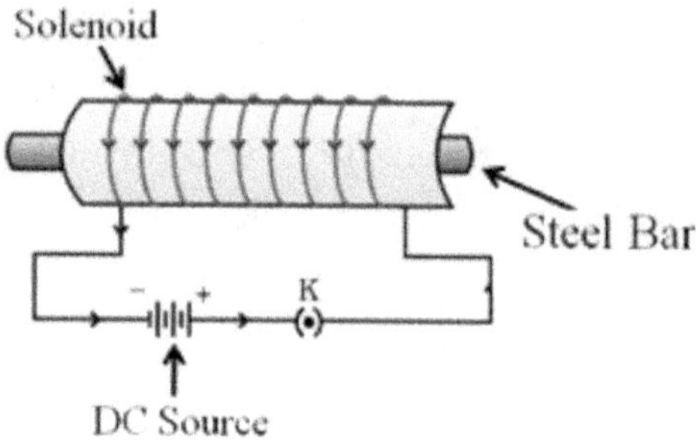

(1)

12. (a) Sexually transmitted diseases (STDs) are infections that are passed from one person to another through sexual contact.

(b) Bacterial STD – Chlamydia, Gonorrhoea

Viral STD – AIDS, Genital herpes

(c) The correct option is d i.e. Covid-19 (1 + 1 + 1)

13. The atomic number of the given element is 13.

Its electronic configuration is 2,8,3

So, it is electropositive in nature

It is also significant that it belongs to group 13 and period 1.

Therefore, atomic number is more appropriate parameter than atomic mass. (1 + 1 + 1)

OR

(a) The element carbon has twice as many electrons in its second shell as in the first shell.

It has 6 electrons. In the first shell K, there are 2 electrons and in the second shell L, there are 4 electrons which can be represented as: (1½)

K	L
2	4

(b) The following are the characteristics of the given elements:

(i) Metallic in nature

(ii) They can form alkaline oxides (1½)

Among the given elements, Strontium has the biggest size. This is due to the reason that as we go down the group, the size of the nucleus also increases.

Section – C

14. (a) Rhizopus and Mucor (1)

(b) The cell wall is the outermost layer which protects the spores against a myriad of environmental aggressions such as UV, temperature etc. (1)

(c) Spore formation mainly occurs in non-flowering plants which is a type of asexual reproduction. A thousand spores are produced by the plants, which further grow into new plants. The organism does not need male and female reproductive organs.It does not involve the participation of both male and female gametes. (1 + 1)

OR

The three examples of contraceptive methods can be:

(i) Barrier method – Condoms, diaphragm etc.

(ii) IUDs

(iii)Emergency contraceptive pills (2)

15. (a) The direction of the force on electron will be towards south. (1)

(b) The direction of force acting on the electron will be into the page. (1)

(c) The correct option is (iv) i.e. zero because the angle between velocity and magnetic field is zero. Therefore, the magnetic force on the particle is also zero. (2)

OR

Fleming's Left hand rule states that if we arrange our thumb, forefinger and middle finger of the left hand right angles to each other, then the thumb points towards the direction of the magnetic force, the forefinger points towards the direction of magnetic field and the middle finger points towards the direction of the current. (2)

Social Science

CBSE

Sample Question Paper 1

TERM II

CLASS X

SOCIAL SCIENCE

Time Allowed: 2 Hours | *Maximum Marks: 40*

General Instructions

i. *This Question paper is divided into five sections-Section A, B, C, D and E.*

ii. *All questions are compulsory.*

iii. ***Section-A:*** *Question no. 1 to 5 are very short answer type questions of 2 marks each. Answer to each question should not exceed 40 words.*

iv. ***Section-B:*** *Question no. 6 to 8 are short answer type questions, carrying 3 marks each. Answer to each question should not exceed 80 words.*

v. ***Section-C:*** *Question no. 9 and 10 are long answer type questions, carrying 5 marks each. Answer to each question should not exceed 120 words.*

vi. ***Section-D:*** *Question no. 11 and 12 are Case Based questions.*

vii. ***Section-E:*** *Question no. 13 is map based, carrying 3 marks with two parts, 13.1 from History (1 mark) and 13.2 from Geography (2 marks).*

viii. *There is no overall choice in the question paper. However, an internal choice has been provided in a few questions. Only one of the choices in such questions have to be attempted.*

ix. *In addition to this, separate instructions are given with each section and question, wherever necessary.*

Section-A

Very Short Answer Questions **2 × 5 = 10**

1. Why was the Rowlatt Act unjust?
2. Explain how roads are classified on the basis of raw material used for their construction. Which of the two is better and why?
3. Why is there an overwhelming support for the idea of democracy all over the world?
4. What is meant by Collateral?
5. Write a note on Mini steel plants.

Section-B

Short Answer Type Questions **3 × 3 = 9**

6. Explain how people are involved with banks.

   OR

   'Multinational Corporations through a number of ways spread their production in the global market.' Comment.
7. Why was Simon Commission set up? Why did the Indians oppose it?
8. Explain the political, social and economic outcomes of a democracy?

Section-C

Long Answer Type Questions **5 × 2 = 10**

9. 'Political parties have a crucial role to play in a democracy.' Elucidate.

   OR

   Name any one country that has a multi party system. Explain its merits and demerits.
10. How has globalisation proven to be advantageous for the consumers worldwide but a disadvantage for the local producers?

    OR

    Explain 'loan from Cooperatives.'

Section-D

Case Based Questions **4 × 2 = 8**

Read the given text and answer the following questions:

11. *'We believe that it is the inalienable right of the Indian people, as of any other people, to have freedom and to enjoy the fruits of their toil and have the necessities of life, so that they may have full opportunities of growth. We believe also that if any government deprives a people of these rights and oppresses them, the people have a further right to alter it or to abolish it. The British Government in India has not only deprived the Indian people of their freedom but has based itself on the exploitation of the masses, and has ruined India economically, politically, culturally, and spiritually. We believe, therefore, that India must sever the British connection and attain Purna Swaraj or Complete Independence.'* 4

11.1 The above extract is an excerpt from________________? 1

11.2 What kind of government do the people wish to abolish? 1

11.3 What did the Indians demand for and why? 2

12. *Since the ancient period, India was one of the seafaring countries. Its seamen sailed far and near, thus, carrying and spreading Indian commerce and culture. These are the cheapest means of transport. They are most suitable for carrying heavy and bulky goods. It is a fuel-efficient and environment friendly mode of transport. India has inland navigation of these as 14,500 km in length. Out of these only 5685 km are navigable by mechanised vessels.* 4

12.1 Which means of transport is discussed in the above text? 1

12.2 Apart from goods, what did the Indian sailors carried along and were able to spread using the means of transport discussed in the above text? 1

12.3 State any two advantages of the means of transport discussed in the above text? 2

Section-E

Map Skill Based Question **1 × 3 = 3**

13.1 On the given outline Political Map of India, identify the place marked as A with the help of following information and write its correct name on the line marked near it.

(A) The place associated with the Civil Disobedience Movement (Salt March)

13.2 On the same given map of India, locate the following:

(I) Narora Nuclear plant

OR

Namrup Thermal plant

(II) Thiruvananthapuram software technology park

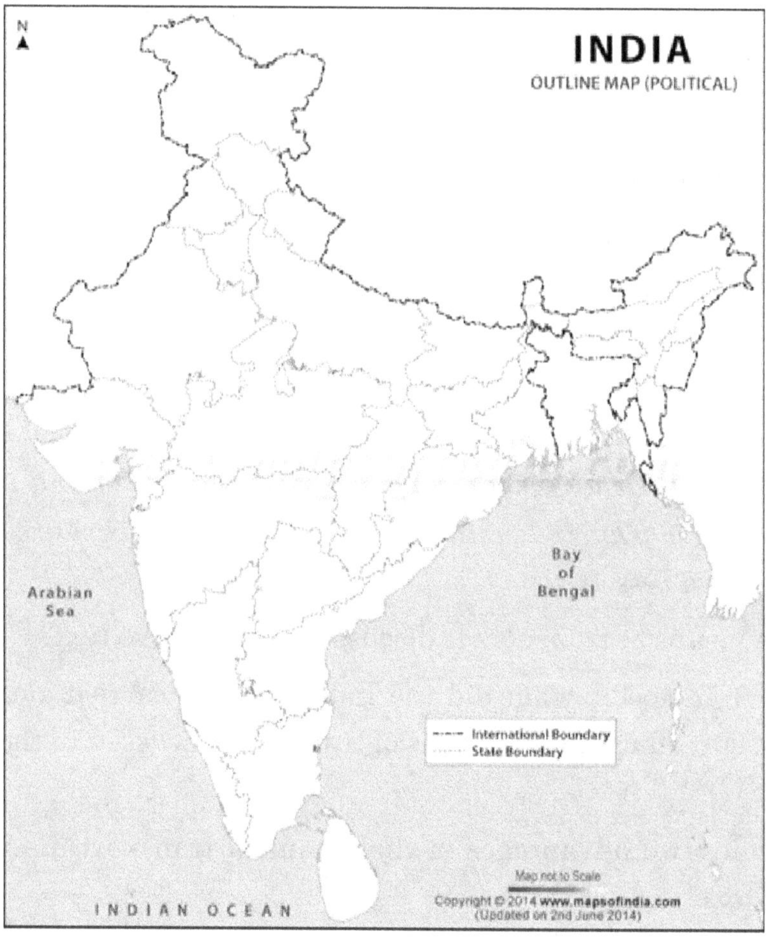

SOLUTION

Section-A

1. The Rowlatt Act of 1919 was unjust because it gave the government enormous powers to repress political activities, and allowed detention of political prisoners without trial for two years. **2**

2. On the basis of raw material used roads are classified as metalled and unmetalled. Metalled roads may be made of cement, concrete or even bitumen of coal, and are therefore more durable over the unmetalled road which may impair during the monsoon. **2**

3. A democratic government is a legitimate government. It may be slow, less efficient, not always very responsive or clean. But a democratic government is people's own government. **2**

4. Collateral is an asset that the borrower owns (such as land, building, vehicle, live stocks, deposits with banks) and uses this as a guarantee to a lender until the loan is repaid. If the borrower fails to repay the loan, the lender has the right to sell the asset or collateral to obtain payment. **2**

5. Mini steel plants are smaller, have electric furnaces, use steel scrap and sponge iron. They have re-rollers that use steel ingots as well. They produce mild and alloy steel of given specifications. **2**

Section-B

6. Banks accept the deposits from the people who have surplus money and also pay interest on the deposits. But banks keep only a small portion (15 per cent in India) of their deposits as cash with themselves. This is kept as a provision to pay the depositors who might come to withdraw money from their accounts in the bank on any day. They use the major portion of the deposits to extend loans to those who need money. In this way, banks mediate between those who have surplus money and those who need money. **3**

OR

Multinational Corporations use the following ways to spread their production in the global market:

(i) MNCs set up production jointly with some of the local companies where they wish to expand their brand.

(ii) MNCs buy the local companies and then expand its production with the help of modern technology.

(iii) Large MNCs in developed countries place orders for production with small producers. **1 × 3 = 3**

7. In response to the nationalist movement that were taking place in India , the Simon commission was set up in Britain to look into the functioning of the constitutional system in India and suggest changes. The Simon Commission was opposed on the ground that it did not consist a single Indian representative, instead all representatives were British. **3**

8. As a political outcome of democracy, we expect an accountable, responsive and legitimate government.

The social outcomes of a democracy are based on the idea of equality. It is expected that social diversities are accommodated and all citizens are provided with dignity and freedom.

As an economic outcome, we expect that democracies must reduce economic inequalities. **1 × 3 = 3**

Section-C

9. It is true that political parties have a crucial role to play in a democracy. This is because of the following reasons:

(i) Parties contest elections: This is the foremost function performed by political parties in a democracy. Parties select their candidates in different ways. In some countries, such as the USA, members and supporters of a party choose its candidates. In other countries like India, top party leaders choose candidates for contesting elections.

(ii) Parties put forward different policies and programmes and the voters choose from them. These policies and programmes are aimed at benefitting the public.

(iii) Parties play a decisive role in making laws for a country.

(iv) Parties form and run governments. The party that wins the elections is endowed with the huge responsibility of forming and running the government. The party needs to ensure that it has capable leaders and policies that are acceptable to the general public.

(v) Those parties that lose in the elections play the role of opposition to the parties in power, by voicing different views and criticising government for its failures or wrong policies. Opposition parties also mobilise opposition to the government.

(vi) Parties shape public opinion. They raise and highlight issues. Many of the pressure groups are the extensions of political parties among different sections of society.

(vii) Parties provide people access to government machinery and welfare schemes implemented by governments. (Any five)

1 × 5 = 5

OR

India.

Merits of a multi-party system:

(i) The foremost advantage of a multi-party system is that it offers a wide variety of choices to its voters.

(ii) This system allows a variety of interests and opinions to enjoy political representation

Demerits:

(i) This type of party system is likely to create political instability.

(ii) If no party gains power and coalition fails to be formed, it can be difficult to form a government. **1 + 2 + 2**

10. Globalisation and greater competition among producers – both local and foreign producers - has been of advantage to consumers, particularly the well-off sections in the urban areas. Globalisation offers a greater choice and an improved quality at a lower cost for several products. As a result, these people today, enjoy much higher standards of living than was possible earlier.

Among producers and workers, the impact of globalisation has not been uniform. Many local producers have been swiped from the market because of globalisation. Moreover, the cost comparison has also led to a decline in consumer share of the local producers. **5**

OR

Besides banks, the other major source of cheap credit in rural areas are the cooperative societies (or cooperatives). Members of a cooperative pool their resources for cooperation in certain areas. There are several types of cooperatives possible such as farmers cooperatives, weavers cooperatives, industrial workers cooperatives, etc. It accepts deposits from its members. With these deposits as collateral, the Cooperative has obtained a large loan from the bank. These funds are used to provide loans to members. Once these loans are repaid, another round of lending can take place. **5**

Section-D

11.1 The Independence Day Pledge, 26 January 1930 **1**

11.2 People wish to abolish a government that deprives the former of their basic rights and oppresses them. **1**

11.3 The Indians demanded *Purna Swaraj or Complete Independence.'* The Indians believed that it was their right to have freedom and to enjoy the fruits of their hard work and have the necessities of life, so that they may have full opportunities of growth. **2**

12.1 Waterways **1**

12.2 Indian culture **1**

12.3 (a) It is fuel efficient.

(b) It is economical.

(c) It is most suitable for carrying heavy and bulky goods. **2**

(d) It is environment friendly. (Any two)

Section-E

13.1 Dandi **1**

13.2

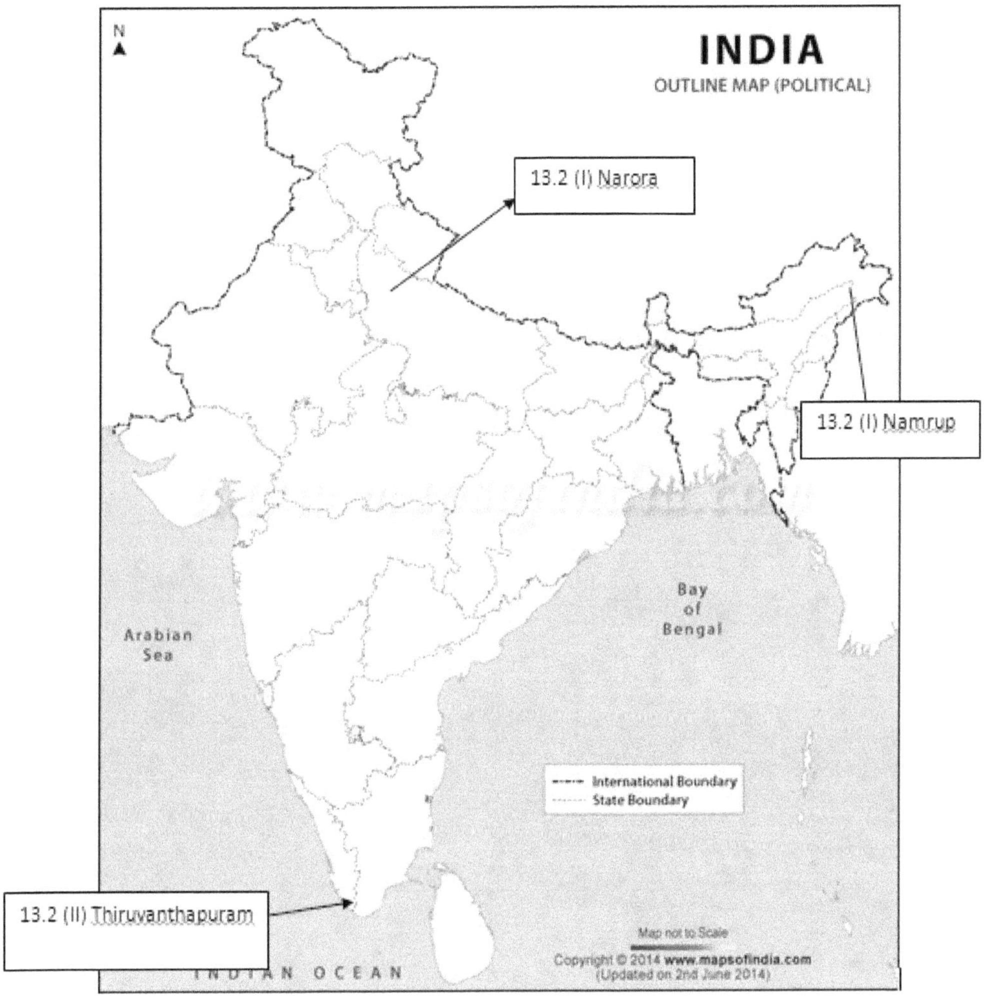

1 + 1 = 2

CBSE

Sample Question Paper 2

TERM II

CLASS X

SOCIAL SCIENCE

Time Allowed: 2 Hours | *Maximum Marks: 40*

General Instructions

i. *This Question paper is divided into five sections-Section A, B, C, D and E.*

ii. *All questions are compulsory.*

iii. ***Section-A:*** *Question no. 1 to 5 are very short answer type questions of 2 marks each. Answer to each question should not exceed 40 words.*

iv. ***Section-B:*** *Question no. 6 to 8 are short answer type questions, carrying 3 marks each. Answer to each question should not exceed 80 words.*

v. ***Section-C:*** *Question no. 9 and 10 are long answer type questions, carrying 5 marks each. Answer to each question should not exceed 120 words.*

vi. ***Section-D:*** *Question no. 11 and 12 are Case Based questions.*

vii. ***Section-E:*** *Question no. 13 is map based, carrying 3 marks with two parts, 13.1 from History (1 mark) and 13.2 from Geography (2 marks).*

viii. *There is no overall choice in the question paper. However, an internal choice has been provided in a few questions. Only one of the choices in such questions have to be attempted.*

ix. *In addition to this, separate instructions are given with each section and question, wherever necessary.*

Section-A

Very Short Answer Questions **2 × 5 = 10**

1. Why did Mahatma Gandhi decide to withdraw the Non-Cooperation Movement?
2. Give an example to show that agriculture and industry move hand in hand.
3. State any two conditions which ensure the success of democracy?
4. Differentiate between Foreign Trade and Foreign Investment.
5. Describe the evolution of pipelines.

Section-B

Short Answer Type Questions **3 × 3 = 9**

6. Write a note on modern forms of money. Why is the modern currency accepted as a medium of exchange?

   OR

   Explain the loan mechanism of banks.
7. Describe the key points about Gandhiji's letter that he wrote to Lord Irwin.
8. Write a note on bi-party system.

Section-C

Long Answer Type Questions **5 × 2 = 10**

9. Write any five features of Bhartiya Janta Party.

   OR

   What factors make democracy a preferred form of government over dictatorship?
10. 'A loan from informal sector is not beneficial in true sense.' Comment. State any one disadvantage of formal sources of credit in India.

    OR

    'The growth in technology sector has accelerated globalisation,' Elucidate.

Section-D

Case Based Questions **4 × 2 = 8**

Read the given text and answer the following questions:

11. The failure of the Cripps Mission and the effects of World War II created widespread discontentment in India. This led Gandhiji to launch a movement calling for complete withdrawal of the British from India. The Congress Working Committee, in its meeting in Wardha on 14 July 1942, passed the historic resolution demanding the immediate transfer of power to Indians and quit India. On 8 August 1942 in Bombay, the All India Congress Committee endorsed the resolution which called for a non-violent mass struggle on the widest possible scale throughout the country. It was on this occasion that Gandhiji delivered the famous 'Do or Die' speech. People observed hartals, and demonstrations and processions were accompanied by national songs and slogans. The movement was truly a mass movement which brought into its ambit thousands of ordinary people, namely students, workers and peasants. It also saw the active participation of leaders, namely, Jayprakash Narayan, Aruna Asaf Ali and Ram Manohar Lohia and many women such as Matangini Hazra in Bengal, Kanaklata Barua in Assam and Rama Devi in Odisha. The British responded with much force, yet it took more than a year to suppress the movement. 4

11.1 Identify the movement discussed in the above ? (1)

11.2 Which famous slogan from Mahatma Gandhi's speech emerged during the planning and execution of the movement? (1)

11.3 Give any two features of the movement. (2)

12. Mass communication provides entertainment and creates awareness among people about various national programmes and policies. It includes radio, television, newspapers, magazines, books and films. All India Radio (Akashwani) broadcasts a variety of programmes in national, regional and local languages for various categories of people, spread over different parts of the country. Doordarshan, the national television channel of India, is one of the largest terrestrial networks in the world. It broadcasts a variety of programmes from entertainment, educational to sports, etc. for people of different age groups. 4

12.1 Justify the name 'mass communication' (1)

12.2 In which languages are programmes on All India Radio broadcasted? (1)

12.3 State any two features of the national television channel of India. (2)

Section-E

Map Skill Based Question **1 × 3 = 3**

13.1 On the given outline Political Map of India, identify the place marked as A with the help of following information and write its correct name on the line marked near it.

(A) The place where the Non-Cooperation Movement was called off.

13.2 On the same given map of India, locate the following:

(I) Singrauli Thermal plant

OR

Surat cotton textile

(II) Kochi port

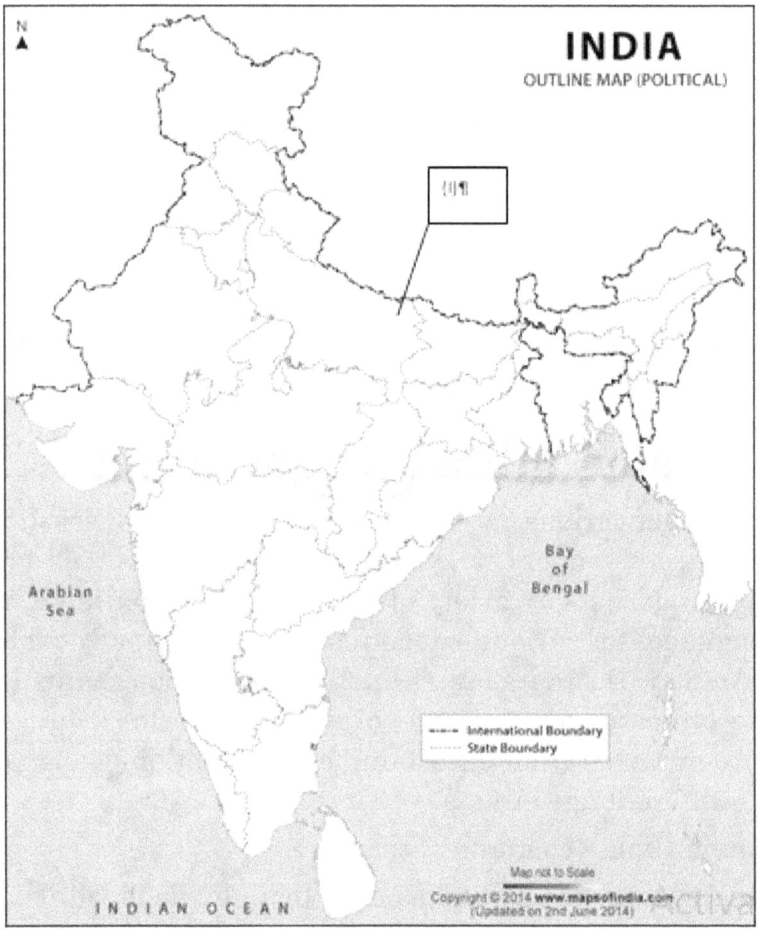

SOLUTION

Section-A

1. In February 1922, Mahatma Gandhi decided to withdraw the Non-Cooperation Movement. This was mainly because:
   (i) Mahatma Gandhi felt that the movement was turning violent in many places.
   (ii) He also felt that the satyagrahis needed to be properly trained before they would be ready for mass struggles. **1 + 1 = 2**
2. The agriculture sector depends upon the agro-industries for products such as irrigation pumps, fertilisers, insecticides, pesticides, plastic and PVC pipes, machines and tools, etc. These products have pumped production and also made the production processes very efficient. **2**
3. Democracy is considered successful when:
   (i) Decisions are taken by elected representatives and not the rich.
   (ii) Elections are held in a free and fair manner.
   (iii) Political equality is practiced. (Any two) **1 + 1 = 2**
4. The process of buying and selling goods and services between two or more than two countries is known as foreign trade.

   When MNCs set up their production units in different countries, they spend money in buying assets such as land, building, machines and other required equipments. This form of investment is called as Foreign Investment. **1 + 1= 2**
5. In the past, pipelines were used to transport water to cities and industries. Now, these are used for transporting crude oil, petroleum products and natural gas from oil and natural gas fields to refineries, fertilizer factories and big thermal power plants. Solids can also be transported through a pipeline when converted into slurry. **2**

Section-B

6. Modern forms of money include currency — paper notes and coins. It is unlike the ancient form of currency as it is not made of any precious metal. And unlike grain and cattle, they are neither of everyday use. The modern currency is without any use of its own. It is accepted as a medium of exchange because the currency is authorised by the government of the country. **3**

OR

Banks keep only a small proportion of their deposits as cash with themselves. For example, banks in India these days hold about 15 per cent of their deposits as cash. This is kept as provision to pay the depositors who might come to withdraw money from the bank on any given day. Banks use the major portion of the deposits to extend loans. There is a huge demand for loans for various economic activities.

7. (i) On 31 January 1930, Mahatma Gandhi sent a letter to Viceroy Irwin stating eleven demands. Some of these were of general interest; others were specific demands of different classes, from industrialists to peasants.

(ii) The most stirring of all was the demand to abolish the salt tax.

(iii) Mahatma Gandhi's letter was, in a way, an ultimatum. If the demands were not fulfilled by 11 March, the letter stated, the Congress would launch a civil disobedience campaign. **1 × 3 = 3**

8. In some countries, power usually changes between two main parties. Several other parties may exist, contest elections and win a few seats in the national legislatures. But only the two main parties have a serious chance of winning majority of seats to form government. Such a party system is called two-party system. The United States of America and the United Kingdom are examples of two-party system. **3**

Section-C

9. Following are the features of Bhartiya Janta Party:

(i) It was Founded in 1980 by Syama Prasad Mukherjee.

(ii) Cultural nationalism (or 'Hindutva') is an important element in its conception of Indian nationhood and politics.

(iii) Its support base increased substantially in the 1990s. Earlier limited to north and west and to urban areas, the party expanded its support in the south, east, the north-east and to rural areas.

(iv) It came to power in 1998 as the leader of the National Democratic Alliance (NDA) including several regional parties.

(v) It emerged as the largest party with 303 members in the 2019 Lok Sabha elections and currently leads the ruling NDA government at the Centre.

OR

The following factors make democracy a preferred form of government over dictatorship:

(i) Promotes equality among citizens- Democracy has legal and constitutional provisions that are made to ensure that all citizens are treated equally.

(ii) Enhances the dignity of the individual- Democracy ensures that the dignity of individuals is not put at stake. Every individual has access to various facilities provided by the government.

(iii) Democracy improves the quality of decision making: Though decisions in a democracy might be delayed as they are taken after much of negotiation and deliberation, yet decisions are aimed at benefitting the maximum number of people.

(iv) Democracy always looks for a middle path that provides a method to resolve conflicts.

(v) Democracy has a great advantage of allowing room to correct mistakes. This helps in taking better decisions too. **1 × 5 = 5**

10. It is correct that a loan from informal sector is not beneficial in true sense. This is because of the following reasons:

(i) Rate of Interest: The rate of interest charged by informal lenders is much higher than what is charged by formal sources of credit.

(ii) Terms and Conditions: The terms and conditions laid by an informal lender are generally harsh and the borrower is left at the mercy of the lender.

(iii) Debt trap: In many scenarios the poor people are caught in a debt trap when they procure loans from informal lenders.

(iv) Supervision: The Reserve Bank of India supervises the functioning of formal sources of loans. However, there is no one who supervises the loan activities of the informal sources of credit.

The formal sources of credit in India still meet only about half of the total credit needs of the rural people. **4 + 1 = 5**

OR

Rapid improvement in technology has been one major factor that has stimulated the globalisation process. For instance, the past fifty years have seen several improvements in transportation technology. This has made much faster delivery of goods across long distances possible at lower costs.

Even more remarkable have been the developments in information and communication technology. Many MNCs are service based companies and are required to communicate with countries across the globe. Internet, mobile phone, etc. has made this very easy and that too at a very nominal cost.

Computers are now used in almost every industry and have made a lot many tasks to be performed easily and quickly. Information technology has allowed the expansion of resources from countries all across the world. This expansion leads to new ideas and products, as well as new ways of doing business. **5**

Section-D

11.1 Quit India Movement **1**

11.2 'Do or Die' **1**

11.3 **(a)** The movement involved mass struggle. **1 + 1 = 2**

(b) It took almost a year for the British to suppress the movement.

12.1 Radio, television, newspapers, etc. are sources of mass communication as they provide information to masses. **1**

12.2 Regional and local languages **1**

12.3 (a) Doordarshan is one of the largest terrestrial networks in the world.

(b) It broadcasts a variety of programmes from entertainment, educational to sports, etc. for people of different age groups.

1 + 1 = 2

Section-E

13.1 (A) Chauri Chaura 1

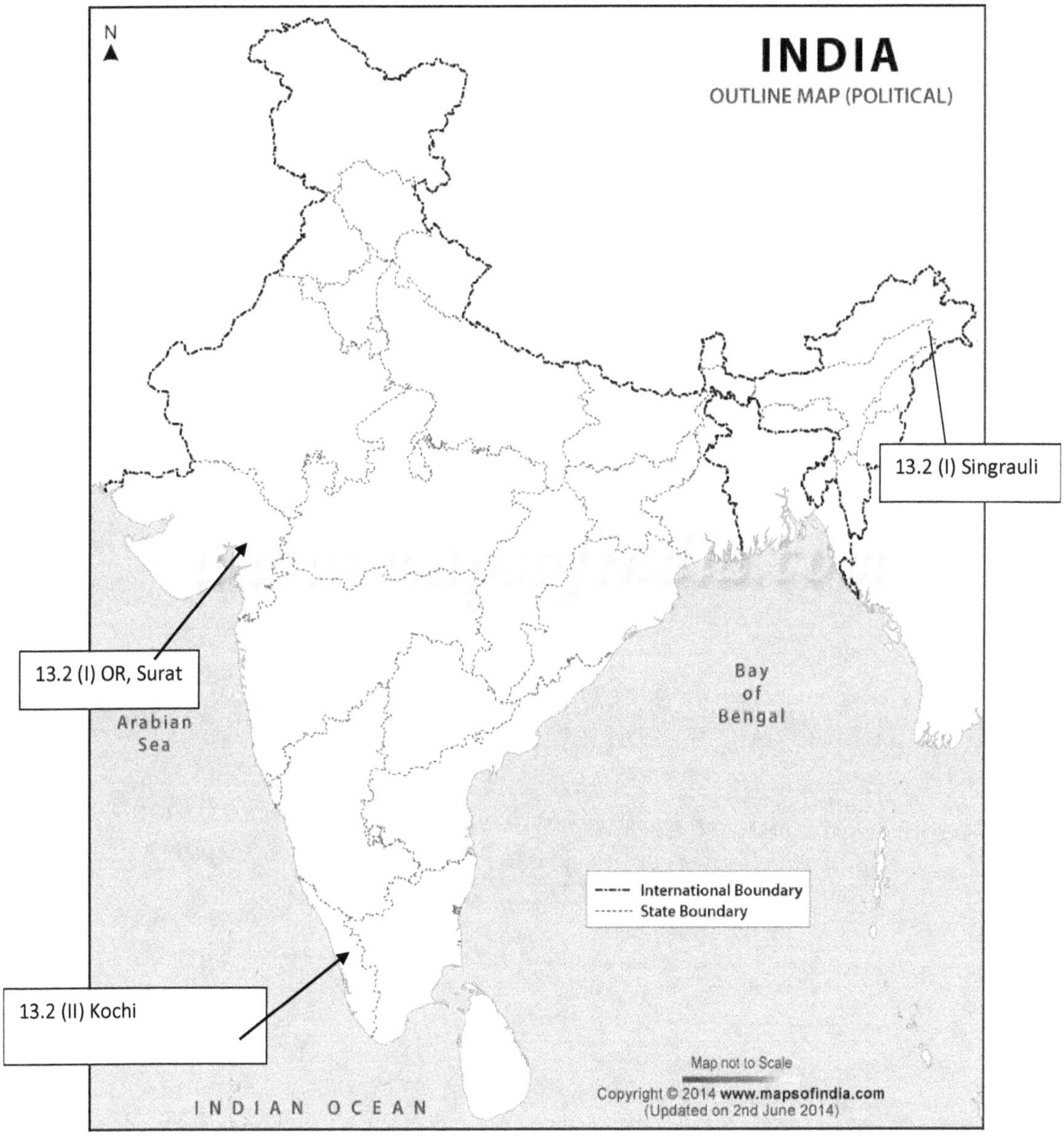

1 + 1 = 2

CBSE

Sample Question Paper 3

TERM II

CLASS X

SOCIAL SCIENCE

Time Allowed: 2 Hours | *Maximum Marks: 40*

General Instructions

i. *This Question paper is divided into five sections-Section A, B, C, D and E.*

ii. *All questions are compulsory.*

iii. ***Section-A:*** *Question no. 1 to 5 are very short answer type questions of 2 marks each. Answer to each question should not exceed 40 words.*

iv. ***Section-B:*** *Question no. 6 to 8 are short answer type questions, carrying 3 marks each. Answer to each question should not exceed 80 words.*

v. ***Section-C:*** *Question no. 9 and 10 are long answer type questions, carrying 5 marks each. Answer to each question should not exceed 120 words.*

vi. ***Section-D:*** *Question no. 11 and 12 are Case Based questions.*

vii. ***Section-E:*** *Question no. 13 is map based, carrying 3 marks with two parts, 13.1 from History (1 mark) and 13.2 from Geography (2 marks).*

viii. *There is no overall choice in the question paper. However, an internal choice has been provided in a few questions. Only one of the choices in such questions have to be attempted.*

ix. *In addition to this, separate instructions are given with each section and question, wherever necessary.*

Section-A

Very Short Answer Questions **2 × 5 = 10**

1. Describe the idea of 'Satyagraha' as stated by Mahatma Gandhi.
2. What is meant by small scale industry?
3. Explain the relationship between democracy and development.
4. "The rupee is widely accepted as a medium of exchange in India." Explain.
5. Why does Chhotanagpur plateau region in India has the maximum concentration of iron and steel industries?

Section-B

Short Answer Type Questions **3 × 3 = 9**

6. Explain the concept of 'double coincidence of wants' with an example.

   OR

   What is Globalization? How can the government ensure fair Globalisation to its people? Give two points.
7. How did World War I proved to be a blow on Indian economy?
8. Explain' Transparency' as an important feature of democracy.

Section-C

Long Answer Type Questions **5 × 2 = 10**

9. Write any five features of Communist Party of India.

   OR

   Write any five features of Indian National Congress.
10. What is liberalisation? Describe any four effects of liberalisation on the Indian economy.

    OR

    'Banks play an important role in the economic development of a nation.' Comment.

Section-D

Case Based Questions **4 × 2 = 8**

Read the given text and answer the following questions:

11. *'I have no hesitation in declaring that if the principle that the Indian Muslim is entitled to full and free development on the lines of his own culture and tradition in his own Indian home-lands is recognised as the basis of a permanent communal settlement, he will be ready to stake his all for the freedom of India. The principle that each group is entitled to free development on its own lines is not inspired by any feeling of narrow communalism ... A community which is inspired by feelings of ill-will towards other communities is low and ignoble. I entertain the highest respect for the customs, laws, religions and social institutions of other communities. Nay, it is my duty according to the teachings of the Quran, even to defend their places of worship, if need be. Yet I love the communal group which is the source of life and behaviour and which has formed me what I am by giving me its religion, its literature, its thought, its culture and thereby its whole past as a living operative factor in my present consciousness ...* 4

11.1 Who delivered the words given in the above text? 1

11.2 What does the speaker demand for? 1

11.3 Pick two sentences from the text to show that the speaker believed in secularism? 2

12. Factors responsible for their location in the Hugli basin are: proximity of the producing areas, inexpensive water transport, supported by a good network of railways, roadways and waterways to facilitate movement of raw material to the mills, abundant water for processing raw form, cheap labour from West Bengal and adjoining states of Bihar, Odisha and Uttar Pradesh. Kolkata as a large urban centre provides banking, insurance and port facilities its export. 4

12.1 Which crop is discussed in the above extract? 1

12.2 Which part of India has concentration of this crop? 1

12.3 State any two reasons that make Hugli Basin favourable for the growth of the crop discussed in the above extract. 2

Section-E

Map Skill Based Question **1 × 3 = 3**

13.1 On the given outline Political Map of India, identify the place marked as A with the help of following information and write its correct name on the line marked near it.

(A) The place where the Congress session was held in Sep. 1920.

13.2 On the same given map of India, locate the following:

(I) Raja Sansi International Airport

OR

Tarapur Nuclear plant

(II) Bokaro

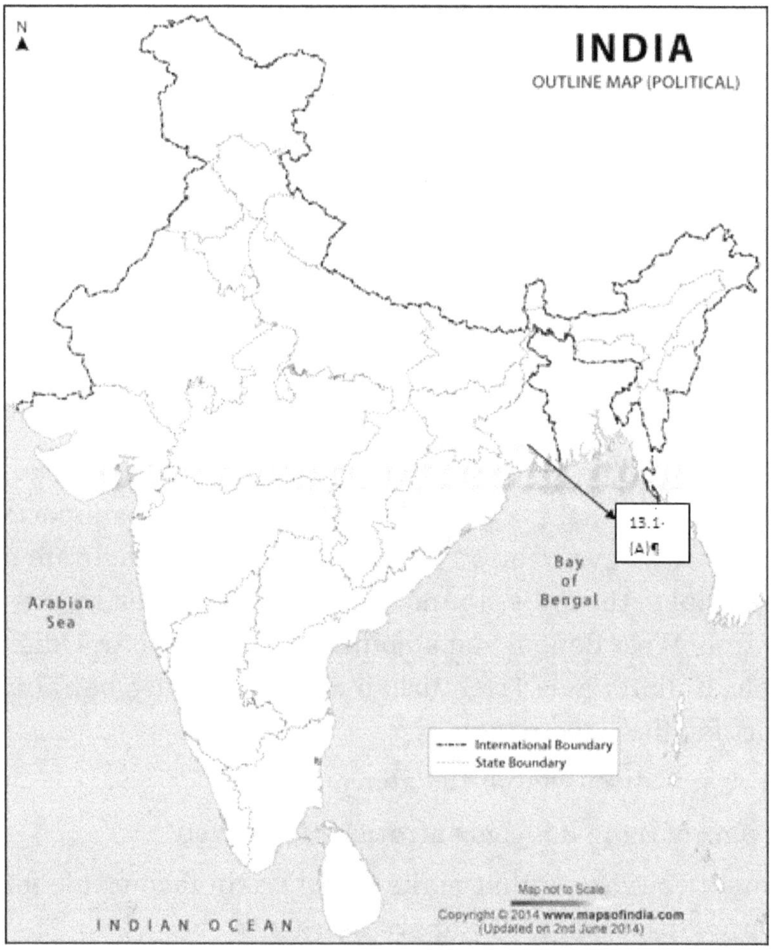

SOLUTION

Section-A

1. The idea of satyagraha emphasised on the power of truth and the need to search for truth. It suggested that if the cause was true, if the struggle was against injustice, then physical force was not necessary to fight the oppressor. 2
2. Small Scale: A small scale industry is defined with reference to the maximum investment allowed on the assets of a unit. This limit has changed over a period of time. At present the maximum investment allowed is rupees one crore. 2
3. Development is a necessity for any nation and depends upon various factors like size of the population, global situation, cooperation from other countries, etc. Democracy needs to ensure that decisions taken lead to development and not any sort of conflict. 2
4. In India, the law legalizes the use of rupee as a medium of payment that cannot be refused in settling transactions. No individual in India can legally refuse a payment made in rupees. Hence, the rupee is widely accepted as a medium of exchange. 2
5. Chhotanagpur plateau region has the maximum concentration of iron and steel industries. It is largely, because of the relative advantages this region has for the development of this industry. These include, low cost of iron ore, high grade raw materials in proximity, cheap labour and vast growth potential in the home market. 2

Section-B

6. Let us say that there is a boy named Amar who is willing to sell his shoes and wants a cricket bat in return. Now Amar will have to look for someone who wants a pair of shoes and can offer a cricket bat to Amar. That is, both parties have to agree to sell and buy each other's commodities. This is known as double coincidence of wants. What a person desires to sell is exactly what the other wishes to buy. 3

OR

The integration between countries through foreign trade and foreign investments by multinational corporations is called as globalisation. The government can ensure fair globalisation by:

(i) Government policies must protect the interests, not only of the rich and the powerful, but all the people in the country.

(ii) Government should support small producers to improve their performance till the time they become strong enough to compete. **1 + 2 = 3**

7. World War I created a new economic and political situation. It led to a huge increase in defence expenditure which was financed by war loans and increasing taxes: customs duties were raised and income tax introduced. Through the war years prices increased – doubling between 1913 and 1918 – leading to extreme hardship for the common people. Villages were called upon to supply soldiers, and the forced recruitment in rural areas caused widespread anger. **3**

8. Transparency is an important feature of democracy. Democracy ensures that decision making will be based on norms and procedures. So, a citizen who wants to know if a decision was taken through the correct procedures can find this out. She has the right and the means to examine the process of decision making. This feature or liberty is often missing in non-democratic governments. **3**

Section-C

9. Features of Communist Party of India:

(i) Communist Party of India was founded in 1925.

(ii) The party is based on the principles of Marxism-Leninism, secularism and democracy.

(iii) It accepts parliamentary democracy as a means of promoting the interests of the working class, farmers and the poor.

(iv) Its support base had gradually declined over the years. It secured less than 1 per cent votes and 2 seats in the 2019 Lok Sabha elections.

(v) Advocates the coming together of all left parties to build a strong left front.

OR

Features of Indian National Congress:

(i) It is one of the oldest parties of the world and was founded in 1885 and has experienced many splits.

(ii) It played a key role in India's struggle for independence.

(iii) Under the leadership of Jawaharlal Nehru, the party sought to build a modern secular democratic republic in India.

(iv) The INC supports new economic reforms but with a human face.

(v) A centrist party (neither rightist nor leftist) in its ideological orientation, the party espouses secularism and welfare of weaker sections and minorities. **1 × 5 = 5**

10. Removing barriers or restrictions set by the government is what is known as liberalisation. Following are the effects of liberalisation on the Indian economy:

(i) Many MNCs have started investing in India. This has created a lot of job opportunities especially for the youth which has proven to be a boon for the economy.

(ii) Trade activities have increased to a large extent due to liberalisation.

(iii) A negative effect of liberalisation is that many small businesses have crumbled. This has impacted many producers and shopkeepers.

(iv) A lot many industries or factories have emerged that mostly work on the patterns of unorganised sector. Due to this many employees face exploitation. **1 + 4 = 5**

OR

(i) Banks keep money of the people in safe custody to be used by the depositors in future.

Section-D

11.1 Sir Muhammad Iqbal **1**

11.2 Separate electorates **1**

11.3

(i) *A community which is inspired by feelings of ill-will towards other communities is low and ignoble.*

(ii) *Nay, it is my duty according to the teachings of the Quran, even to defend their places of worship, if need be.* **1 + 1 = 2**

12.1 Jute **1**

12.2 Hugli **1**

12.3 (i) Availability of various means of transport.

(ii) Availability of abundant natural resources.

(iii) Availability of cost-effective labour from West Bengal and adjoining states of Bihar, Odisha and Uttar Pradesh. **1 + 1 = 2**

(iv) Availability of financial institutions. (Any two)

Section-E

13.1 (A) Calcutta **1**

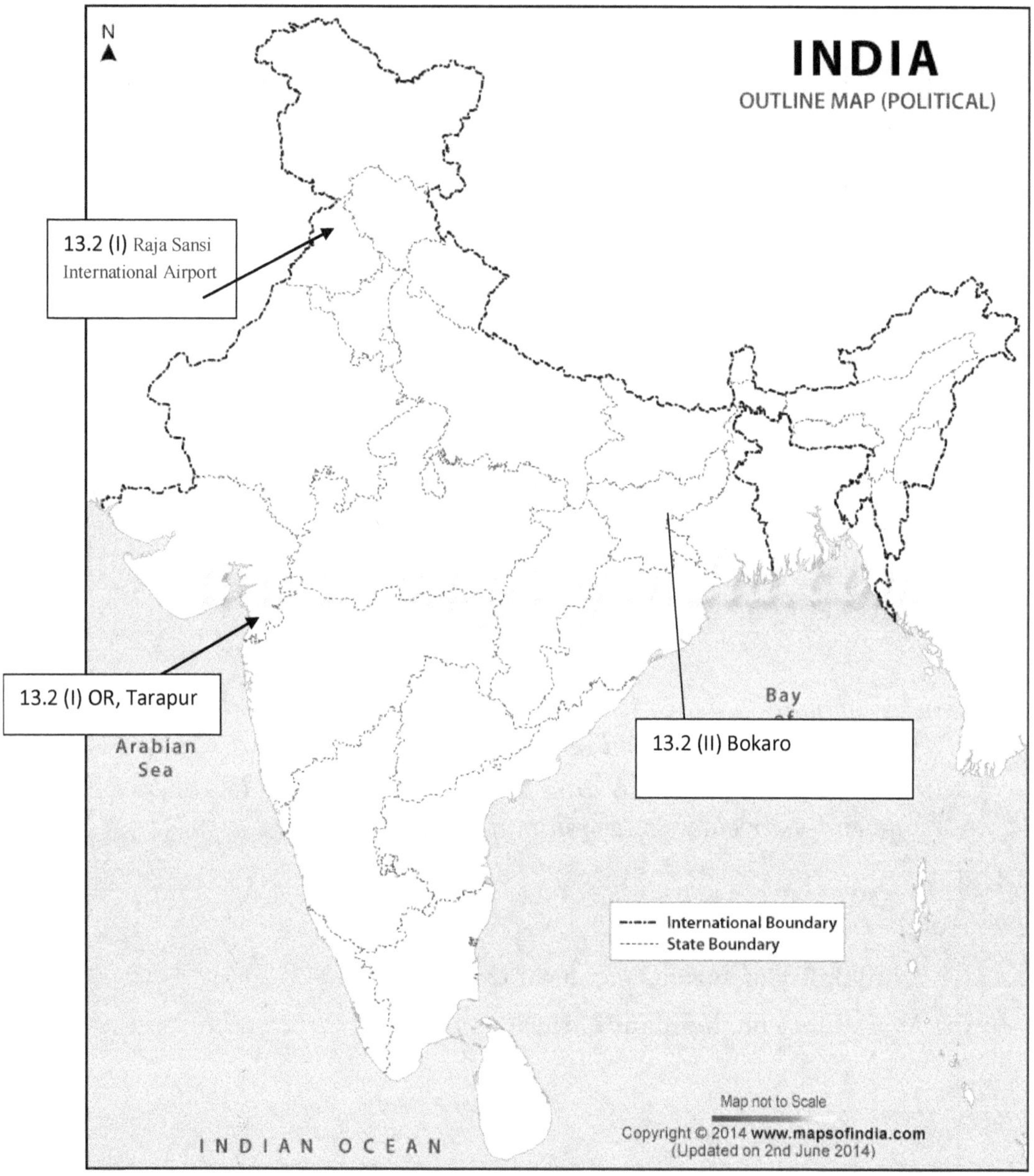

1 + 1 = 2

CBSE

Sample Question Paper 4

TERM II

CLASS X

SOCIAL SCIENCE

Time Allowed: 2 Hours | *Maximum Marks: 40*

General Instructions

i. *This Question paper is divided into five sections-Section A, B, C, D and E.*

ii. *All questions are compulsory.*

iii. ***Section-A:*** *Question no. 1 to 5 are very short answer type questions of 2 marks each. Answer to each question should not exceed 40 words.*

iv. ***Section-B:*** *Question no. 6 to 8 are short answer type questions, carrying 3 marks each. Answer to each question should not exceed 80 words.*

v. ***Section-C:*** *Question no. 9 and 10 are long answer type questions, carrying 5 marks each. Answer to each question should not exceed 120 words.*

vi. ***Section-D:*** *Question no. 11 and 12 are Case Based questions.*

vii. ***Section-E:*** *Question no. 13 is map based, carrying 3 marks with two parts, 13.1 from History (1 mark) and 13.2 from Geography (2 marks).*

viii. *There is no overall choice in the question paper. However, an internal choice has been provided in a few questions. Only one of the choices in such questions have to be attempted.*

ix. *In addition to this, separate instructions are given with each section and question, wherever necessary.*

Section-A

Very Short Answer Questions **2 × 5 = 10**

1. Give a brief about the Khilafat issue.
2. State the major objective of the Golden Quadrilateral Super Highways. In India who is responsible for the implementation of highway projects.
3. Write a note on economic outcomes of democracy.
4. Why did the Indian government put barriers on foreign trade and foreign investment after independence?
5. What is manufacturing? Name the important raw materials used in cement industry.

Section-B

Short Answer Type Questions **3 × 3 = 9**

6. Explain with an example how a transaction takes place using cheque as a mode of payment.

   OR

   Write a note on demand deposits.
7. 'Indian nationalists employed a number of ways to inculcate a sense of collective belonging.' Justify.
8. Describe the three components of a political party.

Section-C

Long Answer Type Questions **5 × 2 = 10**

9. Describe the challenges faced by political parties.

   OR

   Write any five features of Bahujan Samaj Party.
10. How did 'Cargill Foods' become the largest producer of edible oils in India? Explain.

    OR

    What is meant by 'Terms of Credit?' Explain the conditions included in it.

Section-D

Case Based Questions **4 × 2 = 8**

Read the given text and answer the following questions:

11. Gandhiji proposed that the movement should unfold in stages. It should begin with the surrender of titles that the government awarded, and a boycott of civil services, army, police, courts and legislative councils, schools, and foreign goods. Then, in case the government used repression, a full civil disobedience campaign would be launched. Through the summer of 1920 Mahatma Gandhi and Shaukat Ali toured extensively, mobilising popular support for the movement. 4

11.1 Which nationalist movement is discussed in the above extract? 1

11.2 Into how many stages was the movement divided into? 1

11.3 What was the next step of the movement discussed in the above extract? How did students participate in the movement? 2

12. The World's longest Highway tunnel-Atal Tunnel (9.02 Km) has been built by BRO. This tunnel connects Manali to Lahul-Spiti valley throughout the year. Earlier the valley was cut off for about 6 months each year owing to heavy snowfall. The tunnel is buit with ultra-modern specifications in the Pir Panjal range of Himalayas at an altitude of 3000 metres from the Mean Sea Level (MSL). 4

Source:http://www.bro.gov.in/pagefimg.asp?imid=144,And PIBdelhi03October2020 / ncert

12.1 What is the full form of BRO? 1

12.2 What type of means of transport is discussed in the above text? 1

12.3 State two features of the Atal Tunnel. 2

Section-E

Map Skill Based Question **1 × 3 = 3**

13.1 On the given outline Political Map of India, identify the place marked as A with the help of following information and write its correct name on the line marked near it.

(A) The place where the Congress session was held in Dec. 1920.

13.2 On the same given map of India, locate the following:

(I) Marmagao

OR

Tuticorin

(II) Salem

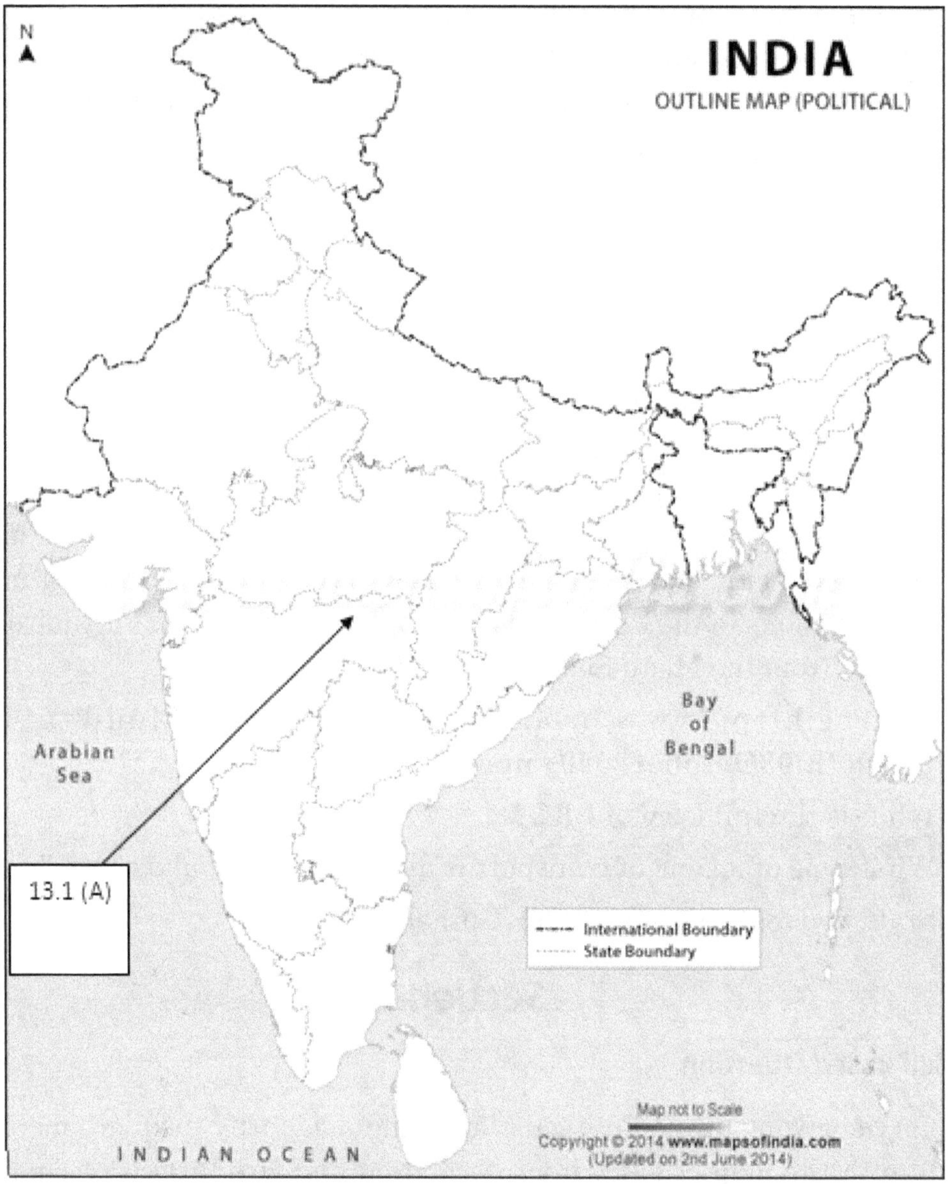

SOLUTION

Section-A

1. The First World War had ended with the defeat of Ottoman Turkey. There were rumours that a harsh peace treaty was going to be imposed on the Ottoman emperor – the spiritual head of the Islamic world (the Khalifa). This was called as the Khilafat issue. **2**

2. The major objective of these Super Highways is to reduce the time and distance between the mega cities of India. These highway projects are being implemented by the National Highway Authority of India (NHAI). **2**

3. The economic outcome of democracy is to reduce economic inequalities. When we consider all democracies and all dictatorships for the fifty years between 1950 and 2000, dictatorships have slightly higher rate of economic growth. The inability of democracy to achieve higher economic development worries us. But this alone cannot be reason to reject democracy. **2**

4. The Indian government, after Independence, had put barriers to foreign trade and foreign investment. This was considered necessary to protect the producers within the country from foreign competition. Industries were just coming up in the 1950s and 1960s, and competition from imports at that stage would not have allowed these industries to come up. **2**

5. Production of goods in large quantities after processing from raw materials to more valuable products is called manufacturing. The cement industry requires bulky and heavy raw materials like limestone, silica and gypsum. **1 + 1 = 2**

Section-B

6. Let us say that there is a bag manufacturer A.K. Sharma who has to make a payment to the leather supplier. He therefore writes a cheque for a specific amount. The Cheque will contain details like date, name of the receiver, amount and A.K. Sharma's signature. Once all the details are verified by the bank, cheque will be processed and within 3 working days money will be credited in the leather supplier's account. The transaction is complete without any payment of cash.

OR

People also have the provision to withdraw the money as and when they require. Since the deposits in the bank accounts can be withdrawn on demand, these deposits are called demand deposits. Demand deposits share the essential features of money. The facility of cheques against demand deposits makes it possible to directly settle payments without the use of cash. Since demand deposits are accepted widely as a means of payment, along with currency, they constitute money in the modern economy. **3**

7. It is true that the Indian nationalists employed a number of ways to inculcate a sense of collective belonging:

(i) History and fiction, folklore and songs, popular prints and symbols, all played a part in the making of nationalism. In late-nineteenth-century India, nationalists began recording folk tales sung by bards and they toured villages to gather folk songs and legends.

(ii) It was in the twentieth century, with the growth of nationalism, that the identity of India came to be visually associated with the image of Bharat Mata. The image was first created by Bankim Chandra Chattopadhyay

(iii) Moved by the Swadeshi movement, Abanindranath Tagore painted his famous image of Bharat Mata in which she was portrayed as an ascetic figure; she is calm, composed, divine and spiritual.

(iv) During the Swadeshi movement in Bengal, a tricolour flag (red, green and yellow) was designed. It had eight lotuses representing eight provinces of British India, and a crescent moon, representing Hindus and Muslims.

(v) Another means of creating a feeling of nationalism was through reinterpretation of history. By the end of the nineteenth century many Indians began feeling that to instill a sense of pride in the nation, Indian history had to be thought about differently. Indians began looking into the past to discover India's great achievements. They wrote about the glorious developments in ancient times when art and architecture, science and mathematics, religion and culture, law and philosophy, crafts and trade had flourished. (Any three)

1 × 3 = 3

8. The three components of a political party are:

(i) The Leaders: A political party consists of leaders, who are mainly responsible for formulating policies and programmes and choose candidates for contesting elections.

(ii) The Active Members: They are the ones who work very enthusiastically for activities like image building, administrative tasks during campaigning, etc.

(iii) The Followers: These consists of those who are ardent followers of the leaders and work under the guidance of the active members.

1 × 3 = 3

Section-C

9. Challenges faced by political parties:

(i) The first challenge is lack of internal democracy within parties. All over the world there is a tendency in political parties towards the concentration of power in one or few leaders at the top. Ordinary members of the party do not get sufficient information on what happens inside the party.

(ii) The second challenge of dynastic succession is related to the first one. Since most political parties do not practice open and transparent procedures for their functioning, there are very few ways for an ordinary worker to rise to the top in a party.

(iii) The third challenge is about the growing role of money and muscle power in parties, especially during elections. Since parties are focussed only on winning elections, they tend to use short-cuts to win elections.

(iv) The fourth challenge is that very often parties do not seem to offer a meaningful choice to the voters. In order to offer meaningful choice, parties must be significantly different. **1¼ × 4 = 5**

OR

Features of Bahujan Samaj Party:

(i) It was formed in 1984 under the leadership of Kanshi Ram with the objective of representing and securing power for the bahujan samaj which includes the dalits, adivasis, OBCs and religious minorities.

(ii) The party draws inspiration from the ideas and teachings of Sahu Maharaj, Mahatma Phule, Periyar Ramaswami Naicker and Babasaheb Ambedkar.

(iii) It stands for the cause of securing the interests and welfare of the dalits and oppressed people.

(iv) It has its main base in the state of Uttar Pradesh and substantial presence in neighbouring states like Madhya Pradesh, Chhattisgarh, Uttarakhand, Delhi and Punjab.

(iv) It formed government in Uttar Pradesh several times by taking the support of different parties at different times. **1 × 5 = 5**

10. Cargill Foods, a very large American MNC, has bought over smaller Indian companies such as Parakh Foods. Parakh Foods had built a large marketing network in various parts of India, where its brand was well-reputed. Also, Parakh Foods had four oil refineries, whose control has now shifted to Cargill. Cargill is now the largest producer of edible oil in India, with a capacity to make 5 million pouches daily. So it is clear how the *Cargill* MNC bought up a local company in India and then expanded its production.

OR

Terms of Credit is a term used for loan activities. Every loan agreement specifies an interest rate which the borrower must pay to the lender along with the repayment of the principal. In addition, lenders may demand collateral (security) against loans. If the borrower fails to repay the loan, the lender has the right to sell the asset or collateral to obtain payment. Interest rate, collateral and documentation requirement, and the mode of repayment together comprise what is called the terms of credit. The terms of credit vary substantially from one credit arrangement to another.

They may vary depending on the nature of the lender and the borrower. **5**

Section-D

11.1 Non- Cooperation Movement **1**

11.2 Three **1**

11.3 Civil Disobedience was the next step of the movement. Students boycotted schools. **1 + 1 = 2**

12.1 Border Roads Organisation **1**

12.2 Roadways **1**

12.3 (a) This tunnel connects Manali to Lahul-Spiti valley throughout the year.

(b) The tunnel is buit with ultra-modern specifications in the Pir Panjal range of Himalayas at an altitude of 3000 metres from the Mean Sea Level (MSL) **1 + 1 = 2**

Section-E

13.1 (A) Nagpur **1**

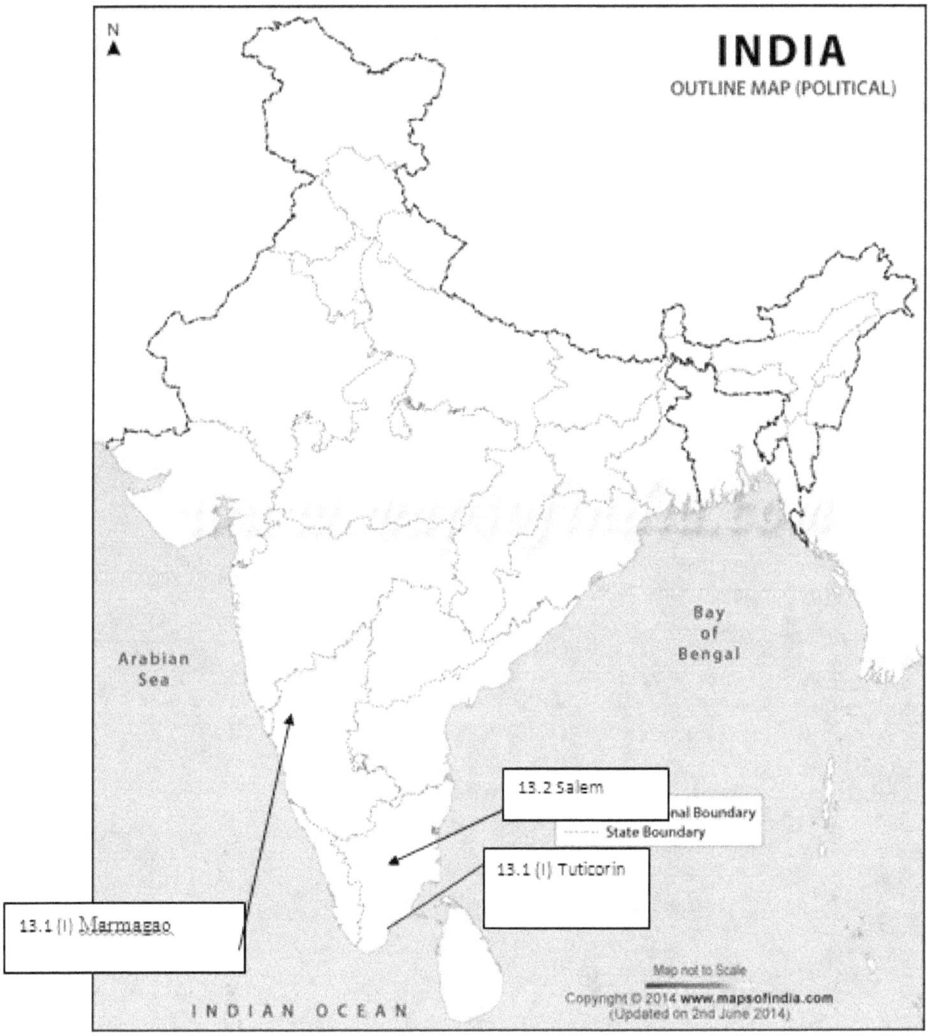

1 + 1 = 2

CBSE

Sample Question Paper 5

TERM II

CLASS X

SOCIAL SCIENCE

Time Allowed: 2 Hours *Maximum Marks: 40*

General Instructions

i. *This Question paper is divided into five sections-Section A, B, C, D and E.*

ii. *All questions are compulsory.*

iii. ***Section-A:*** *Question no. 1 to 5 are very short answer type questions of 2 marks each. Answer to each question should not exceed 40 words.*

iv. ***Section-B:*** *Question no. 6 to 8 are short answer type questions, carrying 3 marks each. Answer to each question should not exceed 80 words.*

v. ***Section-C:*** *Question no. 9 and 10 are long answer type questions, carrying 5 marks each. Answer to each question should not exceed 120 words.*

vi. ***Section-D:*** *Question no. 11 and 12 are Case Based questions.*

vii. ***Section-E:*** *Question no. 13 is map based, carrying 3 marks with two parts, 13.1 from History (1 mark) and 13.2 from Geography (2 marks).*

viii. *There is no overall choice in the question paper. However, an internal choice has been provided in a few questions. Only one of the choices in such questions have to be attempted.*

ix. *In addition to this, separate instructions are given with each section and question, wherever necessary.*

Section-A

Very Short Answer Questions **2 × 5 = 10**

1. Explain the proposals of the Non-Cooperation Movement given by Gandhiji.
2. Differentiate between integrated steel plants and Mini-steel plants.
3. How does democracy produce an accountable, responsive and legitimate government?
4. Write a note on barter system by giving an example.
5. How are industries classified according to their main role?

Section-B

Short Answer Type Questions **3 × 3 = 9**

6. Taking example of a farmer, explain how does credit plays a negative role.

OR

Explain any three advantages of globalisation.

7. Explain the features of Bharat Mata as depicted by Abanindranath Tagore. Explain the contrasting figure of Bharat Mata.
8. What criteria is laid down by the Election Commission of India to recognise a party as regional or national?

Section-C

Long Answer Type Questions **5 × 2 = 10**

9. What is meant by defection? What steps have been taken by the Election Commission of India to reform political parties?

OR

Write any five features of All India Trinamool Congress.

10. How have Self- Help groups acted as an aid to the poor section of the society in terms of procuring loans.

OR

Explain with examples the impact of globalisation in our day to day lives.

Section-D

Case Based Questions **4 × 2 = 8**

Read the given text and answer the following questions:

11. *'It is said of "passive resistance" that it is the weapon of the weak, but the power which is* the subject of this article can be used only by the strong. This power is not passive resistance; indeed it calls for intense activity. The movement in South Africa was not passive *but active ...* 4

11.1 Which ideology of Mahatma Gandhi is discussed in the above extract? 1

11.2 Name the ideology of Mahatma Gandhi that is related to the one discussed in the above extract? 1

11.3 What all does a person practicing the ideology discussed in the above extract needs to know? 2

12. This is the principal mode of transportation for freight and passengers in India. This means of transport makes it possible for people to conduct multifarious activities like business, sightseeing, pilgrimage along with transportation of goods over longer distances. Apart from an important means of transport these have been a great integrating force for more than 150 years. This means of transport in India bind the economic life of the country as well as accelerate the development of the industry and agriculture. 4

12.1 Which means of transport is discussed in the above text? 1

12.2 What aspect of one's life is benefitted through the means of transport discussed in the above text? 1

12.3 State the two advantages of the means of transport discussed in the above text? 2

Section-E

Map Skill Based Question **1 × 3 = 3**

13.1 On the given outline Political Map of India, identify the place marked as A with the help of following information and write its correct name on the line marked near it.

(A) The place where the Congress session was held in 1927.

13.2 On the same given map of India, locate the following:

(I) Chennai (Meenam Bakkam) international airport

OR

Durgapur iron and steel industry

(II) Paradip

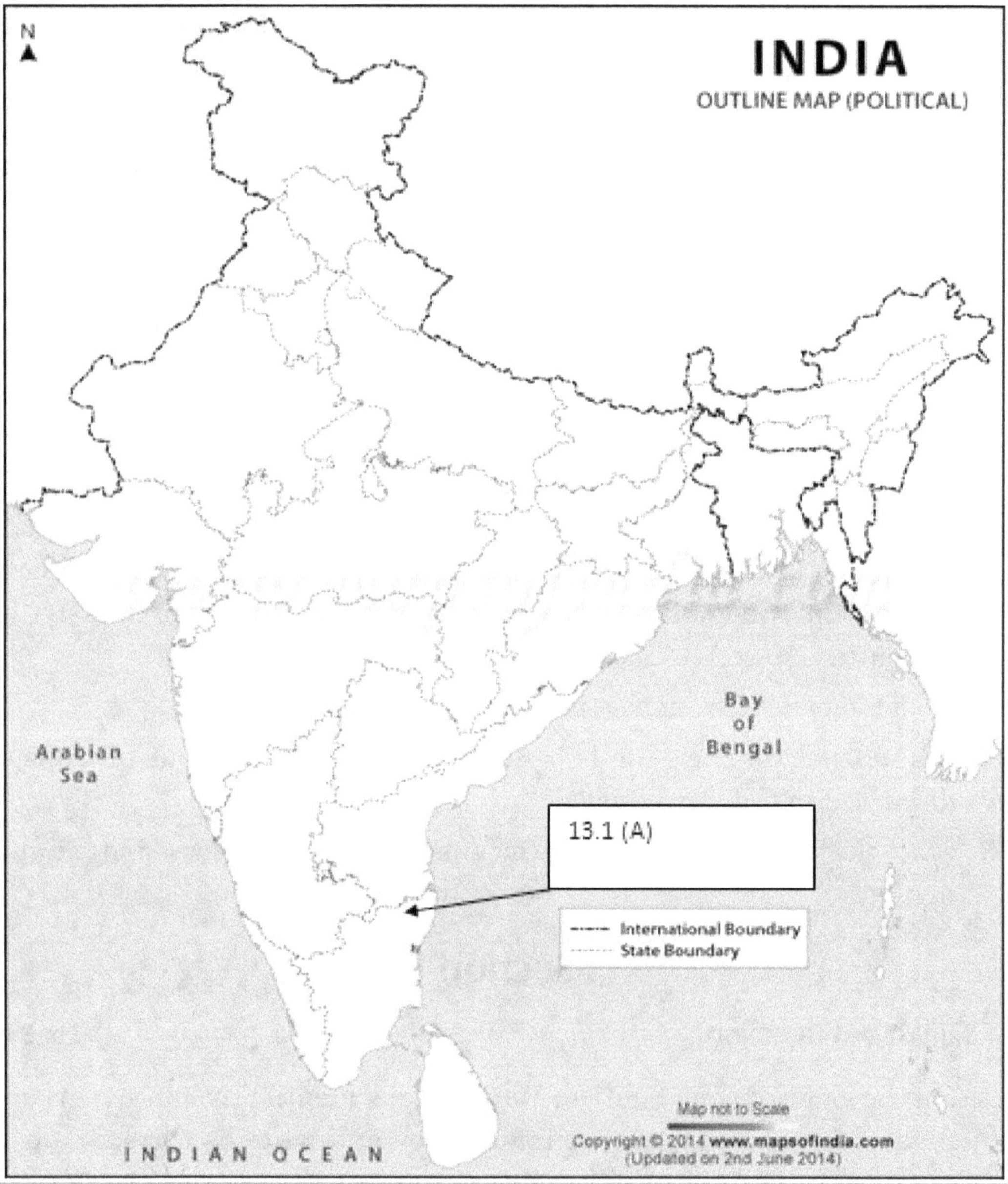

SOLUTION

Section-A

1. Gandhiji proposed that the Non-Cooperation movement should unfold in stages. It should begin with the surrender of titles that the government awarded, and a boycott of civil services, army, police, courts and legislative councils, schools, and foreign goods. Then, in case the government used repression, a full civil disobedience campaign would be launched. **2**

2. An integrated steel plant is large, handles everything in one complex – from putting together raw material to steel making, rolling and shaping.

   Mini steel plants are smaller, have electric furnaces, use steel scrap and sponge iron. They have re-rollers that use steel ingots as well. They produce mild and alloy steel of given specifications. **1 + 1 = 2**

3. In a democracy people have the right to choose their rulers and have control over the rulers. Democracy produces a government, which is accountable to the citizens and is based on the idea of liberation and negotiation. Decision-making is based on norms and procedures and its transparency. **2**

4. In a barter system goods are directly exchanged without the use of money. For eg: there is a farmer who is willing to exchange his crops in exchange for some cattle. Now this farmer will have to look for someone who wants to sell his cattle and in exchange is looking for crops. This process is very cumbersome and in it emerges the problem of double coincidence of wants. **2**

5. According to their main role industries are classified as:
   - Basic or key industries: These include industries supply their products as raw materials to manufacture other goods e.g. iron and steel and copper smelting, aluminum smelting.
   - Consumer industries: These include industries that produce goods for direct use by consumers – sugar, toothpaste, paper, sewing machines, fans etc. **1 + 1 = 2**

Section-B

6. Credit and a negative role: A farmer generally takes loan to meet the expenses related to cultivation activities. He hopes to have a good harvest the sale of which shall help him in repaying the loan easily. However,

the harvest doesn't turn out as expected owing to factors like low rainfall, pest attack, etc. Now next year he again takes loan but the crop is not good and loan repayment cannot be made. This cycle at time continues making the farmer fall in a debt trap. In some scenarios the farmer is left with no other option other than selling a piece of his land. **3**

OR

Globalization means integrating the economy of the country with the world economy. The advantages of globalisation are as follows:

(i) People usually move from one country to another in search of better income, better jobs or better education. In the past few decades, however, there has not been much increase in the movement of people between countries due to various restrictions. However, globalisation has paved way for this movement.

(ii) Globalisation has proven to be a booster for technology. In recent times, technology in the areas of telecommunications, computers, Internet has been changing rapidly. Today due to this development in technology we have been able to connect with people around the globe

(iii) Globalisation and greater competition among producers – both local and foreign producers - has been of advantage to consumers, particularly the well-off sections in the urban areas **1 × 3 = 3**

7. Moved by the Swadeshi movement, Abanindranath Tagore painted his famous image of Bharat Mata In this painting Bharat Mata is portrayed as an ascetic figure; she is calm, composed, divine and spiritual. In the contrasting figure, Bharat Mata is shown with a trishul, standing beside a lion and an elephant – both symbols of power and authority. **3**

8. The Election Commission has laid down detailed criteria of the proportion of votes and seats that a party must get in order to be a recognised party. A party that secures at least six per cent of the total votes in an election to the Legislative Assembly of a State and wins at least two seats is recognised as a State party. A party that secures at least six per cent of the total votes in Lok Sabha elections or Assembly elections in four States and wins at least four seats in the Lok Sabha is recognised as a national party. **3**

Section-C

9. Defection is the act of changing party allegiance from the party on which a person got elected (to a legislative body) to a different party.

The Election Commission of India has taken the following steps to reform political parties:

(i) The Constitution was amended to prevent elected MLAs and MPs from changing parties. This was done because many elected representatives were indulging in Defection in order to become ministers or for cash rewards.

(ii) The Supreme Court passed an order to reduce the influence of money and criminals. Now, it is mandatory for every candidate who contests elections to file an Affidavit giving details of his property and criminal cases pending against him. The new system has made a lot of information available to the public.

(iii) The Election Commission passed an order making it necessary for political parties to hold their organizational elections and file their income tax returns. **2 + 3 = 5**

OR

Features of All India Trinamool Congress:

(i) It was launched on 1 January 1998 under the leadership of Mamata Banerjee.

(ii) It was recognised as a national party in 2016. The party's symbol is flowers and grass.

(iii) The party is committed to secularism and federalism.

(iv) The party has been in power in West Bengal since 2011. Also has a presence in Arunachal Pradesh, Manipur and Tripura.

(iv) In the General Elections held in 2019, it got 4.07 per cent votes and won 22 seats, making it the fourth largest party in the Lok Sabha.

1¼ × 4 = 5

10. In recent years, the concept of Self- Help Groups has emerged largely among women. A typical SHG has 15-20 members, usually belonging to one neighbourhood and each member saves an amount depending upon their ability. Members can take small loans from the group itself to meet their needs and are charged a nominal rate of interest. After a year or two, if the group is regular in savings, it becomes eligible for availing loan from the bank. Loan is sanctioned in the name of the group and is meant to create self- employment opportunities for the members. For instance, small loans are provided to the members for releasing mortgaged land, for meeting working capital needs (e.g. buying seeds, fertilisers, raw materials like bamboo and cloth), for housing materials, for acquiring assets like sewing machine, handlooms, cattle, etc. **5**

OR

Effect of globalisation on the lives of people are :

(i) Due to globalisation, there has been an increased investment in industries such as cell phones, automobiles, electronics, soft drinks, fast food or services such as banking in urban areas.

(ii) Globalisation has created several job opportunities A lot of new jobs have been created. The youth particularly has been able to procure jobs in various sectors and these jobs have allowed the youth to upgrade their skill set. New opportunities for service such as data entry, accounting, administrative tasks are available to many.

(iii) Many local companies that had been supplying raw materials to these industries have experienced a boom. Some have gained from successful collaborations with foreign companies.

(iv) Several of the top Indian companies have been able to benefit from the increased competition. They have invested in newer technology and production methods and raised their production standards.

1 ¼ × 4 = 5

Section-D

11.1 Satyagraha **1**

11.2 Non-violence **1**

11.3 It requires resistance to oppression without using any force. It emphasises the power of truth and the need to search for it. The Satyagrahi could win the battle against the oppressor by appealing to his conscience, by persuading him to see the truth. **2**

12.1 Railways **1**

12.2 Economic **1**

12.3 Advantages of the means of transport:

(i) This means of transport makes it possible for people to conduct multifarious activities like business, sightseeing and pilgrimage along with transportation of goods over longer distances.

(ii) This means of transport in India bind the economic life of the country as well as accelerate the development of the industry and agriculture.

1 + 1 = 2

Section-E

13.1 (A) Madras 1

OR

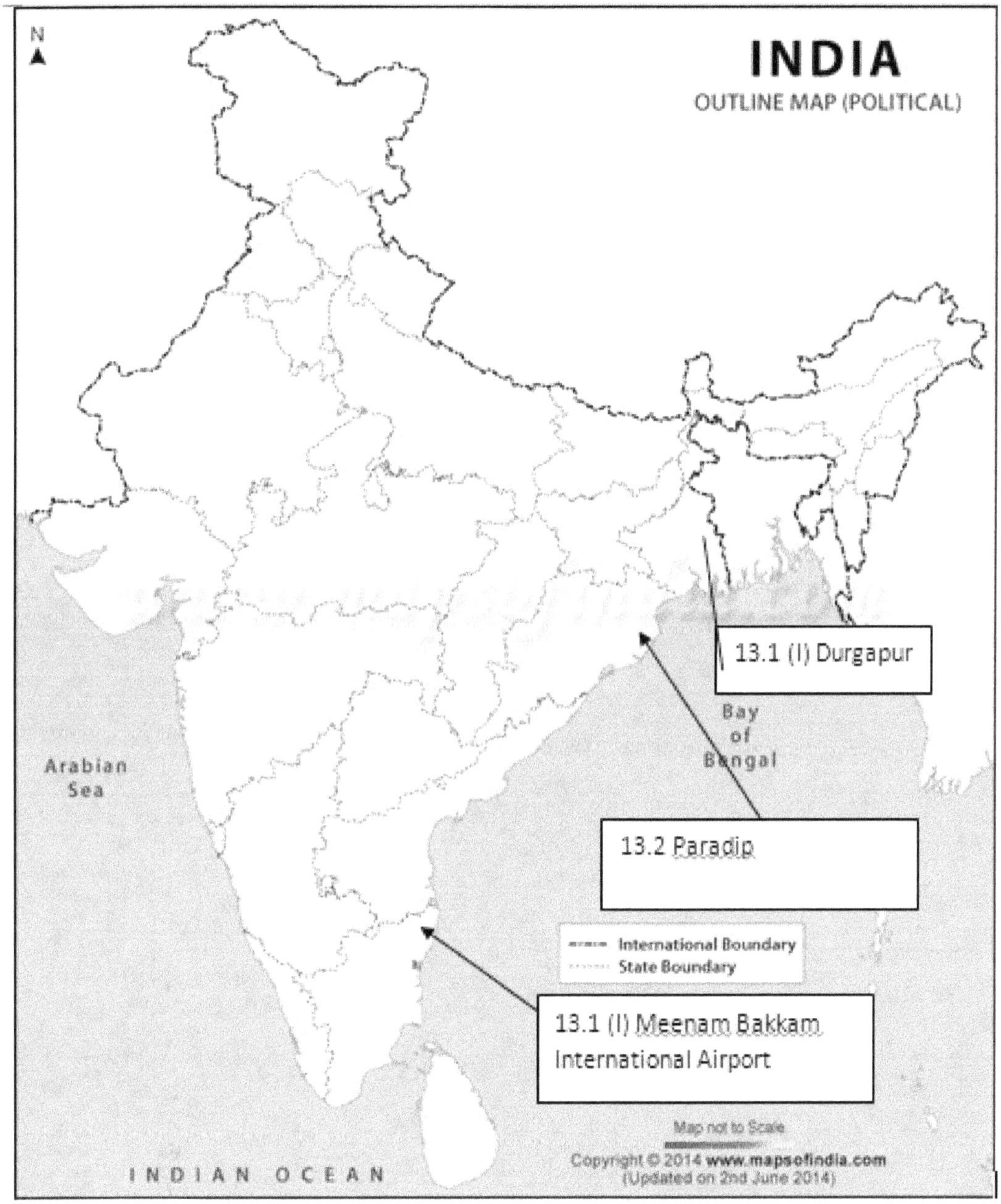

1 + 1 = 2

English Language and Literature

CBSE

Sample Question Paper 1

TERM II

CLASS X

ENGLISH - Language and Literature

Time Allowed: 2 Hours *Maximum Marks: 40*

General Instructions

1. *The Question Paper contains THREE sections-READING, WRITING & GRAMMAR and LITERATURE.*
2. *Attempt questions based on specific instructions for each part.*

Section-A

READING **10 Marks**

Read the passage given below.

1. 1. Children in India live in diverse circumstances and have diverse needs and rights. Along with their need to be educated, healthy and skillful, they need, and have rights to adequate nutrition, to live in a safe and supportive environment, have opportunities to reach their optimal potential and generally lead healthy, joyful and fulfilling lives so that they can be productive and well adjusted citizens of tomorrow.

2. Children in our country face many challenges. Many of them are first generation learners and face myriad problems throughout their schooling. They, due to the socio-economic and cultural determinants may be vulnerable in many ways. Peer pressure and lack of positive role models may prompt them to make unsafe and unhealthy choices. Anxiety and depression amongst the students, to the point of turning them suicidal, have been a cause of concern in the recent past.

3. Girls are more vulnerable and face discrimination at many levels from being unwelcome since birth to being pulled out of school for a variety of reasons. Dropping out of school, low motivation for academics and general disinterest in sports and physical activities too are some of the problems that need to be addressed. Child malnutrition is rampant in most parts of the country. This has an adverse bearing on their cognitive capacities, learning performance and physical capacity.

4. Our children have a right to age appropriate education, skills building, a safe and supportive environment, positive role models, empowerment, and friendly health services and counseling. Well informed and skilled children are likely to make better decisions concerning not only their careers and relationships, habits, physical and mental health, but will be successful and an asset to the society.

5. They also need to understand and deal with emerging issues like newly available career choices, pollution, water and energy conservation, global warming, protection of environment, terrorism and disasters. Dealing with anxiety and depression, negative peer pressure, violence, accidents, are some other significant issues that impact individuals health and also the social, economic and health indicators of the country. Gender sensitivity, prevention of female infanticide and good parenting are some important social issues that all children need to understand. Children require guidance and assistance - both covert and overt- from their Parents, Teachers, peers and society in general to complete the various "tasks" of development and deal with such issues.

Based on your understanding of the passage, answer ANY FIVE questions from the six given below : **1 × 5**

i. What does the author mean by 'fulfilling lives' in Para 1?

ii. Rewrite the following sentence by replacing the underlined phrase with a word that means the same in para 4

Once a person becomes educated he becomes ***useful or valuable*** for the society and henceforth education is important for national development.

iii. State any two reasons why child malnutrition is a huge matter of concern.

iv. Why is guidance a necessity for growing children?

v. List one impact of peer pressure.

vi. How does the writer justify the need for well informed and skilled children?

2. Read the following report on Sustainable Development in Indian states.

1. Himachal Pradesh, Kerala and Tamil Nadu have emerged as the front runners in the race to achieve key sustainable development goals (SDG) like removal of poverty and inequality, while Assam, Bihar and Uttar Pradesh are the laggards in a ranking of states released on Friday by federal policy think tank NITI Aayog and the UN.
2. According to the SDG India Index, the nation as a whole has a score of 58, showing the country has reached a little beyond the halfway mark in meeting the sustainable development goals adopted by India and 192 other nations in 2015. The index covers 13 of the 17 sustainable development goals, including healthcare, gender equality, clean energy, infrastructure, education, peace and building strong, accountable institutions.
3. Four goals, including climate action and sustainable use of marine resources, were left out because of lack of data at the state level.

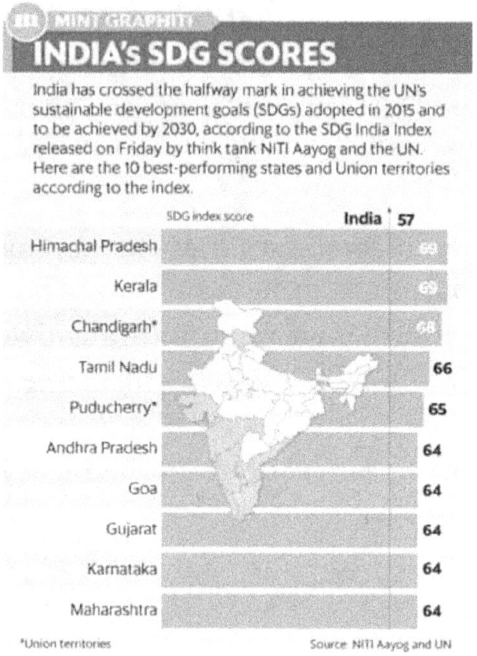

4. Kerala's overall top rank (69) is attributed to its strong performance in providing good health, reducing hunger, achieving gender equality and providing quality education. The rank shows the distance each state has to cover to reach 100-the point at which it fully meets the sustainable development goal.
5. Himachal Pradesh ranks high with a similar overall score in providing clean water and sanitation, reducing inequalities and preserving the mountain ecosystem. Tamil Nadu has a score of 68. Among Union territories, Chandigarh takes the lead with a score of 68 on account of its track record in providing clean water and sanitation. Performance in providing quality education has also helped Chandigarh achieve the high score.
6. Tamil Nadu topped the states in poverty reduction, while Kerala topped in providing quality education, closely followed by Chandigarh and Himachal Pradesh.
7. Jharkhand, Odisha and Nagaland are also among the states that have a lot more ground to cover in the overall rankings.

   The scores represent the current status of achievement in meeting the goals. NITI Aayog chief executive officer Amitabh Kant said that the index, which is also available for reference in the form of an online dashboard, will be updated in realtime. "This will lead to a lot of changes at the grass root level.

(Adapted from: https://www.livemint.com/Politics FctE2j3URJCeP3q Xim8RWI/Himachal-Kerala-Tamil-Nadu-top-UN-SDG-India-index.html)

Based on your understanding of the passage, answer ANY FIVE questions from the six given below : **1 × 5**

i. What reason does the NITI Aayog chief executive officer gives for updating the index online on real time basis?

ii. Which factor, apart from providing clean and sanitation water, has helped Chandigarh score above Tamil Nadu?

iii. What is the remarkable feature of India's SDG scores?

iv. What type of achievement made Tamil Nadu a leading state?

v. How has Himachal Pradesh contribute to the preservation of landforms?

vi. When will a state be considered to have fully met the goals of sustainable development?

Section-B

WRITING AND GRAMMAR **10 Marks**

3. Attempt ANY ONE from i and ii.

i. The chart shows the division of household tasks by gender in Great Britain. Write an analytical paragraph describing the chart given in not more than 200 words.

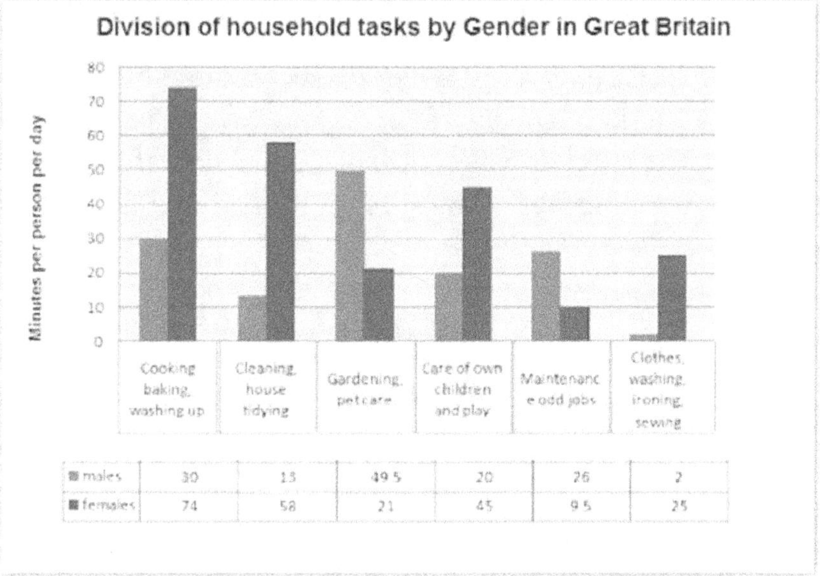

ii. You are Nandini /Vishal, Hostel Warden, Apex Public School, Agra, Uttar Pradesh. Write a letter to the Sales Manager, Uttam Electronics and Domestic Appliances Ltd., New Delhi, placing an order for a few fans, microwaves, ovens and geysers that you wish to purchase for the hostel. Also ask for discount permissible on the purchase. **5**

4. The following paragraph has not been edited. There is one error in each line. Identify the error and write its correction against the correct blank number. Remember to underline the correction. The first one has been done for you. **1 × 3**

	Error	Correction
Community service sensitise people to	to	towards
other's needs and supported inclusive	(a) ________	________
develops of the underprivileged sections	(b) ________	________
with the society. Courses about social	(c) ________	________
work prepares frontline workers to take up		
assignments in social welfare organizations.		

5. Read the conversation between a teacher and student and complete the passage that follows

Teacher : Why were you absent last week ?

Student : I was absent because I was not well.

Teacher : Will you be able to complete your pending work?

Student : I will work hard to complete it.

The teacher asked the student (a).............The student replied (b)...............The teacher was concerned and asked if he would be able to complete his pending work. The student replied that he would study hard to complete it. **1 × 2**

Section-C

LITERATURE **20 Marks**

6. Answer ANY SIX questions in 30-40 words each. **2 × 6**

i. How did Kisa Gotami realise that life and death is a process?

ii. How does Walt Whitman describe the non-materialistic nature of animals?

iii. Write a short note on the title of the poem 'Amanda'?

iv. How was Custard's reaction to the pirate unlike the other pets in the tower?

v. Explain the second argument that took place between Natalya and Lomov.

vi. How did Matilda's life change after she lost the necklace?

vii. The hack driver was a clever fellow. Comment.

7. Answer ANY TWO of the following in about 120 words each. **4 × 2**

i. How is the baker, his dress and his arrival described in the chapter 'A baker from Goa'?

ii. Bholi rejected the marriage proposal of Bhishamber Nath on the day of marriage. Her teacher was proud of this decision. Develop a conversation between the two, based on your understanding of the chapter.

You may begin like this:

Bholi: Ma'am look everyone is surprised by my decision but not you.

Bholi's teacher: Absolutely correct Bholi. That's because I am proud of your decision.

iii. A play is often used as a tool to depict the arrangements that exist in a socicty. With context to the play 'The Proposal', Comment.

SOLUTION

Section-A

1. (i) 'Fulfilling lives' in para 1 means life full of enough opportunities for one to grow as an individual.
   (ii) Asset
   (iii) Child malnutrition is a huge matter of concern because:
      (a) Malnutrition has an adverse impact on cognitive capacities of a child.
      (b) Malnutrition impacts ones physical growth.
   (iv) Right guidance promotes holistic development of a child.
   (v) Children are likely to make unhealthy choices.
   (vi) Well informed and skilled children are likely to make better decisions concerning not only their careers and relationships, habits, physical and mental health, but will be successful and an asset to the society. **1 × 5 = 5**
2. (i) NITI Aayog chief executive officer states that updating the index online on real time basis will pave way for bringing about changes at the grass root level.
   (ii) Chandigarh has provided quality education.
   (iii) It reached a little beyond the halfway mark in meeting the sustainable development goals adopted by India and 192 other nations in 2015.
   (iv) Tamil Nadu was at the apex in context to poverty reduction.
   (v) Himachal Pradesh has made efforts in preserving the mountain ecosystem.
   (vi) When a state reaches 100 points it will be considered to have fully met the goals of sustainable development. **1 × 5 = 5**

Section-B

3. (i) The above graph is a representation of time (number of minutes per day) spent by Britain men and women in doing household chores. While red bar denotes time spent by men, the blue bar represents time spent by women. Cooking, baking and washing activities are the ones in which women spend the maximum time in. Cleaning of house is also an area in which women spend much more time than men which is 58 minutes per day.

   In laborious tasks like gardening and pet care, men spend around 49.5 minutes per day. As the typical mindset goes, the responsibility of taking care of the child is primarily given to the females. Infact, in this category of household chores, women spend double time than that spend by men. While men take care of maintenance and odd jobs, women have surpassed men by spending almost ten times more time than men in laundry related jobs.

Two important conclusions drawn from the chart are : (a) Women are considered proficient with household chores and (b) It is a conservative thought process that women should be involved in household chores while men should be doing maintenance related tasks.

3. (ii) Apex Public School

Gandhi Road Agra

Uttar Pradesh XXXXX

20th January 20XX

The Sales Manager

Uttam Electronics and Domestic Appliances Ltd.

Daryaganj

New Delhi 1100XX

Subject : Order for domestic appliances

Dear Sir

We are pleased to place an order for the following items. Kindly send these at the above mentioned address through transport carefully as per the prices already negotiated.

Name of the Item	Quantity	Brand
Fans	50	Uma
Microwave	20	LGH
Oven	10	ABC
Geysers	70	XYZ

Kindly ensure that all the items are in good condition and preferably bubble wrapped properly . We request you to deliver the above listed items within 15 days of the issue of this letter.

Yours faithfully

Nandini /Vishal

(Hostel Warden- Apex Public School) **1 × 5 = 5**

4.	Error	Correction
(a)	supported	support
(b)	develops	development
(c)	with	of

$1 \times 3 = 3$

5. (a) why he had been absent the previous week.

(b) that he had been absent because he had not been well. $1 \times 2 = 2$

Section-C

6. (i) When Kisa Gotami was unable to find a house where nobody had died, she sat helpless at the wayside watching the lights of the city. As they flickered up and were extinguished again she realised that human lives had the same journey of flickering up for some time and are extinguished again.

(ii) Animals do not yearn to possess worldly things. Whereas, the more humans get, their desires keep on increasing leaving them dissatisfied forever. The absence of this greed in animals keeps them satisfied but its presence keeps humans dissatisfied.

(iii) The poem Amanda is about a girl who is scolded because she does not listen to the advice of her mother. Amanda is irritated by this scolding and she desires to escape the reality by living in an imaginative world. Through this gateway she experiences calmness, away from her nagging parents.

(iv) Each of Belinda's pets ran away and hid. They were scared at the sight of the pirate. Custard jumped in front of pirate and when the pirate missed his bullets, he then grabbed him. Custard faced the pirate and killed him.

(v) Natalya and Lomov, in their second argument, wanted to prove the superiority of their respective dogs. According to Lomov, his dog Guess was superior to Natalya's dog Squeezer. They argued over the price of the dogs, their pedigree, their hunting capability and even the proportions of their jaws.

(vi) In order to repay the loan that Matilda's husband had taken to buy a new necklace, they had to shift to a cheaper room and dismiss the servant. Now Matilda had to do all the household work like that of fetching water, washing the floor, utensils and dirty clothes all by herself.

(vii) It is correct to say that the hack driver was a clever fellow. He could easily deceive the lawyer and took him to several places so as to find Oliver

Lutkins, though the hack driver himself was Oliver Lutkins. Morcover, he was also able to take a lot of money from the lawyer for taking him to so many places. **2 × 6 = 12**

7. (i) The baker is described as a plump man and therefore it is assumed that baking was a profitable profession. In good old days during the Portuguese rule, the baker or bread seller had, a peculiar dress known as "kabai.. It was a single piece long frock reaching down to the knees. These days a pader wears a shirt and trousers which are shorter than full lengths ones and longer than half pants. During the narrator's childhood days, they wore a shirt and trousers of length slightly shorter than the usual ones. The baker used to arrive on the spot with the 'jhang-jhang' sound that was being made his bamboo. The sound would wake the children up and they would run to him in excitement.

(ii) Bholi: Thanks a lot ma'am. But it is all because of your encouragement that today I could take such a strong decision.

Bholi's teacher: Well, you see as a teacher our biggest reward is to see our students grow as good hearted and strong beings. Today seeing you like this I feel so proud and overwhelmed.

Bholi: Yes ma'am. Today everyone is surprised to see me transformed from a timid girl to an assertive one. I am short of words to thank you.

Bholi's teacher: You don't have to thank me. I just did my job.

Bholi: I am so grateful to be your student and I too would become a teacher just like you so that I can also bring about a positive change in one's life the way you brought in mine.

Bholi's Teacher: I wish you all the very best for your future endeavors. My blessings are always with you.

Bholi: Thanks a lot ma'am. I am truly blessed to have a teacher like you.

(iii) 'The Proposal' is a one-act play that highlights the tendency of wealthy families trying to increase their financial status by encouraging marriages that make good economic sense.

Lomov is a rich bachelor who wishes to marry Natalya, the daughter of Chubukov who himself is a rich man. Though Lomov is not really in love with Natalya and the two argue a lot, but he wants to marry Natalya as he feels she is a good house-keeper, beautiful and well educated. Natalya, who initially quarrels with Lomov wants to patch up with him when she comes to know that Lomov had come with a marriage proposal that she finds lucrative enough. At the end of the play, the proposal is finally accepted.

Just like this play, many other plays are made that depict the arrangements that exist in the society. While some plays are too serious, there are some that use satire to present these arrangements. A play acts as a wonderful medium to showcase important issues that exist in a society.

4 × 2 = 8

CBSE

Sample Question Paper 2

TERM II

CLASS X

ENGLISH - Language and Literature

Time Allowed: 2 Hours | *Maximum Marks: 40*

General Instructions

1. *The Question Paper contains THREE sections-READING, WRITING & GRAMMAR and LITERATURE.*
2. *Attempt questions based on specific instructions for each part.*

Section-A

READING **10 Marks**

Read the passage given below.

1. 1. Have you ever failed at something so miserably that the thought of attempting to do it again was the last thing you wanted to do?

2. If your answer is yes, then you are "not a robot." Unlike robots, we human beings have feelings, emotions, and dreams. We are all meant to grow and stretch despite our circumstances and our limitations. Flourishing and trying to make our dreams come true is great when life is going our way. But what happens when it's not? What happens when you fail despite all of your hard work? Do you stay down and accept the defeat or do you get up again and again until you are satisfied? If you have a tendency to persevere and keep going then you have what experts call, grit.

3. Falling down or failing is one of the most agonizing, embarrassing, and scariest human experiences. But it is also one of the most educational, empowering, and essential parts of living a successful and fulfilling life. Did you know that perseverance (grit) is one of the seven qualities that have been described as the keys to personal success and betterment in society? The other six are: curiosity, gratitude, optimism, self-control, social intelligence, and zest. Thomas Edison is a model for grit for trying 1,000 plus times to invent the light bulb. If you are reading this with the lights on in your room, you know well he succeeded. When asked why he kept going despite his hundreds of failures, he merely stated that what he had been not failures. They were hundreds of ways not to create a light bulb. This statement not only revealed his grit but also his optimism for looking at the bright side.

4. Grit can be learned to help you become more successful. One of the techniques that helps is mindfulness. Mindfulness is a practice that helps the individual stay in the moment by bringing awareness of his or her experience without judgement. This practice has been used to quiet the noise of their fears and doubts. Through this simple practice of mindfulness, individuals have the ability to stop the self-sabotaging downward spiral of hopelessness, despair, and frustration.

5. What did you do to overcome the negative and self-sabotaging feelings of failure? Reflect on what you did, and try to use those same powerful resources to help you today.

[Adapted from http://www.huffingtonpost.com/debbic-lyn-toomey/grit_b_12768724.html

Based on your understanding of the passage, answer ANY FIVE questions from the six given below : **1 × 5**

i. What attributes are used to differentiate between humans and robots?

ii. How does mindfulness allows one to come to a calm state of mind?

iii. How can a failure be used for positive reinforcement?

iv. How can we say that Thomas Edison was a man of perseverance?

v. What word is used to describe behaviors or thought patterns that hold you back and prevent you from doing what you want to do? (Para 4)

vi. Which quality, apart from grit, did Thomas Edison possess?

2. Read the following passage on declining number of vultures.

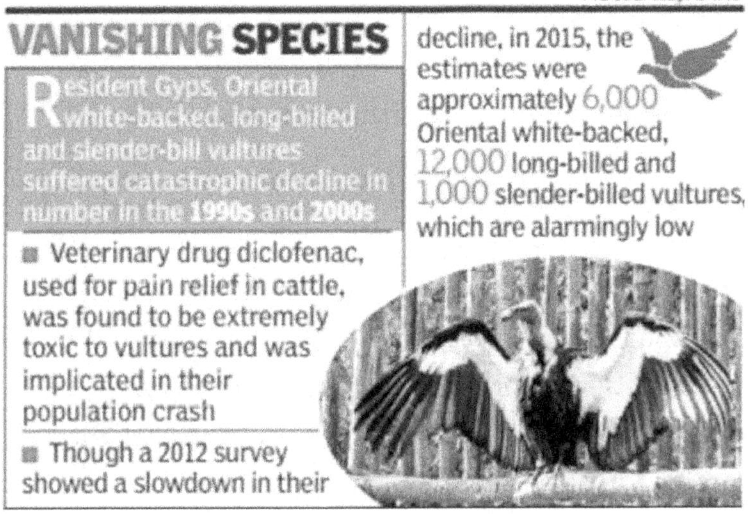
VANISHING SPECIES

Resident Gyps, Oriental white-backed, long-billed and slender-bill vultures suffered catastrophic decline in number in the 1990s and 2000s

■ Veterinary drug diclofenac, used for pain relief in cattle, was found to be extremely toxic to vultures and was implicated in their population crash

■ Though a 2012 survey showed a slowdown in their decline, in 2015, the estimates were approximately 6,000 Oriental white-backed, 12,000 long-billed and 1,000 slender-billed vultures, which are alarmingly low

1. Evolution has designated vultures to be the ultimate scavengers. Enormous wingspans allow them to circle in the air for hours. Their beaks, while rather horrifying, are weak by bird standards, made to scoop and eat flesh.

2. However unappealing they may seem, vultures serve an important role in the ecological cycle: processing dead bodies of animals. Only 20 years ago, India had plenty of vultures-flocks so enormous they darkened the skies. But by 1999, their numbers had dropped due to a mysterious kidney ailment. By 2008, 99.9 percent of India's vultures were gone. It was finally discovered that they had been killed by a drug called diclofenac (a pain reliever along the lines of aspirin or ibuprofen).

3. Indians revere their cows, and when a cow showed signs of pain, they treated it with diclofenac. After the animal died, the vultures would eat the corpse. And though they boast perhaps the world's most efficient digestive system, vultures cannot digest the drug. India banned the use of diclofenac for veterinary use in 2006, but it's still widely used.
4. The near extinction of vultures has caused a disease in the country, as rats and dogs moved in to take their place-spreading pathogens that would have otherwise been destroyed by the vultures.
5. Vultures need large ranges to scan for food and undisturbed areas in which to nest. They also need an abundance of prey species since they rely more on chance than their own hunting skills to eat. All of these things have been reduced by human activity. Meanwhile, there is a dramatic increase in secondary poisoning. Vultures feed on carcasses laced with poison, intended to kill jackals or other predatory carnivores. Or they are poisoned by the lead in animals left behind by hunters.

Based on your understanding of the passage, answer ANY FIVE questions from the six given below : **1 × 5**

i. State an important feature of vultures with regard to their metabolism.
ii. What problems are faced by the vultures during the consumption of their carcasses?
iii. Which species were noticeably at a low count in 2015?
iv. How do vultures manage to fly for long hours?
v. How are vultures an important part of the ecological cycle?
vi. Where do vultures prefer to build their nests?

Section-B

WRITING AND GRAMMAR **10 Marks**

3. Attempt ANY ONE from i and ii.

i. The following pie chart represents the attitude of people towards animals." Write a paragraph in not more than 120 words, analysing the listed responses.

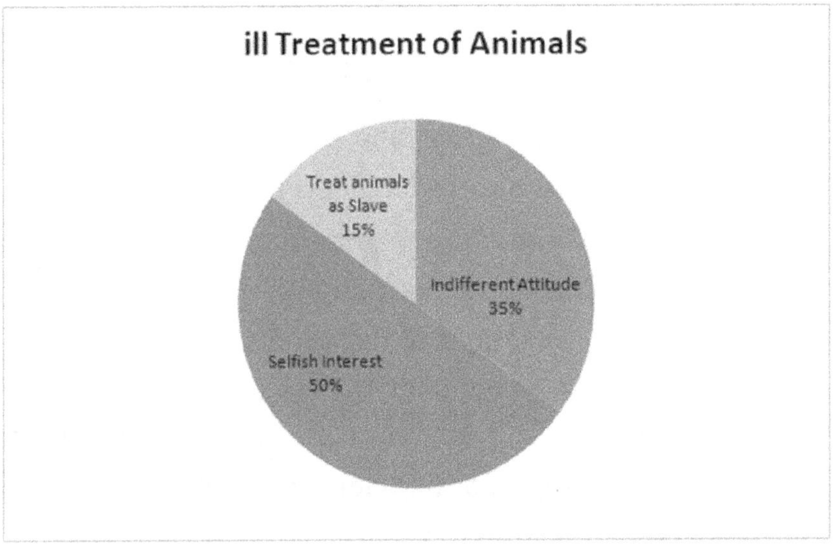

ii. Write a letter to M/s. Oxford Prints, Delhi placing the order for your school library. You are Varun Joshi, Librarian for Zenith School, Sector-20, Chandigarh. Furnish necessary details. **5**

4. Complete the passage below by filling the blank with the correct form of verb given in the brackets. **1 × 3**

Suddenly when the bushes rustled, father wolf dropped to the ground, (a) (prepare) to leap at the predator. Hold on!" cried mother wolf, "It's a mancub!" It (b) (be) a little baby. Father wolf closed his jaws and (c) (carry) him to mother wolf.

5. Read the conversation between a teacher and student and complete the passage that follows. **1 × 2**

Priya: Hi Neha. Where have you been all these days?

Neha: I went to Pune to attend a seminar on environmental degradation.

Priya : How was the seminar?

Neha: Quite informative and worth attending.

Priya asked Neha (a) ________________________. Neha replied that (b) ________________ on environmental degradation Priya wanted to know how the seminar was. Neha told her that it was quite informative and worth attending.

Section-C

LITERATURE **20 Marks**

6. Answer ANY SIX questions in 30-40 words each. **2×6**

i. How are the people of Coorg described?

ii. Describe 'Amanada'.

iii. How did Richard's mother help him develop love for science?

iv. Why was Kisa Gotami in a state of despair? Describe the episode of flickering lights.

v. Why did the first argument occur between Lomov and Natalya?

vi. How was Matilda not like her husband?

vii. Why is Walt Whitman in awe of animals?

7. Answer ANY TWO of the following in about 120 words each. **$4 \times 2 = 8$**

i. 'An underdog sometimes performs beyond expectations.' Taking cues from the poem 'The Tale of Custard the Dragon', comment.

ii. 'The lawyer was easily fooled by the Hack Driver.' Justify.

iii. Give the character sketch of Richard Ebright.

SOLUTION

Section-A

1. (i) Feelings, emotions and dreams are used as attributes to differentiate between humans and robots.

   (ii) Mindfulness allows an individual to stay in the moment by bringing awareness of his or her experience without judgement.

   (iii) A failure is one of the most educational, empowering, and essential parts of living a successful and fulfilling life.

   (iv) Thomas Edison tried 1,000 plus times to invent the light bulb.

   (v) self-sabotaging

   (vi) Optimism **1 × 5 = 5**

2. (i) The vultures have the world's most efficient digestive system.

   (ii) The vultures often feed on carcasses laced with poison putting their life in danger.

   (iii) Oriental white blacked, long- billed and slender- billed.

   (iv) Enormous wingspans allow vultures to fly for long hours.

   (v) Vultures only eat dead animal carcass. They remove bacteria and other poisons in the environment quickly, consuming carcasses before they decay.

   (vi) Vultures prefer to build their nests in undisturbed areas. **1 × 5 = 5**

Section-B

3. (i) Since ages some human beings have been extremely cruel towards animals. The above pie chart shows reasons for this unacceptable behaviour that human beings have displayed. It comes as a shock that 50% of people were cruel towards these innocent lives for their selfish interests. These included making fancy, luxurious outfits, etc. It was observed that 35% of people had an indifferent attitude towards animals and did not really care about their pain and sufferings that animals were made to undergo. Besides, to add to their woes, 15% of people believe that animals are their slaves. Animals were treated in the worst manner possible for financial gains.

   However, those who are cruel towards the animals must be made to realise that animals too deserve the same love and respect that human beings do. Those found harming the wildlife must be strictly punished.

(ii) Zenith Public School

Sector-20, Chandigarh

February 20, 20XX

M/s. Oxford Prints

Delhi- 1100XX

Subject: Order for books

Sir,

We are pleased to place an order for the following books for our school library. The list for the books is mentioned below:

S. No.	Name of the Item	Quantity
1	Jataka Tales	50
2	Noddy Series	30
3	Encyclopedia about extinct species	10
4	Folk Tales across the globe	10
5	The World of Mathematics- Grade 5	6

Kindly ensure that all the books are in good condition and properly packed. We will bear the transportation cost for this order. We request you to deliver the above listed items within 15 days of the issue of this letter.

Thanking You

Varun Joshi

(Librarian) **1 × 5 = 5**

4. (a) prepared

(b) is

(c) carried **1 × 3 = 3**

5. (a) where she had been all those days. **1**

(b) she had gone to Pune to attend a seminar . **1**

Section-C

6. (i) The people of Coorg are described as proud and an independent race of martial men and women who are possibly of Greek or Arabic descent. They have a tradition of hospitality and are known for their valour. They enjoy reciting stories of valour related to their sons and fathers.

(ii) Amanda is a little girl who refuses to listen to her mother's advice because of which she is scolded regularly. She uses her imagination, her wonderland as means of getting away from being angry.

(iii) Richard's mother took him on trips, bought him telescopes, microscopes, cameras, mounting materials and other equipments, and helped him in many other ways. She opened the world of science to him by introducing him to Dr Frederick A. Urquhart of the University of Toronto, Canada.

(iv) Kisa Gotami was in a state of despair because she had lost her son and wanted to bring her son back to life. When Gautam Buddha asked her to get mustard seeds from a house where death had never occurred, she was unable to do so that added to her misery.

(v) During their first argument, Lomov and Natalya fought over the ownership of oxen meadows. While Lomov calls it his own, Natalya argues that it belongs to her family. The two try to put different set of facts to prove the ownership of the oxen meadows.

(vi) Matilda, unlike her husband, yearned for a life of materialism. She always cribbed about not being married to a rich man who could fulfill all her materialistic desires. Matilda was greedy and she loved money where as his husband loved Matilda.

(vii) Walt Whitman desires to live among the animals because according to him animals are calm and self-sufficient unlike human beings. They do not whine and weep about their conditions. Animals always express their love and respect for human beings and spend a life of satisfaction and peace. They are not obsessed about their possessions. **2 × 6 = 12**

7. (i) It is true that at time an underdog performs beyond expectations. Custard the dragon proves this statement correct.

In the beginning part of the poem we see how custard, though has all the physical features of a dragon- like sharp teeth, toes like daggers, spikes on back , scales on the belly, mouth like a fireplace, etc., he does not really behave like a dragon. He is teased and tickled by other animals for his cowardliness that even includes a mouse. He always demands a safe place for himself.

However, tables turn when Belinda's house is attacked by a pirate. While all the other pets are frightened to the core, Custard, the dragon jumped in front of the pirate in order to fight with him. When the pirate fired two bullets upon Custard it missed both the shots. Consequently, the custard gobbled whole of the pirate ultimately leaving no trace of him.

(ii) The narrator- a young lawyer was sent to New Mullion to serve a summon on Oliver Lutkins. The narrator did not know Oliver Lutkins looked like. He met Bill, the hack driver at the station, who promised him to help in finding Lutkins. The hack driver first of all took him to Fritz. They learnt from him that he had gone to Gustaff's barber shop to have a shave. Reaching there, they learnt that Oliver had left for Gray's barber shop. They missed him by just a few minutes. The hack driver him to the poolroom. They missed him there too. After lunch the hack driver took the narrator to the farm of Lutkin's mother. The lawyer somehow managed to save himself from Lutkins mother and Lutkins could not be found there as well. Thus, they missed him narrowly everywhere.

The hack driver charged a heavy amount for the entire days' journey and convinced the lawyer that Oliver Lutkins could not be caught.

The next day when the lawyer returned to New Mullion accompanied by his senior, he was offended on knowing that the hack driver himself was Oliver Lutkins and how the lawyer had become a laughing stock for everyone.

(iii) Richard Ebright was a brilliant student. Since his childhood he had a curious mind. At a science fair he learned that one had to do real science experiments to prove a theory. In his kindergarten years he used to collect butterflies. He also collected rocks, fossils and became an eager astronomer. His mother had also helped him a lot by taking him to the trips and she also bought him a telescope, microscope, camera and other equipments and helped him in many other ways. His mother gifted him a book named 'The Travels of Monarch X' that changed his course of life. At the age of 22 he with one of his college roommate explained the theory on how cells work explaining the DNA theory. His curiosity, first rated mind and a will to win for the right reasons has helped him to become a scientist.

4 × 2 = 8

CBSE

Sample Question Paper 3

TERM II

CLASS X

ENGLISH - Language and Literature

Time Allowed: 2 Hours *Maximum Marks: 40*

General Instructions

1. *The Question Paper contains THREE sections-READING, WRITING & GRAMMAR and LITERATURE.*
2. *Attempt questions based on specific instructions for each part.*

Section-A

READING **10 Marks**

Read the passage given below.

1. 1. One of the great values of punctuality is that it gives discipline to life. We have to get up in time. We have to do things at the appointed time. All these entail certain amount of sacrifice. It dispels laziness and removes our 'take-it-easy attitude'. A disciplined person always gets recognition and social acceptance. He is wanted and appreciated. Therefore, punctuality can make us socially acceptable people.

2. Another significant merit of punctuality is that it provides ample time to do our work correctly and properly. Doing things hurriedly or haphazardly can have disastrous consequences. When we do things in time there is every chance that they end up as fine works.

3. The virtue of punctuality is said to be the key to success. Look at the great world leaders who have achieved fame and success. Punctuality was their hallmark. They kept their promises. Punctuality is a virtue that is appreciated by all. Washington once took his secretary to task for being late. The secretary laid the blame upon his watch. Washington reported: "Then, Sir either you must get a new watch or I must get a new secretary." People like them are ideals whom we should follow in earnest.

4. When individuals are not punctual they cause a lot of inconvenience to others. People have to wait for them and waste their valuable time. Want of punctuality reveals want of culture and is discourteous to the person we fail. Unpunctuality invites trouble and worry. History is full of cases which show that lack of punctuality has caused defeat, loss of kingdom and golden opportunities. It is said that Napoleon lost the battle of Waterloo in 1815 because one of his generals came late. Many people lose good. opportunities of job or promotion when they reach late for appointment.

5. All of us are not born with the virtue of punctuality. We have to cultivate it painstakingly. Only constant vigil and practice can implant this virtue. It calls for a great deal of sacrifice. It calls for courage to

root out laziness and the 'take-it easy attitude'. It demands a disciplined life. That is why very few individuals have the virtue of punctuality. But, know it for certain that it is the surest way to success.

Based on your understanding of the passage, answer ANY FIVE questions from the six given below : **1 × 5**

i. State the two requirements for ensuring punctuality in our lives.

ii. What can be said to be the biggest advantage of completing a work on time?

iii. How does unpunctuality impact ones' life?

iv. What kind of attitude needs to be done away with in order to practice punctuality?

v. What consequences did Napoleon face because his general was late?

vi. What is one sure to achieve by practicing punctuality?

2. Read the following passage on global warming:

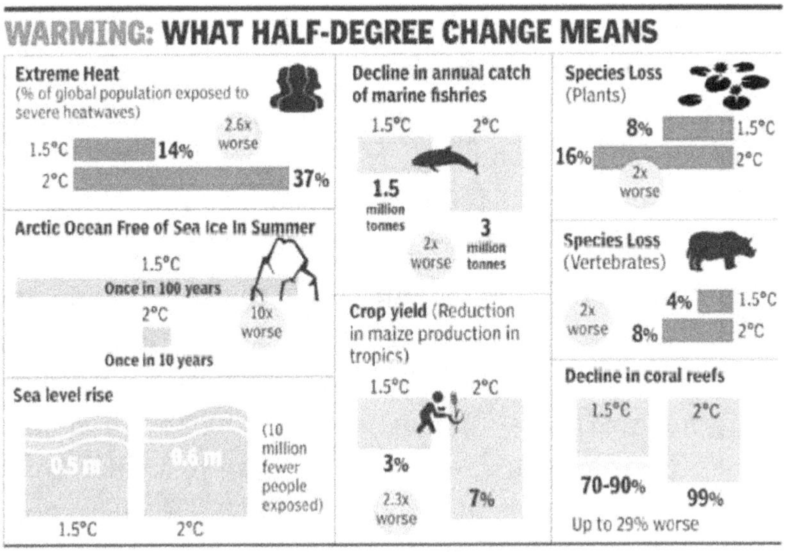

1. The Special Report on Global Warming of 1.5 °C (SR15) was published by the Intergovernmental Panel on Climate Change (IPCC) on 8 October 2018. The report, approved in Incheon, South Korea, includes over 6,000 scientific references, and was prepared by 91 authors from 40 countries. In December 2015, the 2015 United Nations Climate Change Conference called for the report. The rcport was delivered at the United Nations' 48th session of the IPCC to "deliver the authoritative, scientific guide for governments" to deal with climate change.

2. Its key finding is that meeting a 1.5 °C (2.7 °F) target is possible but would require "deep emissions reductions" and "rapid, far-reaching and unprecedented changes in all aspects of society." Furthermore, the report finds that "limiting global warming to 1.5°C compared with 2 °C would reduce challenging impacts on ecosystems, human health and well-being" and that a 2°C temperature increase would exacerbate extreme weather, rising sea levels and diminishing Arctic sea ice, coral bleaching, and loss of ecosystems, among other impacts. SR15 also has modelling that shows that, for global warming to be limited to 1.5°C, "Global net human-caused emissions of carbon dioxide (CO_2) would need to fall by about 45 percent from 2010 levels by 2030, reaching 'net zero' around 2050." The reduction of emissions by 2030 and its associated changes and challenges, including rapid decarbonisation, was a key focus on much of the reporting which was repeated through the world.

3. Global warming will likely rise to 1.5°C above pre-industrial levels between 2030 and 2052 if warming continues to increase at the current rate . SR15 provides a summary of, on one hand, existing research on the impact that a warming of 1.5°C (equivalent to 2.7°F) would have on the planet, and on the other hand, the necessary steps to limit global warming.

   Even assuming full implementation of conditional and unconditional Nationally Determined Contributions submitted by nations in the Paris Agreement, net emissions would increase compared to 2010, leading to a warming of about 3°C by 2100, and more afterwards. In contrast, limiting warming below or close to 1.5°C would require to decrease net emissions by around 45% by 2030 and reach net zero by 2050 (i.e. keeping total cumulative emissions within a carbon budget). Even just for limiting global warming to below 2°C, CO2 emissions should decline by 25% by 2030 and by 100% by 2075.

   (Source: https://en.wikipedia.org/wiki Special_Report_on_Global_Warming_of_1.5_%C2%B0C#:~:text=The%20Special%20Report%20on%20Global,91%20authors%20from%2040%20countries.)

Based on your understanding of the passage, answer ANY FIVE questions from the six given below : **1 × 5**

i. How has global warming impacted fauna?

ii. What is the impact of global warming on water bodies?

iii. What was the purpose of SR15?

iv. The emissions of which gas needs to be brought under control so as to control global warming?

v. Name the crop, the production of which declined due to global warming in the tropic region.

vi. What would happen if warming continues to increase at the current rate?

Section-B

WRITING AND GRAMMAR **10 Marks**

3. Attempt ANY ONE from i and ii.

i. The recent pandemic has had an adverse effect on every facet of life. 'Young Minds' conducted a survey to show how the mental health of young people has been affected during this time.

Write a paragraph in not more than 120 words, analysing the listed responses.

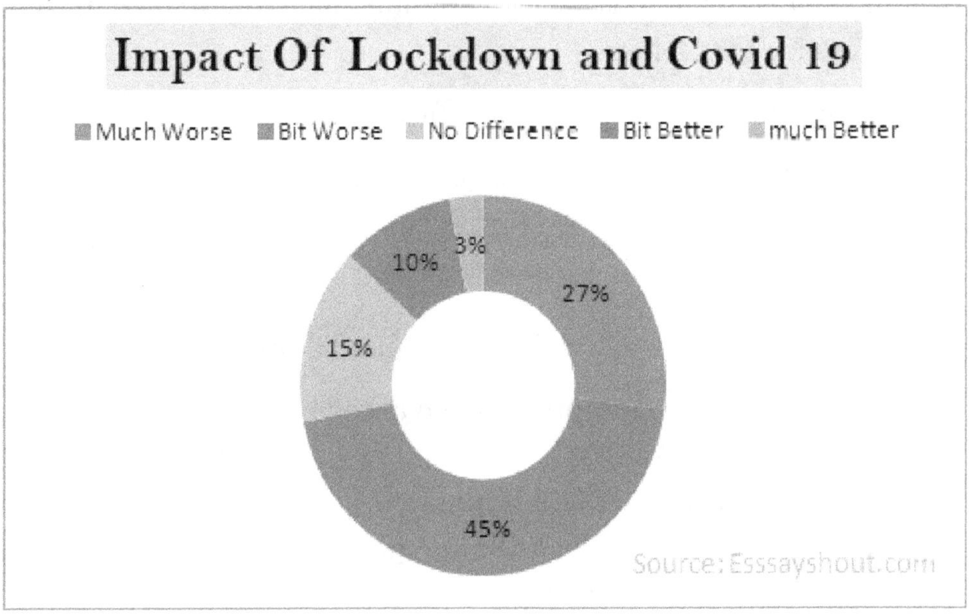

ii. You are Aman/Amita Rai living at 49, S-Block, Model Town, Allahabad-211001. You came across the following advertisement:

Homeo postal class Eng./Hindi. Practicals arranged. Prospectus free. Contact Director, Mavelil Homeo Mission, P.B. 1015, Pattom, Thiruvananthapuram-695004.

Write a letter to the Director asking for detailed information on the courses, duration, fees, assignments, local contact programmes. Request for a prospectus and enclose a self-addressed envelope. **5**

4. Complete the passage below by filling the blank with the appropriate modal: **1 × 3**

Seeing a crow eating a piece of bread, a fox thought how it (a) ..... trick that fellow. It sad, " ..... (b) May I talk to you sir?" The crow merely nodded.' The fox said, 'What a nice bird you are! Your voice is very sweet. I am sure you (b) ________ sing very well. The crow was pleased. Looking at this, the fox said ' Sir, you (c) __________ entertain me with you melodious voice. The moment the crow opened his beak, the piece of bread fell and the fox grabbed it.

5. Read the conversation between Raju and a receptionist and complete the passage that follows. **1 × 2**

Raju: Hello! Is Varun in the office?

Receptionist: Yes, but have you got an appointment?

Raju: No, but tell him that his childhood friend from Agra has come to meet him.

Receptionist: Please wait for a while. I'll inform him now.

Raju greeted the receptionist and asked her (a) __________________. The receptionist asked (b) ________________ . Raju replied that he did not have it, but told her to tell him that his childhood friend from Agra had come to meet him. Then the receptionist requested him to sit and said that she would inform him then.

Section-C

LITERATURE **20 Marks**

6. Answer ANY SIX questions in 30-40 words each. **2 × 6**

i. Describe Amanda's desires.

ii. What are the elders in Goa nostalgic about?

iii. Describe the story about the Kodavu people's descent.

iv. Why did Pranjol's father remark "You have done your homework before coming."

v. How was Custard's behaviour contradictory to his appearance?

vi. What all preparations did Valli make for her bus ride?

vii. Why was Lomov desperate to get married?

7. Answer ANY TWO of the following in about 120 words each. **4 × 2**

i. Comment on the role of Buddha as a mentor in Kisa Gotami's life.

ii. 'Though Coorg is the smallest district of Karnataka, it has rich flora and fauna.' Explain.

iii. 'Bholi evolved as a human being.' Justify.

SOLUTION

Section-A

1. (i) Constant vigil and practice are required for ensuring punctuality in our lives.
   (ii) There is a high probability of producing qualitative work.
   (iii) People who are not punctual are likely to face financial loss in addition to respect.
   (iv) A casual or 'take-it-easy attitude' is to be done away with in order to practice punctuality.
   (v) Napoleon lost the Battle of Waterloo in 1815 because one of his generals came late.
   (vi) Success **1 × 5 = 5**

2. (i) There has been a decline in the number of many species.
   (ii) Global warming has led to increase in sea levels.
   (iii) SR15 report was published with the purpose of providing scientific guide for governments" to deal with climate change.
   (iv) Carbon Dioxide
   (v) Maize
   (vi) Global warming will likely rise to 1.5°C above pre-industrial levels between 2030 and 2052 if warming continues to increase at the current rate.

1 × 5 = 5

Section-B

3. (i) Recently a survey was conducted by 'Young Minds' to understand the adverse effects of lockdown in 2020 during the COVID 19 pandemic. A large percentage of respondents, i.e. 45% said that the 2020 lockdown made them feel a bit worse than the 2019 lockdown. 27% claimed that they felt much worse than the 2019 lockdown and this is an alarming number. While 15% said that the 2020 lockdown did not really impact their mental health, 10% of the respondents said that they felt a bit better and 3% said it to be much better. It is important that in scenarios like these people who feel depressed raise an alarm so that necessary measures can be taken.

(ii) 49, S Block

Model Town

Allahabad 21100X

Uttar Pradesh

10 March 20XX

Maveli Homeo Mission

P.B. 105, Pattom

Thiruvanthapuram 695004

Subject: Inquiry regarding postal homeo course

Dear Sir

This is with reference to your advertisement in the Times of India dated March 8, 20XX regarding the postal homeopathic course, I would like to inform you that I am keen on joining the course and for this I would like have some information.

I would like to know the duration of the course, as well as the total fee. In addition to this, also let me know if any contact programme is held and, if held, of what duration. Kindly send a prospectus to me at the above address. I am enclosing a self-addressed envelope for the purpose.

Looking forward to an early response.

Yours faithfully

Aman/Amita **1 × 5 = 5**

4. (a) could

(b) can

(c) must **1 × 3 = 3**

5. (a) if/whether Varun was in the office. **1**

(b) whether he had got an appointment. **1**

Section-C

6. (i) Amanda has a number of desires. She desires desire to roam in the streets where no one to stop him and she want to become an orphan and a mermaid where she can drift blissfully in the green emerald sea.

(ii) The elders of Goa were nostalgic about the good old Portuguese days, the Portuguese, and their famous bread loaves. The writer says that the eaters of loaves have left but the manufacturers still exist.

(iii) One part of the story is that when a part of Alexander's army moved South along the coast, a few settled there and married amongst the locals and their culture remains alive even to this day. Secondly, because Kodavus wear a traditional garment called 'kuppia' which resembles the 'kuffia' they are said to be descendants of the Arabs.

(iv) Rajvir was very excited about visiting the tea garden and thus, he studied a lot about it before visiting the tea garden. His extensive knowledge about the tea plantation surpassed Mr Barua`s expectations. Hence he remarked that Rajvir has done his homework well before his visit.

(v) Custard had big sharp teeth, spikes on top of him and scales underneath. His mouth was similar to a fireplace, and nose was as a chimney. Also, he had daggers on his toes. Though he had these fierce features, he was a coward.

(vi) Valli saved every penny possible by cutting down on her expenses and resisted all the temptations to save sixty paise for the fare. She gathered all the necessary information from the passengers and neighbours.

(vii) Lomov was desperate to get married because he was almost middle aged man. He suffered from palpitations.He was excitable and always getting awfully upset. The very worst of all was the way he slept - someone would pull him during sleeping. **2 × 6 = 12**

7. (i) Buddha played a commendable role in Kisa Gotami's life as her mentor. When Kisa Gotami's son died, she was in deep sorrow. When she approached everyone possible, a man told her to meet Gautam Buddha as he could help her. With some hope, she went to Gautam Buddha requesting to bring her son back to life. Buddha asked her to look for mustard seeds and the seeds must be procured from a house that had seen no death. Kisa Gotami went to every house but could not find a single house where death had never occurred. Disheartened, she sat at the edge of the road where she saw lights flickering and finally being extinguished. She then realized how selfish she had been. She became conscious to the fact that men were mortal and no one could escape the cycle of life. This was exactly what Buddha wanted her to understand.

(ii) Coorg, or Kodagu, the smallest district of Karnataka, is home to evergreen rainforests, spices and coffee plantations. Evergreen rainforests cover thirty per cent of this district. During the monsoons, it pours enough to keep many visitors away. Coffee estates and colonial bungalows stand tucked under tree canopies in prime corners. The river, Kaveri, obtains its water from the hills and forests of Coorg. Mahaseer - a large freshwater fish - abound in these waters. Numerous walking trails in this region are a favourite with trekkers. Birds, bees and butterflies are there to give you company. Macaques, Malabar squirrels, langurs and slender loris keep a watchful eye from the tree canopy. The climb to the Brahmagiri hills brings you into a panoramic view of the entire misty landscape of Coorg.

(iii) Sulekha was nicknamed as Bholi. At a tender age she fell off the cot that damaged some part of her brain. As a result, she could pick up speech only after she was five years old, but she stammered. She also contracted small pox because of which she had pox marks all over her face because of which she was mocked at by other children. On her first day of school, Bholi was frightened but then she met a teacher who helped Bholi come out of her shell. This filled hope in Bholi and she began to go to school every day.

When Bholi reached a marriageable age, her father said yes to an unequal match for Bholi assuming that there was no boy who would be willing to marry Bholi. On the day of marriage when Bholi's would be groom demanded dowry on the pretext of getting married to her, Bholi refused to get married to this man named Bishamber Nath. The marriage ceremony ended without Bholi getting married. Her father was surrounded by grief and said that now no one would marry her and what would she do in future. To this, she replied that she would take care of her parents when they grew old and would teach in her school. Her teacher who was quietly watching all this felt proud of her decision. Thus Bholi evolved from a timid girl to a girl of bold character. **4 × 2 = 8**

CBSE

Sample Question Paper 4

TERM II

CLASS X

ENGLISH - Language and Literature

Time Allowed: 2 Hours | *Maximum Marks: 40*

General Instructions

1. *The Question Paper contains THREE sections-READING, WRITING & GRAMMAR and LITERATURE.*
2. *Attempt questions based on specific instructions for each part.*

Section-A

READING **10 Marks**

Read the passage given below.

1. 1. The children's literature being produced in India nowadays includes much more than just stories and folktales rich in morals and traditions. The output of its writers and illustrators in a variety of genres and in a plethora of languages reflects India's complex and ever-changing multilingual society. They also break through and go beyond long-standing gender, cultural and social stereotypes. The unique challenges and opportunities Indian children's book creators face-or those in the Diaspora writing about India-help create what one of our interviewees poetically calls the "rainbow-colored horizon" of Indian children's literature.

2. Children's publishing in India is poised for growth in every way. With education becoming a priority area, the demand for books for the growing population of young people can only go up.

3. Traditional retellings have been staple fare for publishers for their very small children's lists as they are 'safe' and they don't have to worry about copyright. More publishers are becoming willing to publish new authors, experiment with new formats, and find synergy with other media that are competing for the mind-space of the urban child. Maybe future books will be inspired by gaming and more merchandise will be inspired by books. Marketing will remain important in creating a positive buzz around books and reading. Books will influence TV and films and in turn be influenced by them. Comics and graphic formats seem poised for the great leap forward. Young Adult Fiction will have a permeable boundary with Adult Fiction.

4. Production standards for children's books will improve as there will be greater exposure to well produced books world-wide. The internet will create new ways to read and share and peer-review books. It may also enable many new talents to emerge as more people will be able to put up their work online.

Based on your understanding of the passage, answer ANY FIVE questions from the six given below : **1 × 5**

i. How do books help in knowing about the linguistic aspect of our country?

ii. What type of work removes the fear of copyright issues?

iii. Which factor that has fuelled the demand for books?

iv. How will internet contribute to the field of creative writing?

v. What noticeable change is seen in the publishing industry?

vi. Why is the author confident about an upgraded version of production standards of children's books?

2. Read the following passage on benefits of papaya:

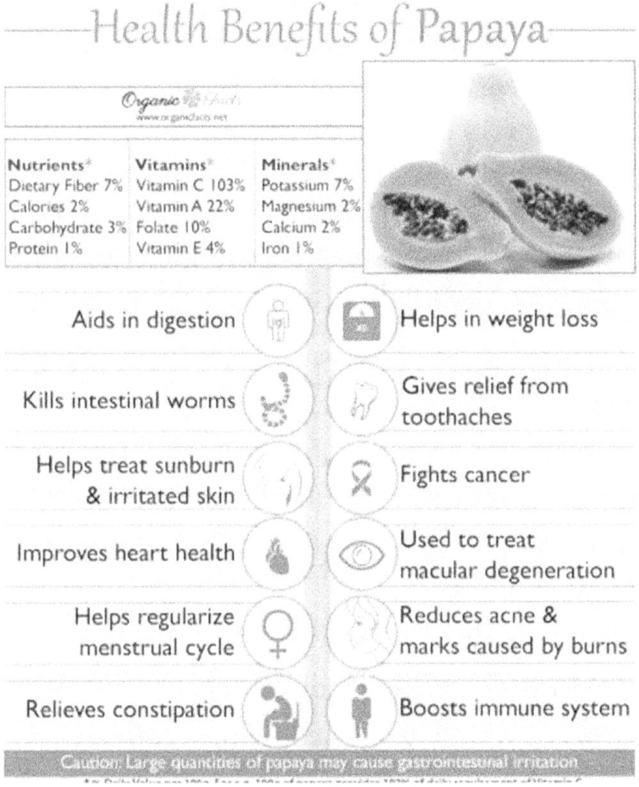

1. Papaya is the healthiest fruit with a list of properties that is long and exhaustive. Papaya favours digestion as well as cures skin irritation and sunburns. You can munch on it as a salad, have it cooked or boiled or just drink it up as milk shake or juice. The most important of these virtues is the protein-digesting enzyme in the milky juice. The enzyme is similar to pepsin in its digestive action and is said to be so powerful that it can digest 200 times its own weight in protein. It assists the body in assimilating the maximum nutritional value from food to provide energy and body-building materials.

2. Papain in raw papaya makes up for the deficiency of gastric juice and fights excess of unhealthy mucus in the stomach, dyspepsia and intestinal irritation. The ripe fruit, if eaten regularly, corrects habitant constipation, bleeding piles and chronic diarrhoea.

3. The juice, used as a cosmetic, removes freckles or brown spots due to exposure to sunlight and makes the skin smooth and delicate. A paste of papaya seeds is applied in skin diseases like those caused by ringworm. The black seeds of the papaya are highly beneficial in the treatment of cirrhosis of the liver caused by malnutrition, alcoholism, etc.
4. A table spoon of its juice, combined with a hint of fresh lime juice, should be taken once or twice daily for a month. The fresh juice of raw papaya mixed with honey can be applied over inflamed tonsils, for diphtheria and other throat disorders. It dissolves the membrane and prevents infection from spreading. The nutrients in papaya have also been shown to be helpful in the prevention of colon cancer. Papaya's fibre is able to control cancer-causing toxins in the colon and keep them away from the healthy colon cells. In addition, papaya's folate, vitamin C, beta-carotene, and vitamin E have each been associated with a reduced risk of colon cancer. These nutrients provide synergistic protection for colon cells from free radical damage to their DNA. Increasing your intake of these nutrients by enjoying papaya is an especially good idea for individuals at risk of colon cancer.

Based on your understanding of the passage, answer ANY FIVE questions from the six given below : **1 × 5**

i. How is papaya helpful in digestion?

ii. How can papaya be consumed?

iii. How is papaya fibre a great medicine against colon cancer?

iv. How is papaya good for the skin?

v. How is papaya used for curing throat related issues?

vi. Which vitamin is the highest in a papaya?

Section-B

WRITING AND GRAMMAR **10 Marks**

3. Attempt ANY ONE from i and ii.

i. The following bar graph shows a comparative analysis of students' performance in different subjects in the terminal exam. Write an analytical paragraph on the variation in the performances of students in about 100-120 words.

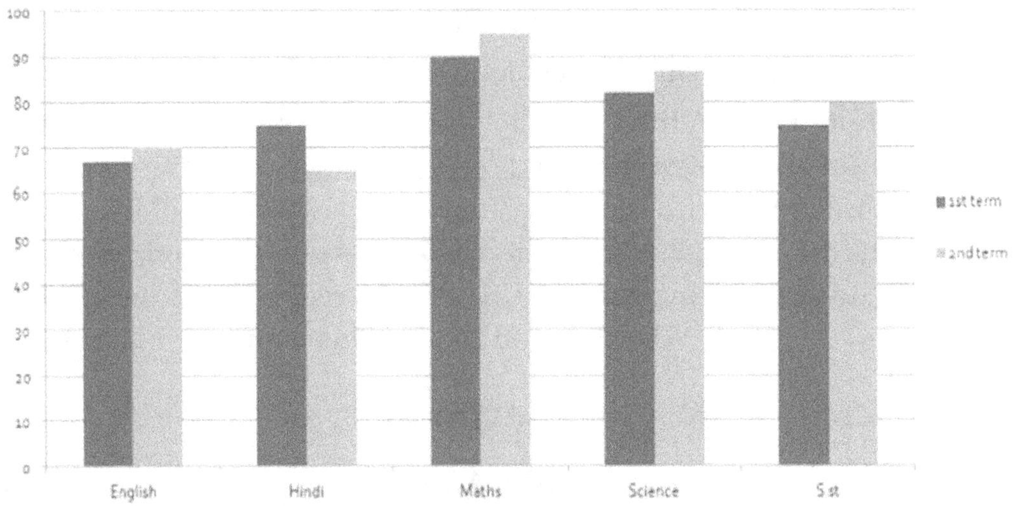

ii. You are Ankit, sports incharge at Blossom Public School Ghaziabad. Write a letter to Sharma Bros. Pvt. Ltd. New Delhi, placing order for sports items **5**

4. The following paragraph has not been edited. There is one error in each line. Identify the error and write its correction against the correct blank number. Remember to underline the correction. The first one has been done for you. **1 × 3**

	Error	Correction
Once there was the guru communicating	the	a
about wisdom to people that came for his	(a) ________	________
darshan within flowers and fruits. One	(b) ________	________
day, the offerings was in plenty, he called	(c) ________	________
the disciple and asked him to cut fruits and		
arrange for their distribution of prasad.		

5. Here is a piece of conversation between Aditya and his friend Gautam. Read the conversation and complete it by choosing the correct option.

Gautam: Hello, Aditya. How're you doing?

Aditya: I am fine.

Gautam: I haven't seen you in several months.

Aditya: Well, I was busy with some personal stuff. I have received a good job offer from a US company.

Gautam: Oh, I see. When are you leaving?

Aditya: I will be leaving for the US next week.

Gautam: You've made it big, mate. I'm really happy for you.

Gautam asked Aditya how he was. Aditya replied that he was fine. Gautam told Aditya that (a)________________. Aditya replied that he had been busy with some personal stuff. He further added that he had received a good job offer from a US company. Gautam inquired when was Aditya leaving for the US. Aditya replied that he would be (b) ________________. Gautam said that he was happy for his friend. **1 × 2**

Section-C

LITERATURE **20 Marks**

6. Answer ANY SIX questions in 30-40 words each. **2 × 6**

i. Why was the Baker's furnace essential in a traditional Goan village?

ii. How did Valli gathered all the information about the bus?

iii. What was the effect of the sufferings of the world on Buddha?

iv. Why does Natalya ask her father Chubukov to fetch Lomov in at once? Why does she accuse her father?

v. What does the poet mean by, "Not one is respectable or unhappy over the whole earth"?

vi. What rare achievement did Richard manage at the age of twenty-two?

vii. Why did the hack driver offer help to the lawyer?

7. Answer ANY TWO of the following in about 120 words each. **4 × 2**

i. The principle 'forgive and forget', helps a lot in maintaining cordial relations with our neighbors. Do you think Anton Chekov conveys this message in the play 'The Proposal'?

ii. Mme Loisel's disposition invites her doom. Comment in the context of the text you've read.

iii. Bholi is a child different from others. This difference makes her an object of neglect and laughter. Elaborate.

SOLUTION

Section-A

1. (i) Books are available in multiple languages that reflects India's complex and ever-changing multilingual society.

   (ii) Traditional retellings

   (iii) Education becoming a priority area has fuelled the demand for books.

   (iv) Internet will enable many new talents to emerge as more people will be able to put up their work online.

   (v) More publishers are becoming willing to publish new authors, experiment with new formats, and find synergy with other media that are competing for the mind-space of the urban child.

   (vi) Production standards for children's books will improve as there will be greater exposure to well produced books world-wide. **1 × 5 = 5**

2. (i) Papaya helps in overcoming the problem of constipation.

   (ii) Papaya can be eaten as a salad, can be cooked or boiled or just be consumed as milk shake or juice.

   (iii) Papaya's fibre is able to control cancer-causing toxins in the colon and keep them away from the healthy colon cells.

   (iv) Papaya helps in treating sunburn and irritated skin.

   (v) The fresh juice of raw papaya mixed with honey can be applied over inflamed tonsils, for diphtheria and other throat disorders.

   (vi) Vitamin C- 103% **1 × 5 = 5**

Section-B

3. (i) The above graph represents the performance of students in different subjects in terminal exams. Some improvement was seen in Maths and Science in the second term with most students scoring higher marks. The scores in Maths and Science were above 80 in the first term. In Maths, most students scored above 90 marks in the second term. Students scored between 60-70 marks in Hindi and English, which means that students need to put in more efforts in the two subjects, especially in Hindi as the students scored less in the second term. There was a marginal improvement in the second term marks in English and Social Science.

   However, efforts must be made to ensure that the overall scores improve in the next academic session, hence proper planning needs to be done so as to achieve this goal.

(ii) Blossom Public School
Ghaziabad- 1100XX
March 25th , 20XX
Sharma Bros. Pvt. Ltd.
New Delhi-1100XX
Subject: Purchase of Sports Items
Dear Sir,

Our school wishes to place an order for sports items in bulk with your company. These items will be used in the activities room, gym, and sports ground of the school starting from the academic sesion of the year 2022-23. List of the items along with their quantity is given below:

Name of the Items	Quantity
Cricket bat	20
Red leather (cricket) balls	20
Football	10
Tennis racket	20
Tennis ball	50
Practice net	8
Volley Ball	10
Badminton racket	30
Shuttle cock	50

Kindly, deliver the order by next week and also ensure that all the items are taken from the fresh lot. Payment of the entire purchase will be done via NEFT .

Looking forward to hearing from you.

Yours Truly,
Ankit
Sports Incharge **1 × 5 = 5**

4. Error Correction

(a) that who
(b) within with
(c) was were **1 × 3 = 3**

5. (a) he had not seen him in several months. **1**

(b) leaving the following week **1**

Section-C

6. (i) Different kinds of breads were important during the different occasions. Bolinhas had to be prepared during Christmas and other festivals. The mothers used to prepare sandwiches on the occasion of their daughter's engagement. So, the baker's furnace was essential.

(ii) Over many days and months Valli listened carefully to conversations between her neighbours and people who regularly travelled in the bus. She also asked a few discreet questions here and there. This way she gathered all the information about the bus.

(iii) At the age of 25, while hunting, one day Buddha saw a sick man, then an aged man, then a funeral procession and finally a monk begging for alms. The sight of these incidents moved him so much that he went out into the world to seek enlightenment.

(iv) Natalya asked her father to fetch Lomov at once as she had come to know that Lomov had come to propose her. She accused Chubukov of driving Lomov out of their home.

(v) The poet means that animals do not pray to God or to ancestors and all of them are equal, hence no one is more respectable than the other. The good values of animals and the lack of social conventions make them happy.

(vi) Richard had a rare honour at the age of twenty-two. He wrote an article with his friend about a theory of how cells work. The article was published in the scientific journal 'Proceedings of the National Academy of Science.' No one had this achievement at such a young age before him.

(vii) The hack driver was none other than Oliver Lutkins himself. He did not wish to take the summons and go as a witness. So, he pretended to be a hack driver. He offered to help the lawyer so that the lawyer would not come to know about him from someone else. **$2 \times 6 = 12$**

7. (i) Anton Chekov does convey the message that the principle of 'forgive and forget' helps a lot in -maintaining cordial relationship with one's neighbours. Initially, the neighbours in the play, Lomov, Natalya and Chubukov were fighting over trivial issues and none among them was willing to give up. They were not paying attention to any of the important issues and wasted their time by arguing over things of no value. These arguments slowly developed into fights and they started hurling abuses at each other. This damaged their relationship with each other.

It was when Natalya came to know that Lomov had come to propose her that she left the topic of argument (Oxen Meadows) behind. She also asked for forgiveness from Lomov and requested him to come to the point. Hence it is mandatory to 'forgive and forget' if one wants to have cordial relationship with others.

(ii) Mme Loisel belongs to a family of clerks. Her existence is quite average. They live on income that is enough for fulfilling basic needs and not luxurious items. She gets married to a clerk and is so caught up with her dreams of materialistic pleasures that she is out of touch with reality of her life. In order to keep up appearances just to flatter her pride, she blows up four hundred francs on a gorgeous dress. And, not contented, she goes on borrowing a necklace from her friend. And, all of this is just to impress the wealthy and the rich with her beauty and glamour (even if on loan). No doubt, her pride is flattered and her wish of fine dining, expensive dresses and jewels satisfied but at a great price. Unfortunately, the necklace has lost and the couple has to give up their entire inheritance and borrow as well to replace it. Repayment of the debt eats away the next ten years of their youth. All the house hold chores and cares of a life of poverty visit them. Hence, her disposition invites her doom.

(iii) Bholi is not like other children. She is slow for her age and stammers when she speaks. Small pox leaves her all covered with pock-marks. As a result, she has to suffer a lot.

Her parents do not even bathe her. She is a neglected child who is considered as a burden. People laugh at her. Children mock her when she speaks. So, she remains silent most of the time. She is low on her self esteem. Society must realise that it is important to accept those who are " different. They too deserve to be treated with love and respect. **4 × 2 = 8**

CBSE

Sample Question Paper 5

TERM II

CLASS X

ENGLISH - Language and Literature

Time Allowed: 2 Hours *Maximum Marks: 40*

General Instructions

1. *The Question Paper contains THREE sections-READING, WRITING & GRAMMAR and LITERATURE.*
2. *Attempt questions based on specific instructions for each part.*

Section-A

READING **10 Marks**

Read the passage given below.

1. 1. The majority of children around the world have at least one sibling. The sibling relationship is likely to last longer than any other relationship in one's lifetime and plays an integral part in the lives of families. Yet, in comparison to the wealth of studies on parent child relationships, relatively little attention has been devoted to the role of siblings and their impact on one another's development.

2. In recent decades, research has focused on sibling relations in early childhood, and the shift from examining the role of structural variables (e.g., age, birth order) towards more process variables (e.g., understanding of their social worlds) has proved to be a fruitful direction. Siblings are viewed as an integral component of family systems and as an important context for learning and development but there are a number of methodological and conceptual challenges to studying siblings from this perspective.

3. In early childhood, four major characteristics of sibling relations are prominent. First, sibling interactions are emotionally charged relationships defined by strong, uninhibited emotions of a positive, negative and sometimes ambivalent quality. Second, sibling relations are defined by intimacy: as youngsters spend large amounts of time playing together, they know each other very well.

4. This long history and intimate knowledge translates into opportunities for providing emotional and instrumental support for one another, engaging in pretend play, for conflict, and for understanding others' points of view. Third, sibling relations are characterized by large individual differences in the quality of children's relations with one another. Fourth, the age difference between siblings often makes the issues of power and control as well as rivalry and jealousy, sources of contention for children, but also provide a context for more positive types of complementary exchanges, such as teaching, helping, and care giving interactions. Broadly speaking, the characteristics of sibling relations sometimes make them challenging for parents, because of the potentially emotional and highly charged nature of the relationship. One issue that arises due to age differences is differential parental treatment.

Based on your understanding of the passage, answer ANY FIVE questions from the six given below : **1 × 5**

i. What is the status of research studies in sibling relations.

ii. Explain about an important characteristic of sibling interaction.

iii. What happens when siblings spend large amounts of time playing together?

iv. What have the recent researches in sibling studies focussed on?

v. When is there a stark difference noticed in parental treatment of siblings?

vi. Give an important feature of sibling relationships in context to its longevity.

2. Read the following passage on Harappan Civilisation.

1. Harappan Archaeological Research dates back to the year 1922 with the advent ofthe finding of Mohen-jo-Daro, the 'mound of dead', in Sindh. Because of its extraordinary urban character, the discovery raised immense interest world-over. Since then, the archaeology of the Harappan Civilization has been growing, both in terms of geographic factors and cultural dynamics. By the time archaeologists found that the Indus Civilization is no longer confined to the Indus Valley, archaeologists have redesignated it as 'Harappan Culture' or 'Harappan Civilization' after the type site namely Harappa (The naming of related sites after the one that was first discovered is a common convention in Archaeology.) discovered in 1921. From 1950 onwards, this study has been occupying paramount place in the archaeology of South Asia and the last twenty five years, in particular, have witnessed excavation of the scores of Harappan sites, which have brought to light the most exciting results. Intensive explorations and excavations of several sites of entire Archaeologists from India and Pakistan, either independently or in collaboration with western scholars, have launched multidisciplinary investigations to reconstruct the spatio-temporal framework of this civilization. The radiocarbon determinations and the evidence of the early food producing cultures in the entire Harappan domain have put this civilization in the perspective of indigenous origins.

2. The manifestation of towns and cities is an urban phenomenon and thus, the first towns and cities were linked with the first urbanization that took place in the fertile valleys of the river Indus, Saraswati and their several tributaries. However, on the basis of excavation, in many of the Harappan sites, it has been confirmed that these towns and cities grew out of earlier villages that existed in the same locality prior to Pre/Early Harappan period. Before 2600 B.C. sites like, Harappa, Dholavira, Rakhigarhi, Banawali, Kalibangan, Rehman Dheri, Nausharo, Kot Diji and many more existed in the form of rural Harappan settlements. Their ideal locational setups were on the threshold, which led to urbanization. Beginning with quite a small population, they grew in size and density to become larger settlements of the region along the major trade routes.
3. Based on the evidence of excavations, the majority ofthe Harappan cities and towns are composed of a series of walled mounds or sectors oriented in different directions. Harappa and Mohen-jo-Daro both have rectangular mound on the west and extensive mounds to the north, south and east whereas the settlement of Kalibangan is confined to two separate mounds with the citadel on the west, represented by a smaller mound and the lower city towards the east, marked by a fairly extensive mound. Citadel was situated over the remains of the preceding occupation to gain eminence over the lower town, which was laid out on the natural plain towards the leaving the gap of over 40 meter between the two. Harappa is remarkably similar to that of Kalibangan in layout having fortifications-parallelogram on plan. Mohen-jo-Daro also appears to have a similar layout, despite the fact that flood erosions have obscured the evidence. The lower town of Harappa and Mohen-jo-Daro spreading out on different mounds also appears to have separately fortified. However, lower town of Kalibangan gives clear indication offortification-parallelogram in shape. In contrast, Lothal and Surkotada follow a different expression for the layout of the settlement. In these two sites, a common periphery wall encloses both the citadel and the lower town. Among all, Dholavira, on account of its unique city planning indeed enjoys a pre-eminent position.

4. Until recently, it was believed that the Harappan civilization along with its spectacular achievements, evolved quite mysteriously and then disappeared suddenly, leaving little or no legacy for later cultures. However, as new sites have been discovered and previously excavated ones were restudied it became apparent that it disintegrated gradually, leaving the field open for the development of subsequent cities.

Important Sites of IVC			
Site	**Excavated by**	**Location**	**Important Findings**
Harappa	Daya Ram Sahini in 1921	Situated on the bank of river Ravi in Montgomery district of Punjab (Pakistan).	▪ Sandstone statues of Human anatomy ▪ Granaries ▪ Bullock carts
Mohenjodaro (Mound of Dead)	R.D Banerjee in 1922	Situated on the Bank of river Indus in Larkana district of Punjab (Pakistan).	▪ Great bath ▪ Granary ▪ Bronze dancing girl ▪ Seal of Pasupathi Mahadeva ▪ Steatite statue of beard man ▪ A piece of woven cotton
Sutkagendor	Stein in 1929	In southwestern Balochistan province, Pakistan on Dast river	▪ A trade point between Harappa and Babylon

Chanhudaro	N.G Majumdar in 1931	Sindh on the Indus river	▪ Bead makers shop ▪ Footprint of a dog chasing a cat
Amri	N.G Majumdar in 1935	On the bank of Indus river	▪ Antelope evidence
Kalibangan	Ghose in 1953	Rajasthan on the bank of Ghaggar river	▪ Fire altar ▪ Camel bones ▪ Wooden plough
Lothal	R.Rao in 1953	Gujarat on Bhogva river near Gulf of Cambay	▪ First manmade port ▪ Dockyard ▪ Rice husk ▪ Fire altars ▪ Chess playing
Surkotada	J.P Joshi in 1964	Gujarat	▪ Bones of horses ▪ Beads
Banawali	R.S Bisht in 1974	Hisar district of Haryana	▪ Beads ▪ Barley ▪ Evidence of both pre-Harappan and Harappan culture
Dholavira	R.S Bisht in 1985	Gujarat in Rann of Kachchh	▪ Water harnessing system ▪ Water reservoir

(Excerpts from: https://www.lkouniv.ac.in/site/writereaddata/siteContent 202003241550006972anil_kumar_HARAPPAN_CIVILIZATION%201.pdf) and

Based on your understanding of the passage, answer ANY FIVE questions from the six given below : **1 × 5**

i. Which site of the Indus Valley Civilisation has fire altars?

ii. Which Indus Valley Civilisation was excavated by R.S Bisht in 1985?

iii. In which Indian state of present day was Banawali located?

iv. What important fact have we learnt about the Harappan civilisation by integrating the newly found and the previous sites?

v. What is an extraordinary characteristic of the Harappan civilisation?

vi. Draw the similarity between Harappa and Kalibangan.

Section-B

WRITING AND GRAMMAR **10 Marks**

3. Attempt ANY ONE from i and ii.

i. The following bar diagram shows the reasons for which parents' have opposed the reopening of schools and to send their child to school amid the COVID 19- Pandemic. Study the bar diagram and write a paragraph in not more than 120 words, analysing the listed responses to the situation.

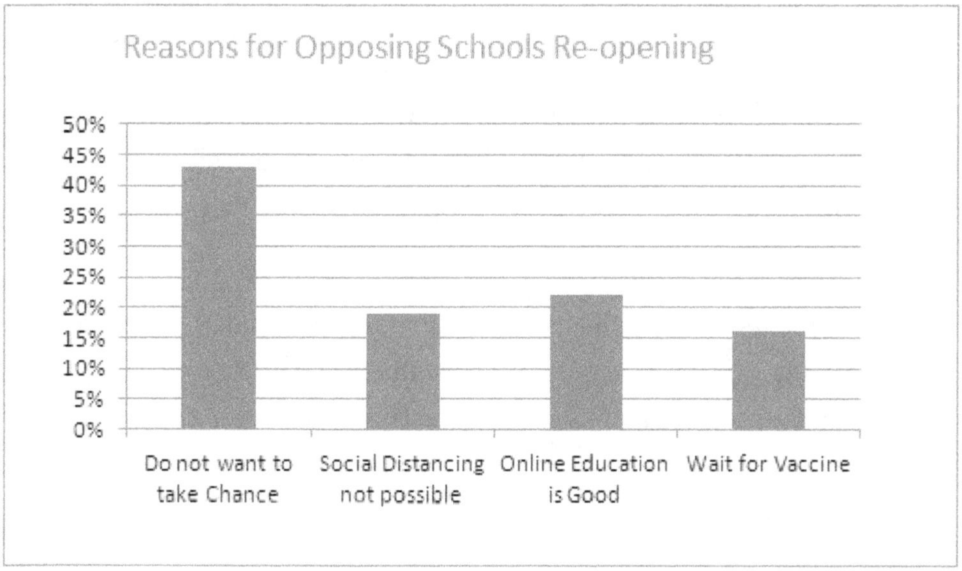

ii. You are Prashant, the Secretary of the Historical Society of Nalanda Senior Secondary School, Bombay. You want to take a group of seventy students of your school on a trip from Bombay to Delhi by a deluxe bus. Write a letter to Global Travels, Bombay, enquiring about their terms and conditions for package tours. You can ask about the duration of the trip, boarding and lodging charges, mode of payment, and discount available if any. **5**

4. The following paragraph has not been edited. There is one error in each line. Identify the error and write its correction against the correct blank number. Remember to underline the correction. The first one has been done for you. **1 × 3**

	Error	Correction
While evening falls, the street gets incredibly	Eg. : When	As
crowded. While music spills out in the	(a) ________	________
houses, mouth-watering aroma steam out	(b) ________	________
from the eateries that cater on the taste buds.	(c) ________	________
of all nationalities.		

5. Read the conversation between a mother and daughter and complete the passage that follows:

Mother : Where were you?

Daughter ' : I was on the terrace playing.

Mother : Please do not go without prior permission.

Daughter : This was the first time ever that I went on the terrace.

Mother : Remember, do not go there alone.

Mother asked her daughter where she had been. The daughter replied that (a)________________. The mother then (b) ______________ The daughter apologised saying that that had been the first time ever that she had gone on the terrace. The mother warned her saying not to go there alone. **1 × 2**

Section-C

LITERATURE **20 Marks**

6. Answer ANY SIX questions in 30-40 words each. **2 × 6**

i. Why did Richard lose interest in tagging butterflies?

ii. What excuse did Loisels put up to explain the delay in returning the necklace?

iii. Why was Bholi fascinated by classroom walls?

iv. How has the Coorgi tradition of courage and bravery recognised in modern India?

v. Where were Rajvir and Pranjol going and why? What did Rajvir see while looking outside from the train?

vi. Describe the interior and exterior of the bus in which Valli travelled.

vii. What happens to Lomov when he is in an excited state?

7. Answer ANY TWO of the following in about 120 words each. **4 × 2**

i. 'Appearances are often deceptive'. Comment on the statement in the light of your reading of the story 'The Hack Driver'.

ii. Personal losses are a part and parcel of life. Instead of wailing on them, we should move on in life. This message of Gautama Buddha has become more relevant in modern times. Do you agree ? Why /why not?

iii. It is not complaining but accepting a situation, the key to happiness in life. Elaborate in context of the poem Animals'.

SOLUTION

Section-A

1. (i) Relatively little attention has been devoted to the role of siblings and their impact on one another's development.

   (ii) Sibling interactions are emotionally charged relationships defined by strong, uninhibited emotions of a positive, negative and sometimes ambivalent quality.

   (iii) Large amounts of time playing together allows siblings to get to know and understand each other deeply.

   (iv) Sibling relations in early childhood.

   (v) When there is a noticeable age gap between siblings, a stark difference is noticed in parental treatment of siblings.

   (vi) The sibling relationship is likely to last longer than any other relationship in one's lifetime. **1 × 5 = 5**

2. (i) Kalibangan

   (ii) Dholavira

   (iii) Hisar district of Haryana.

   (iv) It became apparent that the Harappan civilisation fell apart gradually and not suddenly.

   (v) Urbanisation

   (vi) Harappa is remarkably similar to that of Kalibangan in layout having fortifications-parallelogram on plan **1 × 5 = 5**

Section-B

3. (i) Looking at the bar graph it is quite evident more than 40% of the parents opposed this idea stating that they cannot take any chances or risks with regard to their child's health. Almost 18% of the parents stated that it is nearly impossible to maintain social distancing in school premises.

   There were some, almost 20%, who said that online education was satisfactory enough. Around 15% of parents trusted the vaccine and chose to wait till the vaccine for school going children is launched.

   In a nutshell, schools don't expect to be fully active as only 33% of the parents gave their consent to reopen the schools.

(ii) Historical Society

Nalanda Senior Secondary School

Bombay 4000XX

3 October 20XX

The Manager

Global Travels

New Link Road

Jogeshwari (W)

Bombay 4000XX

Subject: Enquiry regarding package tour to Delhi

Dear Sir

I have received positive feedback about the package tours organised by your firm. Keeping this is mind, I intend to take a group of seventy students to Delhi by a deluxe bus. The trip will be of about 20 days in November. The reason why we want to go by bus is that we want to visit cities en route to Delhi. We plan to see Udaipur and Jaipur on way to Delhi and Mathura, Agra, Gwalior, and Indore on the return journey. We would like to stay at night at these places.

Kindly let us know if 20 days are sufficient for sightseeing in these cities and in Delhi. You will have to arrange for the deluxe bus, our boarding and lodging, and sightseeing. Also, let us know if you can make satisfactory hotel arrangements and what your charges will be regarding this entire trip. We expect the best discount possible as the number of children is large. We would also like the various acceptable mode of payments at you end.

I request you for an early response so that we may finalise our programme.

Thanking You

Prashant

(Secretary- Historical Society) **1 × 5 = 5**

4. (Incorrect–Correct)

	Error	Correction
(a)	in	from
(b)	steam	steams
(c)	on	upon

1 × 3 = 3

5. (a) she had been on the terrace playing **1**

(b) requested her not to go without prior permission. **1**

Section-C

6. (i) Richard raised thousands of butterflies, tagged them and released them to study their migration. But soon, he lost interest because only two of his tagged butterflies were returned to him and they had travelled only seventy-five miles.

(ii) Loisels had lost the necklace and needed time to find an identical one. Thus, Loisels wrote a letter to Mme Forestier with an excuse that the clasp of the necklace was broken and they needed time to get it repaired.

(iii) The walls of the classroom had bright and colourful pictures of a horse, a goat, a parrot and a cow. They all looked familiar to Bholi and were like the ones in the village. That is why she was fascinated to see those pictures.

(iv) The Coorgi tradition of courage and bravery has been recognised by awarding the Coorg Regiment with the maximum number of gallantry awards. Besides, the Coorgis are the only Indians allowed to carry firearms without a licence.

(v) Rajvir and Pranjol were going to Assam as Pranjol had invited Rajvir to spend summer vacation there. Rajvir saw much greenery while looking outside from the train. He was amazed to see the soft green paddy fields first and then the green tea bushes.

(vi) The outside of the bus was painted with gleaming white and some green stripes along the sides. Inside, the overhead bars shone like silver. There was a beautiful clock above the windshield and its seats were soft and luxurious.

(vii) When Lomov is in an excited state his heart beat increases, lips tremble and there is a twitch in his right eyebrow. When he goes to sleep in such a state something pulls him from his left side and he jumps like a lunatic.

$2 \times 6 = 12$

7. (i) It is correct that to say that appearances can be deceptive. People are generally not what they appear to be.

In the story when the young lawyer reaches New Mullion to get a hold of Oliver Lutkins, he meets a hack driver at the station. The driver warns him about Lutkins. He takes him on a tour of the entire village in search of Lutkins. He tells the narrator about his experiences and about the village and its people. The narrator likes him for his helpful and kind nature. The Hack driver takes the lawyer to several people and places trying to show that how much he wants to help the lawyer in finding Oliver Lutkins but by day end their efforts do not reap any results.

He even forgets all about Lutkins. But, the next day he finds out that the hack driver was Oliver Lutkins himself and how, though being a lawyer was easily deceived and had become a laughing stock for many in the town of New Mullion. He realises that a simple and kind person was a trickster in reality.

Therefore we should be careful while dealing with people around us and not judge people based on their appearances.

(ii) Yes, I agree with the message that Gautama Buddha has given about life. In the modem times, people have a lot to explore and move with the world at the same pace. People are way to attached to materialism and have become intolerant. However, if people refuse to understand and accept the practicality of life, they will be always be stressed which will impact all aspects of their life. Moreover emotional pain will worsen their condition. People need to understand that anyone who is born in this world has to leave it on some or the other day. There is no use of being sad or crying over the loss. People should remain calm and composed in such situations. They should face the truth and move on in life.

(iii) The poet Walt Whitman in his poem 'Animals' is in awe of animals. He compares animals to human beings and brings out a set of stark differentiates between the two based of their characteristics and habits. The poet has ranked the animals much higher than humans due to various reasons. The poet is highly impressed with the animals as they do not complain about their situation, they are considered to be much happier than humans. Animals live in natural surroundings, they accept their natural lives. Humans, on the other hand, have never accepted nature, i.e., they complain about it and try to change it, leading to an unhappy life.

4 × 2 = 8

www.ingramcontent.com/pod-product-compliance
Lightning Source LLC
Chambersburg PA
CBHW081306130726
47998CB00010B/2954
* 9 7 8 9 3 9 2 8 3 7 4 8 7 *